Glass House Books

The Lion Behind the Anthill

Gill Shaddick left Britain aged twenty-one to take up a job in Hong Kong and kept on travelling. She met her husband, Mike, in a township in Zambia where she was the only single girl and he the only single guy. Together they embarked on a peripatetic journey living in a dozen countries. They counted cotton bollworms in Egypt, Sudan and Iran, tagged eels in New Zealand, owned a fishing business on Lake Kariba in central Africa and ran a rabbit farm in one of Scotland's remotest corners. Their four daughters, each a constant source of joy, amusement and awe, were all born in different countries.

In 1987, Gill and her family moved to Australia. Months later Mike was diagnosed with Multiple Sclerosis and with that his future plans for overseas contracts disappeared overnight. But travel was Gill's passion and she determined there'd be many journeys ahead, at first with Mike, then backpacking with her daughters and ultimately going solo.

Gill is a distant cousin of Robert Louis Stevenson. His grandfather's clock ticked out the hours as she grew up, which she credits as one reason why, from an early age, she was enchanted by travel and writing.

She is currently working on a new manuscript that traces railway journeys through Siberia and Central Asia, weaving her personal history into the broader narrative. *The Lion Behind the Anthill* is her second book. Her first book, *The Hong Kong Letters*, was published in Melbourne and Hong Kong in 2019.

Glass House Books
Brisbane

Gill and Mike in Kenya

The Lion Behind the Anthill:

A Memoir of Love and Discoveries

Gill Shaddick

Glass House Books
an imprint of IP (Interactive Publications Pty Ltd)
Treetop Studio • 9 Kuhler Court
Carindale, Queensland, Australia 4152
sales@ipoz.biz
http://ipoz.biz/shop
First published by IP in 2025
© 2025 Gill Shaddick (text); IP (design)

All rights reserved. Without limiting the rights under copyright reserved above, no part of this publication may be reproduced, stored in or introduced into a retrieval system, or transmitted, in any form or by any means (electronic, mechanical, photocopying, recording or otherwise), without the prior written permission of the copyright owner and the publisher of this book.

Printed in 14 pt Avenir Book on Caslon Pro 12 pt.

ISBN: 9781923435025 (PB) 9781923435032 (eBook)

A catalogue record for this book is available from the National Library of Australia

Author's Note

I have recorded events from my letters and memories. Some names have been changed to maintain anonymity.

*For Mike with my love and gratitude
for many adventures and many daughters*

Glossary

Chibuku: Sorghum beer
Fellaheen: Name given to an agricultural labourer in Egypt and the Sudan
Honky: A derogatory American term for white people
Hottentot: Historical term for non-Bantu Indigenous people. The preferred term is now *Khoi*
Jellabiyas: Long robes worn in North Africa, usually blue or white
Kaffir: Arabic term for a non-believer, a non-Muslim
Keiff: Cannabis
Kopje: A small hill
Matabele: Bantu-speaking African peoples known also as Ndebele
Mossad: National Intelligence agency of the State of Israel
Organophosphate: Widely used agricultural insecticide
Putsi fly: Also known as mango fly, it lays its eggs on wet clothing. The larvae then penetrate the skin, grow and then erupt out of the skin
Scouse: A native or inhabitant of Liverpool, England
Shongololo: Giant millipede
Tepes: Artificial mounds in Iran dating date back thousands of years BCE
Wog: Offensive term for a foreigner

Contents

Glossary	vi
Chapter 1 – Myself	1
Chapter 2 – Zambia, 1971	4
Chapter 3 – Chilanga Cement	12
Chapter 4 – The Party	24
Chapter 5 – Love in Six Weeks	32
Chapter 6 – African Composition	40
Chapter 7 – Getting Married, 1972	49
Chapter 8 – A Sojourn in Cairo, 1973	59
Chapter 9 – El Minya, Upper Egypt	68
Chapter 10 – Egyptian Cotton	79
Chapter 11 – Khartoum and Omdurman	86
Chapter 12 – Wad Adam in the Gezira	96
Chapter 13 – Bollworms, Birds and Borders	106
Chapter 14 – A Mighty Miscarriage	115
Chapter 15 – The Shah's Iran, 1974	122
Chapter 16 – Exploring Khuzestan	130
Chapter 17 – New Zealand, 1975	137
Chapter 18 – Casablanca Moment, 1976	145
Chapter 19 – Commissioning *Hu Hu*, 1977	153
Chapter 20 – Kariba	162
Chapter 21 – Bumi River	172
Chapter 22 – The Chicken Run	180
Chapter 23 – Galloway, 1978	189
Chapter 24 – The Rabbit Run, 1979	199
Chapter 25 – Back to Africa, 1980	209
Chapter 26 – Geneva, 1984	220
Chapter 27 – Sydney and Swank, 1987	225
Chapter 28 – The Black Dog	235
Chapter 29 – Variations on an Idea	242
Chapter 30 – Waiheke and Other Interludes, 2009	250
Chapter 31 – Blue Gum Lodge, 2010	261
Chapter 32 – Respites and Rescues	269
Chapter 33 – The Long Drop Off	273
Chapter 34 – Rooms to Let	280
Epilogue	290
Acknowledgements	292

The things you think are the disasters in your life are not the disasters really. Almost anything can be turned around: out of every ditch, a path, if you can only see it.
– *Hilary Mantel,* Bring Up the Bodies

Chapter 1 – Myself

He didn't want me to go, so made money the obstacle, but neither did he want to appear miserly. To end the conversation, he said, "The only possibility is selling Mrs Mops."

"Done!" I cried and we stared at each other. My outburst from an uncharted well of aspiration, surprised Dad and astounded me. Was I that fickle? Move over Mrs Mops?

Mrs Mops, a bay mare over 16 hands tall, was my teenage confidant. She dared me to reckless gallops and discreetly kept the secrets I shared as we ambled Oxfordshire bridle-paths. Dad never imagined I would trade her in for a ticket to visit cousins in Australia.

Still, he was hesitant. I paused to eavesdrop at the door when I heard my name.

"Gill's not exactly streetwise. She's never been anywhere on her own. How's she going to get to Italy to catch the boat?"

To my amazement, Mum championed me. "She'll soon be eighteen. She's more resourceful than you think, Alan. She'll manage – there'll be a boat-train from Calais."

I left Dover on a bright Spring day in 1965 but, halfway across, thick fog enveloped the Channel.

"No idea," advised the purser when I asked how long we'd be delayed. "You just stay on the ferry, dear, and go back. You've already missed the boat-train to Genoa."

Instead, I got a train to Paris and met a sweet French boy who said we should elope. I kissed him goodbye and caught a milk-train through Switzerland. The seats were wooden and I sat beside a woman endowed with such enormous hips that I feared if I stood up, I would never see my seat again. A grumpy Swiss conductor protested my ticket was not for his train, and, when I reached Genoa, it seemed that all was lost until a Lloyd Triestino official saw my First-Class luggage label and plucked me out of the crowds and up the gangplank. That thrilling twenty-four hours triggered in me an insatiable appetite for travel.

After my Australian adventure, it was three years before I left the UK again. In 1968, when I was twenty-one, I took off on the Trans-Siberian Express on the way to Hong Kong, where I'd landed a job in an advertising agency.

I spent two glorious years growing up and melting down in a noisy pot of colour and culture and would have been oblivious to the fact that it was almost the last outpost of the British Empire had there not been a great many 'when-wes' in Hong Kong. These were Brits who'd lived a bloody marvellous life in Africa until 1960, when Prime Minister Harold Macmillan signalled that Britain would relinquish its African colonies: "The wind of change is blowing through this continent. Whether we like it or not, this growth of national consciousness is a political fact."

My teenage years had been punctuated by BBC newsreels of independence ceremonies held on white-hot African parade grounds. Flag poles, brass bands and speeches of faith, hope and charity. First Ghana, then a phalanx of others. I'd watched to keep Dad company, and he watched because he'd been an army doctor in Africa during the Second World War.

David Dunlop, one of my workmates in Hong Kong, had lived for a decade in Kenya and filled my ears with tales of empty spaces teeming with wildebeest and of the unforgettable fragrance that rose off the earth when the rains came.

His Africa was seductive: a deeply satisfying place, not hedonistic like Hong Kong. "Ah, Gill, you won't have lived unless you go to Africa."

So, I had to go. Captivated by the idea of an unspoilt continent, lyrical and full of wonder, it's not surprising that when I reached Central Africa, I was out of place, spare and, of course, so white I made the locals blink. In short, I wished myself gone soon after I arrived.

Eventually, I would be grateful for what Africa taught me. Its complexities provoked me to dig deeper into what went before to understand the now. If we don't keep picking away at the past – tapping, burrowing and prospecting – we can get stuck, like sitting plonked alone on a seesaw, feet on the ground. Balancing past and present is a lot more fun, and each rise and fall brings fresh air, a new view.

And, just as a broader understanding of a country comes through its history, understanding its people, through their stories and heritage, is the same.

Chapter 2 – Zambia, 1971

Though I was only twenty-three, my Hong Kong experience made it surprisingly easy to find a job in Africa. I saw Africa as one place, rather than a jigsaw of shades and languages, religions and cultures, each country unique. I was blasé and took the first offer that matched my criteria, which was to work for a black African. The job, financed by Britain's Commonwealth Development Corporation, was as secretary to the chairman of Chilanga Cement, and based just outside Zambia's capital, Lusaka.

I packed up in Hong Kong and returned to England to exchange my wetsuit and thongs for safari shirts and desert boots, oblivious that the move from Asia to Central Africa needed much more than a change of wardrobe.

With my contract came a copy of *The Zambia Tourist Guide* with cliché pictures of big game, African dancers and copper mines. It said that, while Zambians might not have the exuberance of Mexicans, they glowed with goodwill. The exuberant Mexican connection was hard to fathom – Mexico being so very far removed – but I had happily set off for a country where its citizens glowed with goodwill.

My flight from Heathrow to Lusaka refuelled at Entebbe. Cocks were crowing in the distance as I walked across the warm tarmac, excited to breathe in the scent of Africa before reboarding for the last leg of my long journey. On take-off, we banked steeply over Lake Victoria, a huge expanse of freshwater, which had a flat and desolate dawn look.

For weeks, I'd studied a wall map of the three once-British countries of Central Africa: Zambia, Malawi and Rhodesia,

Chapter 2 – Zambia, 1971

linked by old colonial connections, as well as by geography and ethnicity. I wanted to visit them all.

Zambia and Malawi had gained their independence from Britain in 1964, while the white-minority government of Rhodesia had taken matters into its own hands the following year and declared it for themselves.

From my map, I'd dubbed the nation shapes like organs bundled inside the ribcage of Africa: Zambia, a reclining kidney, Malawi, an appendix and, to the south, Rhodesia in the pink shape of a bleeding heart. Just as an anatomy student finds a brightly coloured diagram of the brain turns to a homogeneous grey reality, viewed through the plane window, my coloured maps turned to undulating thorny tan without end.

There was nothing to indicate borders drawn arbitrarily seventy years before by colonial draftsmen when the scramble for Africa began. The 'scramble' was a grab of vast tracts of the African continent by European powers following the steps of early explorers. To avoid war between them, the heist was validated when the nations sat down at the Berlin Conference in 1884 to agree on the division of the spoils. There were two rules. There had to be a request for protection by the territory leader formalised by a paper treaty and there had to be occupation.

Thus began the rush – mainly by commercial interests – to woo the leaders of Africa's interior with guns and trinkets, obtaining marks and seals on paper before carving up the continent. Some borders followed rivers while others were along the straight edge of their rulers. Pencilled lines had made indelible incisions, bisecting stomping grounds, sovereignty, neighbours and habitats. Early chroniclers invented histories and explorers gave modish aliases to places that already had names.

Even when I arrived in the early 1970s, any narratives available in print were written for European consumption with little interest in illuminating positive aspects of African culture and governance. After independence, towns and places reverted to old names and slowly histories were rewritten. Yet the sharpened lead of cartographers endured. No amount of rubbing out could shift border lines; those were there to stay.

Britain's unsolicited gift to its colonies at Independence was a Westminster-style democracy. For Zambia it was an altogether new concept, not something the British had ever practised in the colony. It was a bit like your granny leaving you her favourite armchair and making you promise never to get rid of it, only for you to discover that it didn't fit your décor at all and was terribly uncomfortable.

Zambia gave me a jolt. It was not that Zambia itself was wanting. I had no one to admonish; it was my misstep. I'd left a teeming, booming, multicultural tropical island and arrived on the high empty plateau of Central Africa to a sparsely populated, landlocked country where the first division was by race. There was little sign of the mixed society I'd imagined, largely because, at independence, only 800 Zambians had finished high school and the number of university graduates were estimated to be less than my ten fingers. Landing in Lusaka felt like missing a bottom step.

On arrival, the flight's passengers quickly dispersed from the modern and breezy customs hall, leaving me alone at immigration, where an official took issue with my health documents. A toothpick jiggled between his teeth. Every few seconds, he allowed it to rest on his lower lip and, as it started to fall, flicked out his tongue like a flycatcher's.

Waiting to pick me up, Cynthia, the Australian girl I was replacing, was outside with her friend, Roger, an Englishman. They stood in the sun, beyond the barrier, growing hot and impatient. Roger made stage whispers, "It's nothing that a few

Chapter 2 – Zambia, 1971

greenbacks won't fix."

"What?" I hissed back, "Bribe him?"

"Yeah... just flash a few."

So, I did. Surprising myself. Notching up a first.

The official withdrew the toothpick and scrutinised its bloody tip before he swiped the US dollars into his palm and stamped my passport so hard that the pens on the counter bounced and rolled.

"Thank you," I said breathless, despite no exertion.

He nodded and returned the pick to his teeth.

As we drove off, disconcerted by that strange impasse, I stared out the car window at the flat scrub chromed by an African sky and monotonous as hell.

Disquieted on arrival, I told myself I was just tired; the glow was surely waiting, just as the exuberance was indeed wanting.

Cynthia prattled away, craning her neck to speak to me from the front seat.

"You're taking over my house; it's fully furnished. You'll need to get a guard dog and a car this week. Emson, my houseboy will stay on. He's paid to the end of the month and, if you pay him, too, that'll give him a bonus."

My heels dug down, the skin of my calves sticking to the hot vinyl car seat. It was too much, too soon.

"I don't need a servant," I said, while my brain disputed the need to buy a dog and car together. I didn't like non sequiturs. Was it a one-stop car and dog shop?

The breeze forced through the quarter-light and caught Cynthia's hair, streaming it copper in the sunlight. She was still going.

"Oh gawd! He's halfway through paying for his wife. How awful. I've told him you'll take him on. Why wouldn't you?"

Roger chipped in, "Without him, you'll get cleaned out in a week."

"It's like a social obligation," explained Cynthia, "it didn't occur to me you wouldn't."

Chilanga Village, a soothing flash of cream bungalows under tresses of scarlet and purple bougainvillea, interrupted a straight road that ran through rolling scrub. Home to Chilanga Cement's African executive, expatriates and some government employees, it had a shop, a club, a swimming pool, tennis courts and a bowling green dotted with small brown mounds.

"Once the finest green in the country," Roger remarked, gesturing towards the molehills. "Well, it was before independence. Before the place fell to pieces."

Over the next year, most expats would repeat that exact phrase each time they drove past the bowling club. Those moles triggered some haunting nostalgia for Britain's capacity to create smooth and pleasant greens in lands so far from 'home'.

When we turned into the driveway of a two-bedroom bungalow, I was pleasantly surprised: it was much bigger than I expected. In Hong Kong, I'd shared a shoebox.

Emson, a skinny teenager, greeted us at the house. Cynthia had told him the new madam would take him on. There was no further discussion. I got Emson, the house, the furniture and a new mellow-yellow VW 1300 Beetle, the only car available under the company loan scheme. At least I would get to choose the dog, I thought.

Not so. There was only one at the dog pound, a dumb-looking cross between a Boxer and a Ridgeback. Her sable coat lacklustre, her eyes too far apart, one of them a little milky. We stared at each other.

Her minder, a volunteer, said, "Oh, there's a story there. She was found in the bush and adopted briefly by an English family until she ate the cat. Has a thing about cats. Can't stand them. They said otherwise she's a super dog."

Chapter 2 – Zambia, 1971

I looked at her more closely.

"Did you really eat the cat or just kill it?" I whispered.

Her minder butted in. "Killed. Ate. Same diff, the cat is definitely no more. I think she's actually a sweetheart; bit cowed, though, not sure she's much of a guard dog. Her name's Beauty."

I turned to him in disbelief, and we both laughed.

"Well, it's curtains for her in two days," he said.

Beauty cocked her head. Her good eye was the deepest brown I had ever seen. Like liquid mahogany.

"I'll take her."

Beauty grinned, her stumped tail quivering with excitement.

The next morning, Beauty pottered gingerly out to the struggle of vegetables in my backyard, where she squatted beside a poinsettia tree. My neighbours' dogs, Fritz the Alsatian and Zud the Rottweiler, flew over, skidding to a stop at their fences in a cloud of dust, ferocious and vocal. Beauty bolted past me just as Emson arrived for work. She stood trembling, her wet nose touching the back of my knees.

Emson laughed. "Madam, he is *not* a guard dog."

"He is a *she*," I said.

Minutes later, Andy Malcolm, the Scottish building foreman, arrived with his carpenters to install bookshelves and a telephone. Beauty quivered as the workmen shuffled past.

Andy said because I was such a 'young 'un', my recruiters insisted I have a telephone. He laughed, pointing out the window, "But nae lines up there!"

Surely, I had misunderstood. I watched Andy put a socket in the wall and wire in the phone. Emson picked up the handset with a certain reverence, held it to his ear, then shook the handset as if to prompt a dial tone. I went outside and, sure enough, there were no telephone wires to my house or anyone else's. Not a pole or line in sight.

As Andy left, he offered me one of his young Dobermans, "I dinnae think that dog of yours will give ye proper protection."

I refused politely. He went off shaking his head, "Aye, well, the offer's there."

My telephone was a great icebreaker when I had dinner parties and almost always there'd be a few locals craning their heads to look out my window, wondering if they'd missed a trick.

Beauty didn't walk, she bustled; the ridge of hair that ran up her back in the opposite direction to the rest of her coat was ridiculously wide, more like a landing strip. It reminded me that this pudgy, ugly dog was descended from the ridged hunting dogs, pride of the Hottentots. Unlike so many white men's dogs in Africa, she was no racist, for which I was grateful. She had her foibles – a distant rumble of thunder and she'd dash to the fireplace to scrabble up the chimney, only the back of her shivering hind legs visible. Afterwards, she'd emerge, feeling a little foolish, and run round the house, yapping madly in post-traumatic frolic, spreading soot in all directions. Yet, from the very first morning she greeted me, squirming with pent-up jubilation, I beamed back at her with ridiculous pleasure.

Beauty became my fierce and loyal friend and would, I am sure, have defended me from all comers unless burglers came during a thunderstorm – or with a cat.

In Chilanga, I was whisked into a warm, amiable and self-satisfied expatriate community where the conversation churned over chaotic Zambian politics, ineptitude and shortages. Few could refer to an African without a slur. And it was clear the slang was not only horribly catchy; it was entry to a social league. I balked and pussyfooted, observing, demurring lightly, for I wasn't brought up to make a noise.

"It was originally a Zulu word (or a Xhosa word)."

Chapter 2 – Zambia, 1971

Or,

"It's what they call themselves, for Christ's sake!"

My clucking protests were met with jocularity.

"Ho, ho, you'll come round, Gill, you'll see."

I was also welcomed as a good bet for babysitting small pink babies and toddlers. There, I was adamant. It was, I said, not something I did.

Chapter 3 – Chilanga Cement

I was introduced to Mr Muchangwe, the chairman of Chilanga Cement, on the day I arrived. He'd been one of Zambia's few tertiary graduates at independence. A degree in agronomy from the University of Trinidad had given him government tenure, until tribal or political shuffling had seen him moved from the Ministry of Agriculture to the cement factory. It was neither a promotion nor a sinecure.

He was a tall, fine-featured man with a wrestler's neck. In company, he stood motionless and spoke little. He moved erect, all torso, his limbs strangely rigid. His presence charged the atmosphere around him, making toadies of all his staff, regardless of race. I had the feeling that he observed us minutely and was privy to our innermost thoughts.

On my first day, I cleaned my office and threw out the pile of well-thumbed magazines Cynthia had left me for the 'quiet spells'. It was an airy, sunny space, the anteroom to the chairman's office.

Mid-morning, I knocked and asked the chairman if he needed me. He shook his head, so I went next door to ask Ken, the chief accountant, if he wanted anything done.

"Not really."

Mr Von Baldass? He was our technical manager, a taciturn middle-aged Austrian.

"Thank you, Miss Stevenson. I will keep your kind offer in mind."

Mr Motondo? He was the company secretary, a Zambian of the Lozi tribe from Barotseland. He looked frankly alarmed, "Oh no, Miss Stevenson, we are all very competent."

I went off to see Mr Nkonde in Personnel. He beamed his broad, reassuring smile, "Oh, Miss Stevenson, just relax. There will be plenty of work."

A day or so later, Mr Nkonde arranged a trip to Ndola, in Zambia's north, to visit the Company's Copper Belt operation. No one seemed to think it was exceptional that, only ten days after I'd arrived in Zambia, I was to drive there on my own. Maybe it was just to give me something to do.

"Keep filling up as you go," warned Ken. "Petrol stations run out, and it's a bugger to be stranded."

I bet it is, I thought, trying not to feel apprehensive.

"Oh, and another thing, if you *do* run over anyone, don't stop. Drive on to the nearest police station."

"Run over someone?!"

"Kids, drunks – easily happens in Africa, but don't stop! You could get beaten up or worse."

I was to stay the night in Ndola with the English works manager, Mr Dewey, and his wife.

"Calls himself 'Blue Leader'," Ken said. "Talks wartime slang. Flew kites in the war." And seeing my puzzled look, he explained, "He's ex-RAF. Spitfires, I think. If you want to get on his good side, end your phone calls 'over and out'. He likes that. The man's quite mad."

As I turned to go, Ken said, "And another thing… when he tells you that Baldass is a Nazi war criminal on the run with stolen artworks under his bed, next stop Argentina – it's bullshit."

Beauty and I made an early start to drive the 350 kilometres to Ndola. I sang as I drove and Beauty listened intently with her head first on one side, then the other. She was the ideal companion, solicitous for my welfare, without a word to say.

Ken had scribbled Dew Drop Inn on the map. I thought he was jesting, until I found the board outside the house, swinging, like an English pub sign. A motherly Mrs Dewey came out to greet me.

Her expression froze when she saw Beauty.

"How is your dog with cats?" she asked.

Smudge was black and white, a long-haired, luxurious cat, hailing like her owners from Middle England. I left Beauty in the car with a bowl of water and the windows wound down a fraction.

Mr Dewey arrived to collect me with an American aid adviser already in the front seat. We'd do the works tour together, said Mr Dewey, for he was a bit short on time as there was trouble at the works.

"The kaffirs are being naughty. They've broken the windows at the canteen because there's no bread," he said.

I gulped, staring at the back of his thick red neck. The aid adviser glanced round to catch my eye.

"Not my fault there's no bloody grain in the country," added Mr Dewey, with a grin, for he had enjoyed knocking us both speechless.

The works tour was peppered with more of the same, and, at lunch, the American suggested that Blue Leader should moderate his language.

"Kaffir?" said Dewey. "Just the Arabic term for a non-believer, a non-Muslim, nothing offensive about that. You need to learn the lingo." Then shifting his gaze to address us both, he added, "You're not in Manhattan or Piccadilly now, you know!"

We made mute protest by declining the soft bread rolls served in the executive dining room.

Over breakfast the next morning, Blue Leader gave me the advice I'd been half-expecting.

"Don't let Baron von Bad Ass breathe down your neck. We beat 'em in the last war... He knows the score."

Chapter 3 – Chilanga Cement

I let Beauty out of the car for a stretch in the garden before we made our farewells. She tore around like a mad thing, her claws leaving deep scores on the immaculate lawn, and I was only able to pounce on her when she stopped to dig a hole.

"We imported that turf from England, lass," observed Blue Leader. "Not for a kaffir dog to go chewing it to ribbons."

Beauty and I scrambled for our kite, Mr Dewey cleared us for take-off, flaps up and away.

Bravo Beauty, Bravo.

Before heading back, we stopped at the Works because the chairman had asked me to give the company's training manager a lift to Chilanga.

"That way," said the chairman, "Mr Chisashi will be home a day earlier for his wife and children."

Once in the car, Mr Chisashi fiddled with my radio, surfing the static to arrive at Zairean pop music, then he maxed the volume. He helped me drive, too, lunging across to sound the horn at pedestrians and cyclists. Onlookers gaped at a young white madam in her shiny car, music blaring, honking along the road. I drove out past Ndola's slummy edges with Beauty filling my rear-view mirror, keen to make sure I was on the right route. At first, I imagined it was her muzzle resting on my neck, until I realised it was a soft human caress, not Beauty's moist and bristly snout.

As I removed his hand for the second time, Mr Chisashi said, "Oh, so you don't like to be touched by a *black* man?"

My hands wobbled on the steering wheel as I held my breath behind an overcrowded bus that listed and crabbed round a corner, threatening to dump the passengers' surfing mattresses on its roof. I scrambled to comprehend how my rejecting a married man feeling me up an hour after we'd met labelled me a racist.

I switched our conversation, avowing a sudden interest in Zambian politics. I said I admired KK, President Kenneth Kaunda, the man who had led Zambia's fight for independence. That hit the mark; Mr Chisashi was passionate about politics. He gave a grim laugh. Zambians, he said, had united to get rid of white rule but now there were different ideas on how to run the country. Kaunda was obstinate and didn't want to have to listen to the Opposition. Mr Chisashi reflected, "He will make Zambia a one-party state; everyone will have to be a member of UNIP – his United National Independence Party. Democracy will be but a dream."

He said censorship and intimidation had already started.

"Just like the British – no difference!" he said.

As long shadows slid across the road, his fingers strayed to my thigh, and he suggested we stop and move to the back seat.

"Take your hand away now, and not on your nelly!" I said firmly.

He took back his fingers, which had inched up under the edge of my skirt and stared down hopefully at his crotch.

"My nelly? What is my nelly?"

The dark dropped and we hunched forward, peering blind beyond the pale crescent of my headlights to the strip of pitch ahead. Driving in Zambia was adventure enough during the day, but at night, unlit vehicles, broken down or moving at snail's pace, made it double jeopardy.

"You'll know if there is an accident," said Mr Chisashi, "you mustn't stop."

"Yes, Ken told me, but you could explain…"

"No, no," he insisted, "this is not about the colour of our skins. We never stop at night on the road."

Trucks heavy with grain rumbled in convey under cover of darkness, their drivers only half-awake. The import of grain was

Chapter 3 – Chilanga Cement

a clandestine operation – officially Zambia didn't trade with apartheid South Africa or rogue Rhodesia.

On the open road, lone Africans walked the tarred strip, legless from chibuku – the local sorghum beer – and wild game made desperate attempts to reassert their hegemony on the highway.

We were pleased to be safely back in Chilanga and shook hands at the end of the journey. The drive had forged a featherweight friendship and ever afterwards, when we met, we'd start laughing, and Mr Chisashi would lean in and say, "I am still available."

My interaction with my new boss settled into four nods a day. One in the morning, two at midday, and a final nod at 5 p.m. Once, late back from lunch, I knocked on his door to apologise.

"Miss Stevenson, if you hadn't told me I would not have known." He added, "You don't need to tell me; I don't mind what hours you keep."

"Thank you, Sir," I said, closing the door softly and wondering what on earth I was doing in Zambia.

If there was no job for me, I needed to make one. When I found that every scrap of paper had been treasured since the company's foundation stone was laid in 1949, and filed alphabetically, land-titles with lunch vouchers, I was in my element. Identifying key documents, colour-coding and archiving were my beat. I emerged each day hot, grubby and satisfied at the growing pile of discarded files. Not so Gilbert, the filing clerk, who grew more taciturn as each empty filing cabinet disappeared into storage, shrinking his domain.

Next, I turned to the typing pool, where half the month was spent addressing envelopes for the shareholders' newsletter. I asked the Commonwealth Office for an addressograph machine so the girls could tackle the backlog of copy-typing. Betty, the pool supervisor, feigned indifference. When the personnel manager, Mr Nkonde (a man of permanent good humour) knocked on my office door and ushered in Gilbert and Betty to read out a statement, I was blindsided, the gist being I was a neo-colonial racist who should go back to her own country on the next plane.

As he waved them out, Mr Nkonde turned to me, "Please don't worry, Miss Stevenson, I know you are not a racist."

Devastated, I flew to Ken. He went to find out what was up and came back laughing. Mr Nkonde, he said, was terrified of the ladies in the typing pool, who were all wives of government officials, and it was not in his best interests to cross them. It was obviously not in mine either.

"What Gilbert and Betty actually think is that you are a white whore, only in Zambia, because no one will marry you. Soon, you'll be too old to make babies, which is what you should be doing instead of stripping honest people of their jobs!" added Ken, laughing so hard he started to cough.

I didn't think it was funny at all.

"What will happen, Ken," I said, biting my lip, "if the chairman hears this?"

"Oh, the chairman knows all about it. Told Mr Nkonde you have his full confidence. Delighted with your initiative. And Nkonde's thrilled it's you doing the stirring."

Ken could see I was quite lost.

"Look, Gill, you need to understand…" He paused to refill his pipe. "Chilanga Cement employs as many people as possible and is grossly inefficient. We proudly produce the most expensive cement on the African continent. The demand is sky-high. We sell everything we make to foreign-aid funded customers who don't care how much they pay. So, the company culture is that as long as things tick over, any idea of streamlining operations or efficiency is redundant!"

I apologised, adding, "I get frustrated watching people do boring jobs. I moved too quickly."

"*No*, that's the thing. If you had waited, you would have realised the difficulties and done nothing." He lit his pipe with a match, puffing several times to get it going, before saying quietly, "Most of us get called racists. And it's inevitable if you try to change anything. It's a completely meaningless epithet. There are some bloody awful racists in Zambia and they are not *all* white."

Fortunately, the works office typists, Flossie and Constance, had my back. They were sassy and fun-loving, and not the wives of anyone of note. They'd delighted in the gossip that I'd fallen foul of their antagonists, the stuck-up staff in head office.

It was with their help that I developed a strangely successful relationship with the Union boss. It started after Emson asked if I would collect his new wife from her village.

My neighbour had plenty to say about this trip. Cheery, rotund and permed, Peggy hailed from Yorkshire. She ran the village shop, played bingo, went to church and took an overly keen interest in my wellbeing. Her conduit to my life was through her house servant, who took tea with Emson.

"Don't you go driving off into the bush with that houseboy of yours to fetch his wife; put your foot down or he'll take you for a mug."

Ignoring her advice, I set off with Emson to his wife's village. The dirt road to Lilayi turned onto smaller and smaller tracks, getting rougher and ruttier, my VW bouncing over dry stream beds and gullies. Just as the thick bush clawed us almost to a halt, we were clear of it and a plain stretched out, honeyed in the afternoon light. Emson pointed towards the indigo hills of the escarpment where a smudge of smoke rose from some huts.

We drove on, cloud-play shifting light over whispering grasses and the hills beyond. Emson was excited. He chattered away, explaining how his wife was helping her mother to pound 'mealies'. Mealie maize, a flour made from corn, was a Zambian staple cooked into a thick porridge called *sadza* and eaten with relish made from meat or fish and vegetables.

It was almost dark by the time we reached the tiny village. Some women and children sat round a fire with just one man – a thin tall figure, all sinew and limbs – the village headman. He rose from a dilapidated deckchair, clapping his hands together in greeting, a wide, well-nigh toothless smile on his weathered face.

After a brief conversation with the women, Emson turned to me, a little downcast, "My wife has gone to fetch water, Madam. She will come soon."

The headman beckoned me to sit on the ground next to him. For nearly an hour, I sat watching the twisting flames of the small fire, the flickering shadows overwrought yet soothing, while Beauty happily joined the scratching chickens, snotty children and scabby pie-dogs that skirted the perimeter of the village. Quite suddenly, three girls filed around one of the huts, each with a water bucket on her head. They seemed to have walked out of eternity, unruffled and enduring, then they spotted me, dissolved into giggles and vanished.

The old man smoked the pungent tobacco Emson had brought him, while the women chatted on. The headman reached for a pile of dried corn husks, deliberately throwing them high into the night air above the fire, showering mealie dust that ignited like glitter. I was mesmerised, not noticing the chill gathering at my back until Emson came to squat beside me, flicking a stick at stray embers. "She is refusing. African wives very silly. I told her to come now, or I will get another wife."

Chapter 3 – Chilanga Cement

The headman frowned. He spoke and one by one, the women got up, left briefly and returned. After their efforts at persuasion failed, it was the headman's turn. He lifted himself out of his chair, each bony limb moving autonomously before regrouping, once he was upright.

It was getting late, and I was worried that Peggy would round up a search party. I'd seen her lace curtains twitch as we left.

Eventually, the headman returned, followed by two girls; the oldest looked about twelve.

"Madam," said Emson, standing and stretching out his hand to help me up, "we can go now."

"Yes, Emson, but where is your wife?"

"That is she," he said, indicating the taller girl.

"But Emson, she is too young."

"Oh, no, Madam, she is right age. She is my wife. The other one is her sister. She will come, too."

Driving home was easier than I thought it would be, for my headlights picked out the track in stark relief. The girls giggled happily the whole way.

As a married man, and my employee, Emson was entitled to a house in the company township but there were no houses as no one ever moved out, even if they left the company. I didn't think that was fair, so I talked to Mr Nkonde who said it was a very sensitive issue but had no solution for me. I started pestering the other African executives about how I could get a house for Emson.

Ken asked for a word with me. He'd heard that I was on the warpath about township housing. Mr Nkonde was nervous as he thought if anyone had the capability of bringing the whole workforce out on strike it was me. Ken said I should drop the matter; it was not our business to interfere. But when I explained that Constance suggested I go to the Union boss, Ken said,

"Hmm… not a bad idea. He's got a reputation, but I find him pretty reasonable."

"What's his reputation?"

"Oh, he's a bit of a racist thug."

Getting up to leave, I said, "We should get on well then."

Ken's bellow of laughter followed me out the door.

The Union boss was Mr Phiri Banda, a heavy middle-aged man with pockmarked jowls. On that first meeting, he leaned back in his chair, squinting at me. He listened, then stubbed out his cigarette, got up and, unhooking his hard hat, said there were no houses available.

Feigning innocence, I'd endeavour to bump into Mr Banda at the Works, or turn up at smoko time. I liked the humour that sparked round the men at smoko, where black and white artisans sat around on crates and benches in the sun, chatting together, drinking sweet milky tea from enamel cups. Soon Mr Banda started to smile even as he shook his head at my approach. After a few weeks, I felt a friendly clap on the back and his voice said, "OK, Stevenson, before you ambush me again…"

I turned, and we both laughed. Emson had his house.

(At Chilanga Cement most people were known by their second names, and I was often addressed as 'Stevenson'.)

Mr Banda became a useful ally, as did Mr Chisashi, for my run-in at Head Office would not be the last time I was labelled a "white whore" at Chilanga. And, each time, the news would fly around the Works, and my friends would have my back, consoling me with mirth and tea. The Union Boss knew that I was given contentious issues to sort out and I, with nothing else to do, was stupid enough to try.

Meanwhile the chairman impressed the government with his fast-track Zambianisation, the replacement of expats by locals, and impressed himself with the number of expatriate staff he commanded. He cleverly achieved both by fudging forms. When I questioned a quarterly return showing my position filled by a Zambian national, he simply said, "To me you are a Zambian," and gave me a rare smile.

Chapter 4 – The Party

I liked the chairman, but he had no job for me, and despite my efforts to be interested in grades of gypsum and limestone, cement manufacturing did not hold me in its thrall. I was desperately lonely, with little social life past married couples. I did push myself out to join clubs and The Amateur Dramatic Society and the Squash Club filled some evenings each month, yet, had I been in Luton or Leeds instead of Lusaka, I'd have seen more diversity. These clubs were solidly expat. The Yacht Club was the most fun and yielded many happy, gin-riddled Saturdays with a bunch of amiable old farts seeking out a site on the banks of the Kafue River for a new clubhouse.

"Too close to the village; everything will get nicked."

"Too far from anywhere, we'll never get staff."

"Too many hippos."

The hippos were lugubrious and ridiculous, water shafting off their heads as they ruptured the still surface, scaring the life out of us, bobbing by in little boats.

The words, "Most dangerous animal in Africa", floated through the air at every sighting. It never varied. Repetition was a white-man-in-Africa thing. Not a broad range of motherhoods, but consistent.

After six months, I was done. I'd declined several jobs to take the Zambian position. One, an American oil company in Libya, said to write to them if I changed my mind.

Well, my mind was changed. I wrote the letter and, to hedge my bets, I took the advice of an old boss, "Get a piece of paper so you don't get paid peanuts working for men with half your brains!" and sent a second letter to a correspondence college.

Chapter 4 – The Party

Three envelopes arrived in my letterbox on the same day in early September. An accounting course, an invitation to make-up a foursome on a camping trip and the offer from Tripoli. I laughed at the sky surmising some cosmic shift. Study could wait; yes to camping, and yes to Tripoli. A new priority was to fast-track some travel, so I asked Connie, a local expat, to join me for a road trip to Malawi.

That weekend, there was a party in the village; an older couple were getting engaged. Although I wanted to put in an appearance, I walked towards the music that flowed from the big house on the hill, with some trepidation for I knew Pete – a divorced Scouse from Liverpool whose wife had gone back to Merseyside with their kids – was going to be there. He'd serviced my brand-new car and cleared out snakes from my garden, which Peggy doubted were in residence. To thank him, I'd invited him for a meal from time to time but was careful never ever to sit on the sofa or anywhere he could sit beside me.

The last time I'd seen him at the Club, beer-bold and self-sorry, he'd waved his bottle of Lion lager in my direction, "Bloody frigid bint!" he'd shouted. "Look, but don't touch, that's 'er."

"Shut your trap, Pete, before I do it for you," growled a voice from the gloom.

As I walked toward the flaming bamboo torches that lit the driveway, my beating heart took courage from the spearheads of liquid gold pirouetting into the velvet night. I relaxed a little – loveliness does that.

Carpe diem. I took a short-cut through the garden, my legs brushing grasses, disturbing white moths that fluttered with me towards the lights on the veranda. Martin, our computer guy, beckoned me over to a little group from the office. Someone put a drink in my hand, and I slotted easily into the conversation. I was sitting facing open French windows, so I could not avoid seeing a tall guy pause in the doorway, scan the veranda, and then head straight for me. He held a beer in one hand and with the other, picked up a chair, spun it and threw his leg over the seat. Resting his arms on the backrest, he said, "Hello, I'm Mike, and you must be Stevenson. The whole of Chilanga has said I have to meet you."

I didn't let on that I knew who he was, too. Peggy had said, "Have you met Mike? He's single. Got a really dry sense of humour. Drives a beat-up old Ford."

And Ken too, "Have you come across Mike yet? The young tsetse guy who comes into the village every few months?"

"I don't think so."

"Oh, you'd know if you had. He cuts his hair once a year. It was an Afro at last sighting. Wears bangles. And very short shorts."

"Nope, sounds as if he'd be hard to miss." And, I thought, not my type.

Yet, before me, was a tanned, clean-shaven guy with classic good looks, dressed conventionally in a navy blazer. There *was* something weird, though, about his hair. It was very long and shot straight back to erupt in a mob of curls. There was a bit of a dandy about him. An entomologist from Devon, he'd worked for three years in Barotseland, in Zambia's Western Province.

I told my story, that having been in Zambia for six months, I was moving to Libya in the New Year.

Guests moved in and out of our lively circle, save Mike who did not leave my side except to fetch refreshments from the buffet. Once, with a slight jerk of his head, he asked me sotto voce, "Is he a friend of yours?"

I looked inside and saw Pete, leaning on the bar, glaring at us.

When Mike asked me to dance – and then to dance every dance – Connie, inexplicably burst into tears, and left. Peggy kept winking at me and seemed terribly pleased with herself.

Mike and I left with other stragglers at dawn, and he invited me for breakfast. His house was the standard Chilanga bungalow. I'd driven past it every day. On the coffee table were copies of *Private Eye*, Britain's left-leaning, satirical magazine. My Dad equated it with *Socialist Worker* or the *Morning Star*.

The walls were smudge grey with sully pink ceilings. The TV listed short of the foot on one leg. Mike saw me look at it and said, "Oh it's broken."

I wondered why he didn't throw it out, and if he'd chosen the colour scheme. Ambiance is important to me; I'd delighted in furnishing my house simply. Dried seed pods and grasses collected on my walks graced fat-bellied African clay pots. I was pleased with the rough carvings made by a rheumy-eyed old man who sat surrounded by wood shavings and tins of boot polish on the corner where the road turned off to Chilanga. Andy Malcolm grumbled before he turned them into table lights. And I'd made cushion covers in vibrant colours echoing bougainvillea.

There was there was nothing lovely in Mike's house. An X-ray of his chest curled round a tack on one wall, while Sellotape fastened a torn picture of John Wayne to another.

I left Mike to go sailing that morning, agreeing to meet in the afternoon for a walk to the bulrush ponds. Beauty was young enough at heart to frolic with Mike's Alsatian, George, still a puppy, all paws and ears. We spoke of Africa. Mike's Zambia was the one where thorn-trees and baobabs hosted fish eagles and long grass hid guinea fowl, warthogs and impala. He ran an international rattle-bag of pilots and engineers who flew in for the tsetse spray season. The crop dusters sprayed insecticide on swathes of Zambian countryside in the fight against tsetse, a large biting fly that was endemic in much of Africa, decimating cattle herds and spreading sleeping sickness among villagers. The spray team, a close-knit group of men, bummed around the bush together and, between spray runs, propped up the bars of whatever joint was lucky or unlucky enough to have them, drinking huge quantities of Zambian beer.

We had an early supper at my house. Mike left at dusk; he needed a few hours' sleep before he set off in the small hours of the morning to get back to work. I walked a little way down the hill to the tennis courts with him, the barking hounds restless as it was late for good boy scouts to be about. The air was soft, and soon the dark would drop like a shutter. Mike wrapped his arms, his long, long arms, around me. I leaned into him tired, content and happy. He took a strand of hair, pushing it gently behind my ear, and kissed me, "I don't know when I'll be back. We're over three hundred miles out."

Although our time together had been so short, I'd changed my first impression. It helped to learn his truly strange hair was an experiment with hair-straightener he'd bought from an African store and applied liberally to the front of his scalp, to stop the blonde corkscrew curls falling in his eyes. I'd laughed at that. I'd laughed a lot. He was actually rather nice… But I wanted no misunderstanding, so I put my hands on his shoulders to blurt out that I was going on a blind date, camping, in case he came back and found my house empty. I heard the words vibrate in my throat, sounding quaintly presumptuous.

Mike rocked back on his heels. Then he laughed, "Don't let the grass grow under your feet on my account, I won't be back for weeks," and off he went, whistling to his dog, and disappeared with scarcely a backward wave, George bounding after him, his coppered fur hijacking the last light of the day.

I stood bewildered. Beauty whimpered; she wanted to follow George. She jumped up and I caught her paws.

"Well, sod you, Mike Shaddick," I said softly, *"Don't let the*

Chapter 4 – The Party

grass grow... I won't."

Two days later, I was home for my lunchbreak, reading my book when I heard barking. I glanced out the window. There was Mike walking up the drive with Beauty leaping up to greet him.

"Madam," Emson called. "There is a man to see you."

Mike twirled a red rose and passed it to me awkwardly.

"Had to come back to Chilanga unexpectedly. Something came up."

I believed him.

"Wondered, since I'm here, if you'd like dinner tonight?"

There was never a dinner like it before and there could never, ever be one again. Mike had booked a table by the dance floor of Lusaka's Ridgeway Hotel. As the night wore on, the other diners disappeared from view, leaving only the band playing and the African waiters, hovering, attentive, wreathed in smiles.

Did we have four courses or was it five? No number of courses would have sufficed for all we had to say. Mike ordered a different wine for every course. I don't remember what we had with the entree, but the wine we drank with our steak was French, Champagne with the strawberries and Crêpes Suzette, a glass of Noble Rot with our cheese, and of course a Cognac with our coffee.

Mike took my arm as we walked across the carpark, still talking, and we were still talking when the floodlit smokestacks of Chilanga Cement came into view belching clouds of pale dust into the night. Then he was gone again.

I did go camping and met an interesting, complex, nice guy. He asked me to dinner, but he was too late. And my trip to Malawi with Connie? That was a little strained, for, at the mention of Mike's name, Connie fell pointedly silent.

It was Mike who'd told us both not to miss the Luangwa National Park in Eastern Zambia on our way home. We reached the viewpoint in late afternoon and watched the game coming down to the river to quench their thirst after a long, hot day. The water, translucent blue-green, fringed with sandbanks, curled across the bush like swirls on an artist's palette. It was one of the most beautiful sights I had ever seen.

We were booked in at the resthouse but on arrival, found our accommodation had been commandeered by government ministers, not an uncommon occurrence in Zambia. The warden took pity on us and had camp beds put up in his office, a building set a little apart from the resthouse. There was one problem: a lion. It was hanging around the camp area at night. There had been spoor outside the office several times, and an attack at the game rangers' village nearby. The warden was awaiting permission to shoot it. The warden said he would escort us to the toilet block at 9 p.m. but, after that, we should keep the windows and door shut until he came in the morning. Try that. I attempted distraction – swatting insects, patching holes in the mosquito nets with sticky tape – by candlelight in the hot stuffy room. There was nothing I could do, though; I needed another wee.

"But you went already!" said Connie.

We gingerly opened the door and Connie stood with a torch while I sprinted the interminable distance to the toilet block. Did the lion lurk there at night? Did he lap from the toilet bowls? If I was in the cubicle, would he launch himself from above or lie in wait at the door? It was the quickest wee ever, which was, perhaps, why I woke a couple of hours later, sweating, itching, and dying for another.

As soon as the toilet block beckoned through the misty blush of dawn, I was off like a shot. Somehow, the idea that I'd see the man-eater made it OK. Connie had a cast-iron bladder and made a stately exit with her pink towel and portmanteau-

Chapter 4 – The Party

sized toilet bag sometime later, accompanied by the warden.

It was still early when we left the park and, after twenty minutes or so, we pulled up to let a herd of giraffe cross the dirt road ahead of us. Emerging out of scrub, unconcerned, they moved slowly, with grace and dignity, consecrated by the early rays of sun. I felt I had witnessed the dawn of life itself that morning. We sat watching, stilled, hardly breathing, until they disappeared out of view. Then, suddenly, I was itching to get home.

The following day the first rains of the season arrived. They swept over the land, pounding the gasping dry dirt to mud, liberating a balm of optimism and promise from the shed flowers, toil and sweat, dung and cinders, of an old, old land. The libation drummed an incantation. Beauty and I danced in the garden, panting together in the unforgettable sweet damp fragrance of Africa.

With the rains, Mike arrived and swept me into his arms. There was no discussion, and he never stayed more than a day or two. Once he was gone, I had no way of knowing when he would be back. Just a glorious arriving. I'd hear footsteps on the stairs outside my office, and my heart would stop waiting to hear his voice calling greetings to Mr Motondo and Mr Nkonde, and he'd appear at my office door, sweaty, dusty and eager for me to finish work early. Or I might arrive home to find him cooking in my kitchen. Or in my shower.

One day, I found a total stranger in the bath, "I'm Stewart, I work with Mike... he said you wouldn't mind – his hot water's on the blink!"

Chapter 5 – Love in Six Weeks

Whenever Mike left Chilanga, the very sun would dim. I had always been a bit awkward in my skin. I blamed my mildly Presbyterian upbringing and one rotten headmistress. Neither suggested having a high opinion of self was worthy, so I got on with life and walked ahead without too much self-absorption. At school, lessons transited my brain rather than took lodgings. Mike, on the other hand, was classically well-educated, retentive of knowledge, and self-assured. I likened him to a Greek god – bronzed, corkscrew curls and long limbs – he was gorgeous. Mike unwittingly unnerved me for he didn't need anything. He had an answer for bloody everything. What would a Greek god see in me?

One evening, Peggy's voice, calling out to borrow eggs, interrupted my thoughts. I went out to meet her.

"Mike's been in Chilanga a lot. Not like before when we saw him once in a blue moon. I asked him why? He said it's just temporary, has paperwork to catch up on because of his promotion."

"Oh," I said, "really?"

The conversation unnerved me. And that night, I determined to take hold of myself, slow down this mad romance. I focused on visions of Tripoli and my new life looming in North Africa. The Mediterranean, here I come. Bright lights and desert nights. A rich mix of ethnicities and history. Leptis Magna, Phoenicians, Greeks, Romans, Turks, Berbers and Moors, and Italians.

And then Mike was back. He invited me to lunch with friends. His car was in dock, so would I drive him to the Greek vegetable market? On the way, Mike reached over and put his hand affectionately on my knee. It's surprising I didn't swerve and kill us. The combustion of that moment could easily have done it. I said nothing, yet from thereon, I was lost, powerless to withdraw.

The vegetables and meat bought, we went home where Mike cooked, engrossed in that alchemy, until his friends arrived.

Nick, Mike's fellow entomologist, was a shade uneasy.

"Ahh…" he said when he met me. He'd been wondering why his white-men-drinking-beer-in-Africa time had been curtailed by Mike's dashes back to Chilanga.

Dick and Marilyn, both from Yorkshire, had met Mike years before on the banks of the Zambezi near Sesheke, where they were high school teachers.

"He was sitting in the deep shade of a huge acacia tree next to a beaten-up government Land-Rover, looking for all the world as if he had just trekked the length of Africa. His blond, curly hair was like a beehive and he was brown as a berry. He looked glum," said Dick pausing for a swig of beer.

"We, of course, enquired of a fellow honky why he sat looking like the wild man of Borneo desolate under a tree and he answered, 'The pontoon's buggered… I've been here three days'."

Dick and Marilyn had also come to cross on the pontoon, and with no sign of repair in sight, the three of them returned to Sesheke.

Marilyn chipped in, "We offered him tea but that did little to raise his spirits. He suggested an early-morning beer might hit the spot. So, we sat and drank beer for a week until the pontoon was repaired, and we've been friends ever since."

Dick told me more about Mike that day than I would have heard from the man himself in a year. How his schoolmates had nicknamed him 'Prof' because he knew more than the teachers. How his kind and hapless father, George, after years cajoling headmasters to keep the rebellious teenager at school, had to keep turning up at the local nick on Sunday mornings to bail Mike out after minor misdemeanours.

"Like what?" I said, astonished.

"Oh," said Dick, "stuff that Marilyn and I – we are a couple of years younger and, shall we say, more mainstream – didn't know was possible without hellfire and damnation. Borrowing cars without the owners knowing, and then running over a policeman's foot once, which didn't go down well."

Now Dick started laughing, "Evidently, the final time when the police came to the door to say Mike was at the station, George said, 'Well enough, you can keep the bugger'."

Dick said it was the first time they had ever met anyone who drank neat Scotch at six in the morning, "Just to keep the cold out, Mike would say, although the temperature in Barotseland seldom dipped much below thirty degrees."

Others arrived. All ex-grammar school with university degrees and quick wits. I felt out of my depth.

I wept into my pillow that night. If this was love, I didn't want it. I hardly knew him. I didn't fit.

The next morning was Sunday, and I came back from taking Beauty for her morning romp to the bulrush ponds to find Mike making coffee in my kitchen.

"I really want you to see Kanja. Can you get the day off work tomorrow?"

I knew Kanja was the village on the Zambezi River where Mike had lived in the bush before his promotion.

I took a day off work, and Don, a Canadian pilot, flew us to Kanja in one of the spray planes. On approach, he aborted the landing, shouting above the aircraft noise to Mike that there were too many anthills on the grass airstrip.

Mike shouted, "They're just molehills; they're soft."

Chapter 5 – Love in Six Weeks

"Do you get moles in Africa?" said Don, turning to me in the seat beside him.

I was about to tell him about the Chilanga bowling club when Mike shouted from behind us, "Buggered if I know, but they're not hard like anthills, trust me, I built this bloody strip."

"OK, Mike, on your head be it," said Don, gently pushing down the joystick.

I held tight, squeezed my sphincter and closed my eyes. Mike's hands gripped my shoulders and he shouted, "Bonzo!" as we hit the dirt. When I opened my eyes, we were bumping along the grass strip with Africans streaming towards us, whooping and laughing. The villagers swarmed round Mike, telling him their news while Don and I brought up the rear.

Mike's old house, set a little apart from the rondavels of the village, was a small concrete square, its flat roof heaped with untidy thatch. Inside the door was a paraffin chest freezer. Mike shot for the pot when he first arrived in Kanja, butchering small buck for meat until, scouting around the side of a great anthill, he'd come face-to-face with a very large lion.

"I don't know who was more surprised, him or me. We both bolted. The lion's reaction was a dead ringer for mine! In that moment I knew we were made of the same stuff; we had a common destiny. After that, I couldn't shoot anymore, so the game scouts kept me stocked with meat."

That meant Mike never knew what he'd find in his freezer. Once, the head of some poor Duiker, a small antelope, stared up at him. And sometimes the paraffin ran out and everything went off and stank the house out.

"When the river rose, I could fish from my veranda," said Mike looking fondly at the Zambezi. "I was so happy living here, there was only one thing it needed – someone to share it with. I was bloody lonely in Paradise."

Before we took-off, Don walked the strip, kicking the molehills flat. Mike asked that we fly low along the river, over the horseshoe falls of Nyonge, and circle past the Sioma mission where he'd gone when loneliness overwhelmed him. There he could drink warm Scotch with the Irish fathers and return with a hangover to keep him occupied for the next few days.

"There used to be two, but one decided he preferred girls to God and left," said Mike. "And then there was only one."

And we flew over the mission hospital, where he'd gone for rabies vaccine after he'd been scratched by a kitten having a fit. He'd needed a daily shot for two weeks but as it was too far to go to the hospital, he took the vials of vaccine home to his problematic paraffin fridge. He'd injected his abdomen each day with a long needle – a very painful exercise. Mike said he only persevered because he'd read Wilber Smith's *When the Lion Feeds*, where Duff, one of the characters, contracts rabies from the bite of a jackal and goes slowly mad whilst tied to a post. Mike also pointed out the village where his favourite chief lived, the one who had given him the elephant hair bracelet he wore, and another village, where the chief had put an ivory bangle on his wrist – the bangle he had already given to me.

When I drove home from work a few days later, Mike's car was in the shadow of his carport. I knew something was up. I hadn't been his first stop; he hadn't come looking for me. I knocked on his door. He was slouched on his sofa. Said he'd just driven back from Choma, had a thumping headache that ran up the back of his neck, but was glad I had called in as we needed to talk. My stomach convulsed.

"Sit down."

Not even the offer of a drink. As Mike did not invite me to the sofa, I pulled up a dining chair and perched, my ankles twisted round the legs and my arms straight, hands gripping the

Chapter 5 – Love in Six Weeks

chair seat either side. I had no idea what was coming.

Mike looked up, "Relax," he said, without conviction.

"There are a few things you need to know about me."

His words sounded rehearsed.

"After Uni, I took a break. Got a job driving trucks. Made good money and partied hard with a bunch of friends. We all experimented that summer," he said.

"Experimented?" I queried.

He didn't elaborate but kept to his script. It had started at music festivals, smoking pot, taking LSD and munching magic mushrooms. It had been fun.

"At the end of the summer, everyone got proper jobs, except for me and my mate Badger. We were in too deep. We'd 'crossed the Rubicon' and started using heroin."

They'd dropped into a grubby underworld which in hindsight, he said, had no redeeming features. It took two years before Mike pulled himself up and got help.

"I was lucky that I had a good family to go back to. After rehab, I went to University in Trinidad to do my master's," he said. "I knew I had to make a clean break, be broke and be busy."

"And Badger?"

"He got out too."

He finished the conversation, in much the same way as it had begun.

"I have been clean ever since. I just wanted you to know."

I started to get up to go to him but he held up his hand, "First, you must go and think about it. I understand if it changes things between us. Please give yourself time."

Mike's confessional of skeletons over, I went home, poured myself a large gin, called Beauty and walked into the bush with my glass in hand to sit by the bulrush pond. Beauty dashed ahead. When I arrived, she was paddling, snuffling for voles that had already heard her belly flop and were long gone.

A gentle wind rustled through a mealie patch nearby and, turning my head, I could see the blue smoke of cooking fires rising in the distance. African women ambled along the path carrying pots and baskets on their heads with effortless ease, chatting to each other and smiling shyly at me. Their children grinned and waved.

I thought about what Mike had told me.

I, the most conservative, logical, demure damsel, had found more than a hippie. He knew how square I was. I'd never smoked a joint. I'd never got drunk past merry. He could have anticipated that I'd be aghast. He was beyond my experience, outside my realm. It wasn't that I was starstruck in the way everyone loves a bad boy. He was just the most gentle, exciting, funny, madcap of a man, and, if that was his past, then I understood why he was so different to anyone I'd ever encountered.

A mosquito whined in my ear.

"Come on, Beauty," I said, "let's go."

Beauty leapt out of the water, forcing me to jump quickly to avoid a spray of bilharzia-laden droplets. She ran ahead, pausing to check whether we were going to my house or Mike's. Finally, she slowed and skittered beside me, lifting the purple jacaranda blossoms that littered the road before she ran up to Mike's door, pushing it open with her nose.

He was sitting on the sofa just where I had left him an hour before. He rose to his feet and stood. I put my arms around his waist and lifted my lips to his, and he squeezed me so tight I could not breathe.

The next day, we went for a swim in the unlovely cement pool at the Club. I was floating in a black inner tube when Mike's head broke the waters, and he said, "How does the idea of getting married grab you?"

I am all for ambiance. It was a bloody awful place for a proposal.

Chapter 5 – Love in Six Weeks

I said I needed to think about it. We walked to my house in silence. I showered, put on make-up and a strappy little number, and walked through to the kitchen where Mike stood, brewing coffee and communing with Beauty who seemed to know that something momentous was afoot.

"Yes," I said. Anything else was simply out of the question.

Mike pulled me out into the noonday heat, and we ran up the dirt road knocking on the doors of the houses in the village, with Mike shouting, "We're engaged! Gill's going to marry me!" It seemed I was the only person who was surprised.

Mr Motondo gave me a big hug and said, "Your boyfriend is *my* friend, Shadwrack, the good man. I am very happy."

Shadwrack, the good man: it sounded biblical.

A few doors up was Ken's house.

"Stood to reason," he said. "You are the only single girl, and he's the only boy."

I protested that there had been more competition than that, so he added, "Missionary types and divorcees don't count."

When Anne, his wife, hugged me, she said, "Oh, Gill, I envy you! There'll never be a dull moment with that man."

Her prediction was joy to my heart.

Chapter 6 – African Composition

In the weeks that Mike and I had been wrapped up with each other, a political shift had gained momentum. The black expectations of overnight change and the white predictions of inevitable disaster squeezed President Kaunda like a vice. His solution was, as Mr Chisashi had predicted, a one-party state, and this discussion was on everyone's lips.

Bands of men roamed the townships press-ganging everyone into joining UNIP, Kaunda's Party.

Mike arrived home to find them at his house, chasing his house servant, Eddison Banda, around the garden. Eddison was a middle-aged, hard-working man, and Mike liked him a lot.

"Trespass!" Mike roared at the intruders. George started barking madly. The men fled.

Mike poured himself a cold beer and settled down with the newspaper until the screaming started next door.

Eddison and Mike rushed over just as Smithy, a burly white mechanic, rocked up in his ute. The UNIP men were beating his house servant's wife with sticks and a rolled umbrella. Smithy leapt into the fray, shouting "Bugger off!" while Mike and Edison grabbed the poor girl out of the mêlée. This time, the UNIP men stood their ground, surrounding Smithy, demanding *his* UNIP card.

"I'll get it, you bastards," said Smithy, and disappeared inside to return with a revolver in one hand and a machete in the other. The UNIP gang scarpered to the black township nearby where they would have an easier time of it and never came up to the top end of the village where I lived.

I was nervous, questioning whether Mike and Smithy could get into trouble. Mike said the UNIP collectors were

Chapter 6 – African Composition

opportunistic thugs and doubted whether the money collected even got back to party headquarters.

I'd hear more stories about Smithy when Mike and I spent our first Christmas together at Gwena, an old government resthouse on the shores of Lake Kariba.

There was no electricity in the tumbled-down, dry-stone cottage. Its sagging thatch was held together by cascades of plum, heliotrope and magenta bougainvillea. Gwena had settled gently into its twilight years. The wheezing wicker chairs were tipsy on the slumped flagstones. An ancient bath on a plinth was yellowed with rusty stains that disappeared by candlelight. Its neglect made Gwena all the more magical.

That Christmas, Gwena embraced us like some elderly kin; doddering and creaky yet warm and winsome. We were joined by Mike's friends, Nick, Dick and Marilyn, and a couple of other guys, a teacher and a vet. Time passed slowly, a lazy mix of spotting game, water-skiing and tiger fishing. Each sunset was the same but never the same. At each pale opal dawn, fishermen paddled out quietly from the nearby village, their canoes hewn out of single tree trunks.

Marilyn cooked a magnificent Christmas dinner on a wood-fired stove by the light of guttering candles and oil lamps.

The following day when I helped Mike and Nick launch the ski-boat, I heard Nick say, "Doesn't she know?"

Mike whipped round, "Shut up, Nick."

Nick laughed in mock astonishment.

"What are you talking about?" I asked.

"About a rock!" said Nick, shaking with laughter.

With a sharp intake of breath, Mike hit the paddle on the water, splashing him. "Later, Steve," Mike said to me. (Mike nicknamed me 'Steve' or 'Stevie' not long after we met.)

That evening after the candles were lit, Mike was cornered. The tale began when Mike had a few beers with Smithy, his

Chilanga neighbour. Smithy was buying contraband gold bars from a Congolese guy. The heavy ingots were all embossed with the words 'Union Minière', the stamp of the Belgian mining company with a virtual monopoly on Congo gold. Smithy had them stowed beneath his floorboards. He needed to convert the gold into cash and asked if Mike could help. Mike spoke to Nick, and they made a plan to install a false compartment in Nick's Land-Rover, drive through the neighbouring Portuguese colony of Mozambique and ship the vehicle to Lisbon where they'd convert the ingots into cash. Mike was highly enthusiastic about the proposition. He had asked me to marry him, so the extra money would not go wrong. Then Mike had a thought: did the Congolese guy do diamonds? Smithy said he'd find out. A meet-up was arranged in Lusaka.

Nick took up the story. "Mike asked me to be his wingman. He drove and I sat in the back with the money. We pulled up outside the Lusaka Hotel, and two shifty Congolese dudes climbed in, one beside Mike and the other with me. 'Drive!' says the guy in the front."

Nick started to laugh, pausing to fill his glass. "We weren't suckers. We weren't going to be hurried. Mike did a circuit round town. The guy in front took a huge rough-cut diamond from a very grubby handkerchief. Mike examined it briefly, taking his eyes off the road for as long as it takes to make a professional assessment of a five-carat diamond, and nodded to the guy to hand it to me for a second opinion. I agreed it looked OK, and the deal was done."

By now, Nick was snorting with laughter.

"After we dropped the dudes off, we drove round the block a few times to make sure we weren't followed… in case they wanted it back!"

Mike and Nick celebrated at the bar of the Intercontinental Hotel.

After a couple of beers, Mike said, "Let's get a jeweller to cut

Chapter 6 – African Composition

it, and then Gill can choose the setting."

The jeweller removed his eye loupe to glance at the proffered gem, "Quartz," he said, and returned to his work.

"No, check, it's rough cut," urged Mike.

The jeweller sighed and turned his chair to examine it more closely.

"Terrible piece," he said, "if you want quartz, you can buy good stuff."

News of the fake diamond did not augur well for Smithy's stack of gold ingots. The poor man sat uncharacteristically quiet watching Mike drip nitric acid onto one of the bars. It fizzed, releasing tawny fumes of nitrogen peroxide. The metal turned blue. Smithy had a pile of worthless copper under his floorboards.

"I'll be ready for the fucking bastards the next time they come," said Smithy, leaping up and running his hands through his hair. But they never returned. Some bush telegraph warned them the ruse was up.

After our Christmas at Gwena, we all drove to the Chirundu border post and crossed the Zambezi River into Rhodesia. We'd see in the new year of '72 in Salisbury, Rhodesia's capital and then split up to take separate holidays.

Although I could not imagine a better 'diamond' than the legendary piece of quartz, Mike insisted on a "proper" ring. I only looked in one shop because Mike had a terrible headache. We drove on to the Eastern Highlands, renowned for its spectacular scenery of forest-clad mountains, waterfalls and gorges. While Mike slept, drugged with painkillers, I held my hands at 10 to 2 on the steering wheel, watching my 'diamond' flash in the sun.

The following night, we decided to celebrate at a well-known Portuguese restaurant on the Mozambique border. Months back, there had been a couple of ambushes on the road. Later, they'd be recognised as the beginning of the struggle for black majority rule.

We asked the manager of our campsite if the road was safe.

"It's OK as long as you don't stop," he assured us.

We enjoyed excellent earthy food on terracotta pottery. Geckos played in the shadowy thatch of elephant grass above while a capricious breeze flickered the candles that showered wax down fat-bellied Mateus Rosé bottles onto tablecloths of red gingham. It was nearly midnight when the restaurateur farewelled us. He warned, "Insurgents fake accidents to get drivers to stop – don't stop for anything."

The warning made us nervous, and the *vino tinto* made us brave. Mike drove fast on the dark forest road. About halfway, on a downhill stretch, Mike swerved onto the dirt to avoid a body sprawled across the tar strip, then accelerated up the hill ahead and pulled over.

"Was that a trap?" I said, my heart leaping around my chest.

"Well, if it was, it was suicidal. I damn near ran over him."

We swapped seats so that I drove, switching off the headlights and coasting back towards the prone figure while Mike coached me, "If it's an ambush, promise not to stay. Step on it to the restaurant, and they'll radio in the army."

I pulled up and kept the engine running while Mike leapt out and knelt low listening to the man's chest. Then Mike jumped up, grabbing the guy under the arms, dragging him well off the road and propping him up against a tree before jumping back into the car.

"Go!"

I drove off with my heart pounding, "Was he alive?"

"Yes, breathing well, not injured. Reeks of beer." Mike laughed, "He's going to have a terrible hangover tomorrow, but at least he won't get run over."

Chapter 6 – African Composition

We sped back to Umtali on a blast of adrenaline, and the next day we were back at the border. To keep up morale, the Rhodesian government ensured the shops were full of imported goods, despite sanctions. We'd shopped for Nesquik and knitting wool, Scotch and flour; treasures we could not buy in Zambia. The white Rhodesian border guards were stiffly polite but could not hide their resentment.

It was hard to watch expats like us carting hard-won goodies out of the country.

I was surprised at how pleased I felt a few minutes later when the Zambian guards leapt up from where they'd been lounging in camp chairs, their faces wreathed with smiles as they said, "Welcome home, Madam."

I thought about how I'd laughed at the paragraph in the Zambian tourist guide, which said that while Zambians might not have the exuberance of Mexicans, they glowed with goodwill. These lovely guys had both.

A few days later, Mike asked me to help him with a car drop. Nick, who had been on holiday to the Serengeti National Park, had asked Mike to park his Land-Rover at Lusaka Airport ready for him to drive home when he got off his late flight from Arusha.

Mike drove Nick's Land-Rover and asked me to follow in my VW. The final stretch of road to the airport was a narrow and straight tar strip that ran for miles across empty scrub. Up ahead, I saw shapes shimmering in the heat that began to squirm and heighten, coalescing into a slalom of oil drums and figures as I got nearer. A police road-block. Mike's vehicle had government number plates so was waved through. I was flagged down. The young constable pointed to my windscreen. I knew the problem. The suction on my registration disc hadn't withstood the heat on the bumpy road. I stretched down, grabbed the disc and slapped it back on the windscreen.

"Sorry, Constable," I said.

Out of the corner of my eye I saw another policeman rise from his camp chair. Moments later, he leaned into my window. He had mirror sunglasses and spoke loudly, for his words were not meant for me alone.

"Eh, how can we condone this? And you, you are a European woman!"

I apologised again when a shout from the eager constable focused all five policemen on my back tyre.

I got out and joined them. The tyre was badly worn.

"Ahh… and now this!" said the senior policeman, winding up. "You are white, and you think you can do this?"

I had no excuse. "Officer, I do apologise…"

He cut me off.

"You think that to say sorry is enough! It is your attitude that is the problem. Because of the colour of your skin, you think you can drive in Zambia with no registration and a tyre like that!"

It was disconcerting not to be able to see his eyes but rather a reflection of myself. Repeating apologies, I said, "My boyfriend, the one in the government Land-Rover… He's at the airport, he will help me change the tyre."

The policeman pursed his lips, raised his chin and looked heavenward, his mirror lenses flashing me an arc of corn stubble and blue sky, then pivoted his head forward until I was again looking at myself.

"OK, you go and do it, or I will arrest you, and you will spend a night in jail!"

I drove off glancing in my rear-view mirror till the shapes behind fused and folded back into the yellow corn grass. Nick's Land-Rover came flying down the road towards me. Mike pulled over and jumped out. God, he was good looking.

"Stevie, I am sorry I was slow turning back. I was bloody

Chapter 6 – African Composition

lucky they waved me through. I don't have the papers for this Land-Rover and, if they'd checked, you'd have had to bail me out for stealing a government vehicle! I never thought they'd nab you."

"It was my own fault. I've got a ropey spare that I should have swapped after my last puncture."

We drove in tandem through the airport's dilapidated wire mesh gates, forever open and askew, sewn to the ground by rough grass and stray mealie stalks.

I parked and started to unpack the jack.

"Bugger that!" said Mike. "We need a drink."

Lusaka Airport was always deserted in-between flights. There was no one in the bar, not even a barman. Mike rapped on the wood. Then, with a wide grin he said, "Self-service!" and threw his long legs over the counter. He took two beers from the fridge and put a kwacha note on the till.

Before he could hop back, the barman arrived, "Boss...!"

"It's OK, just thirsty, you can serve us the next round."

"Come on," I said, "the light's nearly gone, we need to get the tyre changed."

"Na, don't bother, I'll get the workshop to do it for you in the morning."

"I'll get arrested!"

"Let's have another drink, they'll pack up at nightfall, and I'll get the tyre changed tomorrow."

We left after dark. Mike drove, the VW headlights picking out the tar strip and little else.

"Look," I said. "Up ahead, torchlights. They're still there!"

"Oh, bugger! Hold on tight!"

"What...?"

Mike flashed the headlights, blew the horn and put his foot down. Just as we closed in, he switched off the headlights and sped through, weaving between the oil drums that gleamed in the light of a campfire and swinging torches.

Mike was roaring with laughter as he flicked the lights back on.

I was breathless, pressed back against my seat by speed, surprise and terror.

"You could have got us killed or killed someone!" I screamed.

"They're traffic cops. They'll only have today's mealie-meal in their holsters and anyhow, you *never* stop at a roadblock in Africa after dark. Never. They'll be on the local brew, pissed, bored and trouble!"

"It doesn't matter!" I protested.

"Look, they knew we were coming through when I blew the horn and flashed our lights. No one in Africa ever stops at night roadblocks. God, I swear there was a guy in mirror sunglasses and it's dark! Poor blighters, I'll bet no one's remembered they're there!"

By this time, we'd reached the highway and turned towards Lusaka, where concrete poles supporting huge florescent lights made the world look suddenly normal again. Mike turned to look at me.

"Hey, I didn't scare you, did I? Sorry, Steve, I wouldn't ever let anything happen to you. I love you *so* much."

My heart missed another beat.

I never knew what this man would do next. And yet how could I ever imagine anyone in his place. He was possibly as much cowboy as Greek god.

Chapter 7 – Getting Married, 1972

Mike was at the end of his contract, but he'd been offered a second stint in Zambia. He'd found his niche. He had his tribe of odd-bods and misfits out in the bush as well as African chiefs. And each year the spray team gathered, flying their aircraft in from all over the globe, and Mike was in his element, directing the team.

I did not want to stay in Zambia and be part of a white society living in Africa.

Mike respected that but felt he was making a contribution.

"In a few years, Zambian entomologists will be doing my job, and that's as it should be. It's just that right now there are none, and I have this extraordinary opportunity to live here. In my view, there are oafs and pillocks everywhere, and the percentage is pretty constant, regardless of race."

In the end, Mike agreed that we would do something new. We talked of all the places we could go. I wanted to go back east; Mike had never fancied Asia. In the end, we left it to fate.

Hellbent on leaving, I was, in hindsight, a wrecking ball.

In the new year, I told the chairman that I was leaving Zambia to get married. A week later, Mr Nkonde breezed into my office with his big smile even wider to give me news of a substantial pay rise. I apologised, handing back the envelope, embarrassed that he did not know that I had resigned.

Mr Nkonde waved towards the chairman's office door, "You must speak to the chairman, Miss Stevenson," and off he went, leaving me mystified.

I knocked on the door and entered, one of the rare times I was even in his office.

The chairman said, "If you deserve a pay rise, and you do, then you are entitled to it whether you have given notice or not. Thank you, Miss Stevenson."

And with that he put his head down, and I was dismissed, stuttering my thanks as I backed out the door.

There was a raft of farewell gatherings as the spray season drew to its close.

After one with all the pilots and engineers at Lusaka's Intercontinental Hotel, we got back to Mike's house to find Eddison sitting upright on the doorstep, the moonlight glinting on a huge metal cleaver. He'd heard intruders and had chased them off wielding his meat axe. Burglars were fair game compared to UNIP thugs.

The robbers had dropped the loot and the police, who were stationed just round the corner, had gathered it off the driveway. We thanked Eddison and set off to the police station.

The constable in charge was drunk, very drunk. In the gloom, behind the wide counter on a dusty wooden shelf, were Mike's record player, speakers and the contents of his cocktail cabinet.

"Good evening. I am Mike Shaddick," he said, pointing to his stuff on the shelf, using the Nyanja word for possessions, "I'm here to collect my katundu."

"Eh, Mista Shadwick, we cannot give it back to you because it is required for *evidance*," said the policeman with a burp.

"The thieves didn't get away with anything and you haven't a hope in hell of catching anyone, so I'll just take my stuff," said Mike.

The policeman swayed gently, burped again and said, "No, it is *EVI-DANCE!*" quite loudly this time.

Mike screwed up his eyes and peered at the bottles on the shelf.

"Struth, look at the levels of my Scotch!"

Chapter 7 – Getting Married, 1972

Turning to the policeman, Mike bellowed, "It's my bloody stuff, and you're drinking the evidence."

With that, Mike leaned across the counter, grabbed the policeman by his lapels and pulled back. The constable, unsteady on his feet and taken by surprise, slid across the smooth surface like a landed fish. Mike did not expect to make such a big haul so easily and almost lost his balance, hanging on for dear life to the lapels he had grabbed, pulling the man further. The policeman's bloodshot eyes were wide, his mouth opened and closed in surprise, involuntarily belching Johnnie Walker.

"Let go!" I screamed, and Mike released his hold.

The constable slid back onto his feet on his side of the counter. A single fly-blown light bulb swayed gently. Both men were paler now: the African grey, Mike ashen. They breathed heavily. My future spiralled. Would Mike be arrested? Would I marry him in captivity? Did I even want to marry him? Would I be charged as an accessory to assault?

Ignoring me, the two men glared at each other; the colour returning to their faces. Both straightened their lapels. Then each nodded at the other. Mike spun on his heel and left.

I could think of nothing to say except, "Goodnight, constable," before I ran out.

The following evening, there was a loud knock on Mike's door. It was the constable and his sergeant.

"Oh, my God," I said under my breath.

"Mista Shadwick, we have brought you back the *evidance*."

The levels on the Scotch bottles were miraculously restored – albeit a paler drop. The trio joked, as men do. Yes, it is difficult to catch felons; no harm was done, what can you do?

"Please come in and have a drink," said Mike.

The constable slapped his thigh and laughed loudly. "Eh, Mista Shadwick, we policemen cannot drink on duty!"

"See, Steve," said Mike, as he gently closed the door, "you didn't need to get so upset. We were both in the wrong and we both knew it."

For the short time we had left in Chilanga, every time the constable and I saw each other, we both waved over-enthusiastically in greeting.

There were loose ends to tie up before we left Zambia. I needed a home for Beauty. George had been easy to place; he was young and a sought-after breed. There was only one taker for Beauty – a German expat – and I didn't take to him at all.

Sensing my hesitation, Mike told me to make it quick while he got her leash. I hugged her tight, then ran off to throw myself onto my bed. When I heard the car drive off, I wept, burying my head in my pillow. Moments later, Beauty cannoned onto the bed, pushing her nose to my face, licking my tears.

"I knew you felt he wasn't good enough for Beauty," said Mike. "If we can't find better, we will take her with us."

Andy Malcolm stepped in and said he knew an old Boer farmer who wanted a dog for his wife, so we drove out into the scrub for over an hour to find the farm. It was a simple homestead, and the couple were quite elderly and friendly in a reserved way. She spoke no English, but her husband had a bit. He said she just wanted companionship, not a young dog that needed exercise. There was just one question I had to ask. He chuckled, translated what I had said and his wife laughed. She hated cats. Beauty took to her immediately.

Mike and I took three weeks holiday on the way back to UK; the longest continuous time we had spent in each other's company. I boarded our plane with two black eyes I'd gained after playing squash with Dick. His racket had flown from his sweaty hand to smack me across the nose.

Chapter 7 – Getting Married, 1972

Our first stop was Kenya. Nairobi and a life-threatening Rift Valley taxi ride to Kisumu. On to Ethiopia, where horsemen galloped from some wild past to overtake our jeep labouring across deserted plains to visit Coptic churches. In Syria, we were discomforted on a grey day wandering the dingy shambles of the Street Called Straight in Damascus, where Arab traders looked down their long noses, swept off their stools and shadowed us, their incessant heckling refusing us a moment of ease.

Happier in Lebanon visiting the colossal ruins of Roman Baalbek and charmed by the country's biblical coast, we stood together overlooking Tyre's ancient hippodrome, the largest ever unearthed. The site was deserted save for a capricious wind that blew spurts of sandy grit against our legs, the same grit once churned by the wheels of chariots egged on by the roar of twenty-thousand spectators. Sidon's Sea Castle outshone a competitive coastline tangle of half-complete contemporary construction.

We were oblivious witnesses to the end of Beirut's golden age. Although the Civil War would not start for another three years, the city was edgy, so we stayed upmarket in the Phoenicia Hotel. Sous la Mer, its subterranean bar, had a glass wall separating it from the swimming pool. I ran to change and dived down to blow kisses to Mike through the glass. Mike stood gorgeous; smiling, happy, propping up the bar, waving back.

Each day, I anxiously regarded the fading bruises from my black eyes, for I was soon to walk up the aisle. Mike's face was changing too. I am not a fan of facial hair. I don't mind a day's bristle, but I'd met Mike clean-shaven. Mike's long hair had been a small challenge, but this new look was a bigger one. I tried being casual.

"What's with the beard?"

"Ahh, yeah, it's a bit wispy, just give it time."

I tried again the next day. "I'm not sure about the beard."

Mike tilted his head, looking in a mirror. "Umm, it's a bit mottled, wonder where the ginger bits come from... something my parents didn't tell me," he chuckled.

I watched tiny bubbles of foam from his beer and crumbs from his toast attach to his moustache, And kissing…

We flew from Beirut to Frankfurt for our last night on holiday. Getting ready for dinner, Mike commented on his whiskers.

"Do you think if I dyed them, I would look less piebald?"

I asked him to shave. Well, maybe I did not ask – I threw a hissy fit. I couldn't reconcile the man I'd fallen for, long-haired but dapper, with the shaggy head of a piebald pony.

At breakfast, I was still at it. Mike drank his coffee slowly and then excused himself. There was a titter as he returned to the dining room. He had shaved off just the left half of his beard and moustache. I was speechless. Mike stirred amusement and strange looks all the way back to England by train and ferry. Thankfully, he did not have the nonchalance to meet my parents like that. He shaved at a petrol station, by which time I was frantic and fawningly grateful.

We had only ten days in England before the wedding. All I had to do was to meet Mike's parents and get a wedding dress. Mum, who had organised everything else, was calm about the dress until with a week to go, she began to crack. The fates rewarded my optimism. I caught the train up to London, stepped off the tube at Marble Arch and my dress was in the window at C&A, 'Coats & 'Ats', as everyone called the chain, a cheap store that knocked off upmarket designs. It was a white crochet number, exactly what I wanted. Next a dress for my niece, Anne-Marie, who was to be my flower girl. I wanted her dress to be deep pink to match my bouquet of fuchsias. Mum said she thought

Chapter 7 – Getting Married, 1972

this late in the day anything pretty would do. We made a list of bridal shops. It was on the stand of the first one.

"Very unusual colour, isn't it?" said the shop assistant. "It's just a one-off, so I don't have any other sizes."

The size was perfect, and the style was a mirror image of my crochet number.

Mum laughed out loud. "Someone looks out for you!" she said.

Dad was not as relaxed. He baulked when I showed off the white knee-high boots I'd bought. Mum said that a small concession was required as she had already had to calm him down after I'd modelled a straw hat instead of a veil.

On the eve of the wedding, Mum and I shopped for boring sandals. Then we stopped for a drink at the pub. Mum said she had no idea why I was so relaxed. I'd told her I'd have walked up the aisle in a white towel for a toga so happy was I to marry my Greek god. And, I thought to myself, I'd have liked to wear boots, too, for my cowboy.

On the morning of the wedding, after everyone else had left the house for the church, Dad plied me with sherry while the limo ticked over outside. We agreed there was so much to be said and yet we didn't need to say a word. As Dad filled my glass for the third time, I said we really had to go, putting aside my last Amontillado and hugging him tight.

Guests said they had never been to a happier wedding. It was June 1972.

Next, Mike needed a job. An unexpected surfeit of biologists took him by surprise. Despite the rejection letters, we relaxed that lovely summer. We punted on the Cherwell, toasting ourselves with champagne and strawberries, then moved to Devon and rambled over Exmoor, visiting iconic pubs. We even pottered around Europe in the warm, honeyed light of autumn.

There was a job promised by a Swiss company in the new year. If nothing else turned up, there was always that. But, as winter gathered itself grey, wet and dark, we shirked family and friends and all their embarrassing questions, moved to a crummy bedsit in London's Earl's Court and signed up with temp agencies.

A few days before Christmas, sitting close to the gas fire in our bedsit, a slim envelope slipped from the fistful of redirected Christmas cards. I was busy appraising robins and Santas, berries and Balthazars, when I heard Mike murmur an expletive. There was no job with the Swiss company, which cited unforeseen re-organisation.

We left London early in the afternoon to drive to Devon for Christmas. I packed the car while Mike poured boiling water down the windscreen, flashing bright clear fingers into the frost which had not lifted all day. We drove in silence. Unusual for us. About halfway, the sun, taking its thin light early to bed over Dorset, shot beams of silver over fallow fields of pewter and up to the edges of leaden clouds.

Mike said, "Look. A silver lining. Is that a sign for us, Steve?"

"Mike, I have an idea," I said. I was always awash with ideas.

I had an inheritance from my grandparents. There might be enough to buy a small guesthouse. The car ate up the miles as my mouth ran away with me. We didn't need experience. Most places like that were run by couples. We could live where we liked. Be free.

I stopped talking. I twisted in my seat to face Mike. He was quiet. Had he heard?

"Well, a bloody sight better than Earl's Court. You know, that might just work."

We drove strangely detached from the world, wrapped by a blanket of grey fog coiling around us. The warmth of possibilities took hold, and we gabbled together the rest of the way.

Chapter 7 – Getting Married, 1972

In the new year, we pointed our pale blue Citroen Diane north to towns and villages with beguiling names. Our budget limited us to cheap lodging houses, so steeped in stale cigarette smoke and spilt beer that we couldn't envisage living in them. The further north, the more we could buy, so we kept going, over the border into Scotland, and further. Past Loch Rannoch and Inverness. Inevitably, but to our surprise, we arrived at John O'Groats. We could go no further. Or could we?

On a clear blue morning, our car was skilfully hoisted in a rope net and loaded onto the Orkney ferry. And there at the end of the rainbow, we found our dream. A small inn with its own trout lake. The Barony on the shores of Boardhouse Loch in Birsay was about thirty minutes from Kirkwall, the Orkney capital. We shook hands on the deal with the charming owners and headed south in high spirits to sort out our affairs. As we drove, tyre-hum singing our song, we devised menus, ways to win over the locals. I redecorated – out with those stags' heads; Mike would stand for the local council. He'd plant trees, change the landscape. We'd hire a live-in manager and go travelling. We were euphoric when we arrived back in Oxford.

The wrought-iron gates of my parents' house were open to greet us on a lovely March spring day. Mum came out of the kitchen door in her blue-striped housecoat, smiling and waving a buff-coloured telegram. Glued oblongs of white paper spelled out, START IMMEDIATE WITH THE EGYPT/SUDAN TEAM.

The Swiss company had offered Mike the job after all. Suddenly anxieties about our lives in Orkney arose. Would we drink ourselves under the bar? Did we have enough money? Would the locals accept us? We sat, both lost in thought for a few moments, and then Mike said, "Steve, Sudan's a bird in the hand..."

I had to agree.

Orkney catapulted away.

The North Sea oil bonanza arrived in the Orkneys two years later. For locals it was like winning the lottery.

Chapter 8 – A Sojourn in Cairo, 1973

Mike's new job was in the Sudan, working as an entomologist during the cotton season and buttering up local officials for the rest of the year, but first we had two months orientation in Egypt.

I felt nervous because Mike's work permits didn't include me. I enjoyed working, I didn't want being a wife to be a job. The Company indicated that the local agents would know a way around the paperwork. (This would turn out to be wishful thinking. The local agents regarded Mike's appointment as a threat to their perks, and they certainly were not going to smooth the path for a wife.)

We had a stopover in Cyprus for Mike to consult with a UN cotton expert. The company booked us into the Ledra Palace Hotel in Nicosia. Fortuitously, it was our first wedding anniversary. So enchanting was the hotel's legendary beauty that we promised ourselves another visit.

Sadly, that was not to be. A year later, the hotel became a war zone, repeatedly swapped between Greek and Turkish forces, eventually becoming a UN headquarters.

The following year, the same fate awaited the stunning Phoenicia Hotel in Beirut where we had stayed on our way home from Zambia. True to its name, the Phoenicia rose again after Lebanon's Civil War, but the Ledra Palace Hotel never had that chance. Today, the building is no longer habitable, although UN peacekeepers still use its swimming pool.

We were young, never imaging those places wouldn't wait for our return. As we took off for the short hop cross the Mediterranean to Cairo, we only had eyes for our next adventure.

Named after a mythological punch-up between Egyptian gods Horus and Seth, Cairo – Khere-Ohe – means 'place of combat'. The drive from the airport said it all; so frenetic was the traffic that Mike and I could not discern on which side of the road Egyptians drove. Surging in perpetual skirmish around the city, ancient over-crowded buses, jointed in the middle, overtook each other heedlessly, like demented rollercoasters, dodged by swarming taxis and bulging minibuses. Flat tyres, collapsed suspensions, blown indicators were *de rigueur*. Human combatants travelled as easily outside vehicles as in them, their jellabiyas vibrating and beating like ailerons, all to the fanfare of horns, bells, and metal on metal whine. Raucous babble and engine revs were peppered by the primordial reverberations of spitting, coughing and hawking. Clouds of shadow-blue exhaust hung in the air already thick with dust. Wooden carts, livestock and all manner of pedestrian humanity brimmed in every space not taken by mechanised conveyances.

We would muse that the traffic enlivened a whole city sunk in a sombre mood. We'd arrived in June 1973, on the anniversary of the 1967 Six-Day War with Israel. The humiliation of the defeat, still raw, would be keenly felt for generations. Egypt's social revolution and President Nasser's Cold War allegiance to the Soviet Union hung like a pall over the city, even though recent elections had delivered a new president, Anwar Sadat, who would change allegiances and look westward.

The country remained on a war footing. Sand-bagged sentry posts were at street corners, and concrete anti-blast walls obstructed the entrance to every building. Windows were streaked in inky-blue blackout paint and taped against blast. Photography was not permitted and our letters home, and theirs to us, were censored. The closure of the Suez Canal, a retaliatory move by Nasser at the beginning of the Six-Day War, was a constant reminder that there was unfinished business with Israel.

Chapter 8 – A Sojourn in Cairo, 1973

None of this suited the complex, warm-hearted and easy-going Egyptians. Cigarette smoke rose lazily from sentry points where guns rested carelessly on sandbags. Bridges across the Nile were guarded by bored-witless soldiers who juggled with their weapons, twirling, throwing and catching them to pass the time.

"Don't worry," said Mike. "They wouldn't do that if they were loaded." But I was not at all convinced.

We checked into the Hilton Hotel in time for dinner with the company team. The restaurant boasted panoramic views over the Nile. When we returned to our room, there was a message from Mr Z, the company's Egyptian agent. Mike, on probation, was not entitled to stay at the Hilton. Although we didn't mind somewhere less pretentious than a five-star hotel when poverty was so pervasive in the city, it still felt awkward for Mike, who'd taken a step backwards when he accepted the job, and was shaken by the year of unemployment in the UK.

The next morning, a taxi drove us over a bridge to our new hotel, on an island in the Nile. On approach, the building looked terribly grand, and we wondered if there had been some mistake. We were ushered from the bright sunlight through the doors of the Omar Khayyam Hotel, blinking as our eyes adjusted to the dim interior, our nostrils flaring at the fetid air, its mustiness clammy and intrusive. We gaped. From the soaring ceiling of the huge foyer hung a massive, begrimed chandelier, more than a little askew, with only two bulbs still working. Ahead, a monumental marble staircase soared up and split into two. I glanced around, taking in the gilded lily-livered mirrors, foxed velvet drapes and dusty potted palms. The carpets were threadbare, and the sofas sagged. The staff, delighted to welcome us, were dressed in fezzes, their long maroon robes bizarrely held together with safety pins and odd bits of string and cord, stiff with stains and, by the nose, never washed.

While Mike was diverted to an incongruous Formica reception desk, circa 1960, I set off up the staircase on my own. A maid followed me and pushed open a series of huge double doors to dim acres of reception rooms, windows shuttered and blinds drawn. Here and there a curtain rail had collapsed, light spilling in through grimy windowpanes. I could make out a scattering of hideous veined marble tabletops on gilt pedestals and clusters of grand red plush furniture. The upholstery had succumbed to rodents, their pathways clear trails on a floor otherwise covered with a deep layer of undisturbed dust.

The hotel was originally a palace built by Khedive Ismail to accommodate guests visiting Cairo for the inauguration of the Suez Canal in 1869. Invited monarchy and dignitaries from around the world gathered to celebrate the success of an engineering feat that had taken more than a decade to build.

Ismail 'the Magnificent' had a penchant for palaces. He enjoyed lavish, sumptuous entertainment. Dancing bears, fire-eaters, a silver-gilded acrobat who walked a tightrope with a baby lashed to each ankle, and a magician who disgorged twelve live chickens were considered frankly excessive by some European visitors who, instead, opted for the ballet or an opera by Verdi, put on at the new opera house also built for the occasion. Fantastic dinners, the porcelain exquisite, the menus prepared by Europe's leading chefs, were served by the flickering light of scores of silver candelabra and finished with cake pyramids and Turkish coffee. The khedive was in his element and enormously enjoyed the whole shebang. It all caught up with him in the end when Egypt's debts, outrageously exacerbated by easy loans from greedy European banks, lead to intervention by the hard-boiled Brits who had him deposed in favour of his son, Tewfik. He died in Ottoman exile while trying to guzzle two bottles of champagne in one draft.

Chapter 8 – A Sojourn in Cairo, 1973

The palace had transitioned to a hotel in 1894 when it opened as the rather splendid Gezira Palace Hotel. It wasn't all stuffed shirts and tea dances. Andrew Humphreys, in his book, *Grand Hotels of Egypt*, describes young ladies in evening dress tobogganing down the marble staircase on tin trays. After a brief spell as a military hospital in World War I, the palace partied on, hosting fabulous receptions for Egyptian aristocracy entertaining guests from all over the world until Egypt's revolution rather put a dampener on that sort of thing, and it was nationalised along with a lot else in the 1960s. A decade on, it was rheumy and rheumatic, fetid and faded, but, by God, it was still a palace.

We were shown out to the gardens, which had fared better than the palace with the passing of time, where a huddle of prefabricated cabins served as ensuite bedrooms. A porter fumbled for the light switch. A single lightbulb revealed the meanness of the accommodation. Two metal beds, grey sheets, a rail for clothes and one broken chair. I stuck my head into the shower cubicle. I saw a small tremor as miniscule wildlife scuttled to shelter under a flap of plaster peeling off a wall sodden with decay and damp.

"No," said Mike, "this room is not suitable."

That, I thought, was an understatement.

The second and third rooms were scarcely better, but they did at least have windows. We took the one where the air-conditioner worked, although when Mike turned it on, it roared and rocked the flimsy cabin. Salivating like an angry beast, it pulsed condensation down a pipe that ended just short of the floor in a greenish puddle of moss and slime.

We tore off the dirty bedsheets and called for the cleaners. Mike sprayed everything in sight with a pump-action spray that he requisitioned from a surprised gardener.

"Only one thing for it, let's have a drink and give the insects time to die," said Mike. As the waiter took the top off Mike's beer, the whole neck of the bottle snapped. I sat reading some brochures and found that Agatha Christie had stayed in the Gezira Palace in 1910 as a nineteen-year-old chaperoned by her mother. They were on a mission, unsuccessful, to find Agatha a husband.

"I doubt if Agatha stayed in the pre-fabs," I joked.

"No, but I feel we could set a murder here," said Mike. "Or two."

That first night we ate in the crumbling splendour of the dining room. It had been a long day, and we pushed the metal beds together and slept, despite the demon-din from the air-conditioner. At 11 p.m., we were jolted awake by bright lights and pulsating music that blasted and surged through the window, turning the space into hell's box room.

Mike sat upright shouting, "What's the devil's going on!" his face flashing from green to red to yellow.

The Omar Khayyam Nightclub was the hotel's principal money-spinner. Mike stormed off to see the manager, who wrung his hands and explained he had had our best interests at heart when he showed us the first room without a window. The next morning, we woke up violently ill with food poisoning. "Gut-rot", as Mike so aptly described it, that would afflict us on and off for the whole time we spent in Cairo.

After Mike started work, I roamed Cairo alone. I was happy to call in my Dad's wartime recollections. Walking Cairo in his footsteps was a sublime sharing of place between the tides of time. Passers-by looked familiar, the breeze rustling the fronds of the date palms blew intimate caresses at my cheek. The Nile slapped against the stone wall of the Corniche with a chummy suck. I made real the illusions that connect us, stirring

Chapter 8 – A Sojourn in Cairo, 1973

an excitement so strong that I felt the past lingered just ahead waiting for me to catch up. This was the way to share place. Had Dad been there, he would have fretted about all that had changed, and I'd have fallen hostage to his disappointment. This way, I walked Cairo un-alone, enthralled and with a smile on my lips, just as the very mention of Cairo had brought a smile to Dad's.

He'd enjoyed a wartime stopover thirty years before, billeted at Shepheard's Hotel in the centre of a brightly lit city that swarmed with officers and men from Allied forces. It has been said that the battle for Egypt, the Desert War, was "fought from Shepheard's terrace". The hotel was run by elite Swiss hoteliers who recruited the very best soft-footed Egyptian waiters and strong Nubian warrior stock for porters. Delicacies included imported grouse and Khartoum ducks, served on silver salvers with a choice of wine from vast well-stocked cellars. Nightly dances were held in the garden behind the hotel.

An eclectic mix of refugees from Europe, patriotic volunteers from the Empire and local beauties were happy to dance the night away with officers in uniform, ambassadors, war correspondents and Egypt's wealthy elite. Open-air cinemas, cabaret, cheap cigarettes and an abundance of all good things were available to the officer class who walked Cairo with their flywhisks and swagger sticks. There was also a delicious air of intrigue. A belly dancer had been arrested, the paramour of a German spy who lived on a houseboat on the Nile. Agatha couldn't have written it better.

Rommel, the German General, had taken the shine off things when he pushed his troops almost to Cairo and a wave of disorderly panic known by the laconic British as 'The Flap' swept the city. But after Rommel was stopped at Al-Alamein, the British officer class continued the good life with excesses that fostered discontent and sedition, not just in Egypt's infant nationalist movement but among their own other-ranks.

I could not visit Shepheard's, for it was gone, among many old icons burned down on Black Sunday 1952 by rioters protesting Britain's military presence that was officially guarding the Suez Canal, but in truth was just reluctant to go. The Gezira Club, an elite sporting establishment founded in 1882, had survived Black Sunday. Dad had spent a lazy afternoon on the terraces after a game of tennis. I'd already walked past the Club several times when Mike and I received an invitation from Mr Z to join him there one afternoon. Mike said Z was making amends for turfing us out of the Hilton.

The activity that day was pigeon shooting. Clay pigeon shooting did not sound wildly exciting. Nevertheless, I was thrilled to take a seat on the terrace. We exchanged pleasantries and drank gin slings. It was only at the last moment we found this was no mock diversion. In the firing pits small boys crouched down and released live birds for their fatal rush for freedom. The carnage went on interminably, the noise and slaughter contrasting bizarrely with the cool and elegant surroundings. I left in tears.

Another evening, Mr Z invited us to dinner at the Hilton with the team. Once we'd crossed a bridge over the Nile, it was only a short walk there. In daytime, there were hawkers and beggars on the patch of dirt-once-was-grass. In the evening, the space was teeming with families. Children were everywhere, jumping and skipping over the prone and infirm laid out on sleeping mats near small cooking fires. As we walked, hundreds of fingers reached out in supplication; small children flocked to us and clustered, blocking our path. We were unnerved by the softness of the petitioning bodies, wispy with rags, like downy moths in the dusk. We took a taxi back, unwilling to walk again.

Chapter 8 – A Sojourn in Cairo, 1973

The mass of humanity was still there, small bodies rushing and fluttering to the cab, hitting themselves against the window glass.

Mike was sceptical about the commercial research conducted on the company's experimental farm. And irritated when he found the tedious, painstaking job of collecting bollworm eggs was done by small children, while older boys stood watch with whips. Little girls acted as human scarecrows, shaking stone-filled tins in the hot sun. Mike told the girls to sit in the shade and only run out when the birds flocked in. Mr Z told Mike his interference was impertinent. Mike put his objections to child labour in writing. A furious Mr Z censored Mike's comments in his consolidated report for the Swiss head office.

Whenever Mike could take time off, and when we were fit enough to do so, we explored Cairo, visiting Coptic churches and a Jewish synagogue. We took myriad pills to stop diarrhoea – or the constipation that followed – to stop the cramping, to kill bacteria, parasites and fungus. We regarded all food with suspicion. In particular, anything served at the Omar Khayyam.

Just as our time in Cairo was coming to an end, Mike's Swiss manager, came to Cairo for a night. It transpired that he had no idea we were not staying at the Hilton. The company had been billed for it. He frowned and then remembered vetoing the expense of accommodating provincial officials as he believed them only useful to Mr Z in one of his nefarious sidelines. He could not take up the matter with Mr Z who'd been called out-of-town on family business.

We decided the experience of the Palace was far more memorable than any Hilton, so it served us well.

Cairo. Such an old tapestry of tongues and races, rent and reworked with a slew of incongruous threads and stitches.

The Cairo of our affection will survive us all. Extraordinary Cairo.

Chapter 9 – El Minya, Upper Egypt

After Cairo, our next stop was five-weeks of insecticide trials at a cotton project near El Minya in Upper Egypt, a hundred and fifty miles up the Nile.

We travelled by train and, as we moved through the outskirts of the city, Cairo's mountain range of rubbish overshadowed our carriage. Shifting embankments of refuse pulsed, teeming with life. Smog, seeping from slow combustion within, mingled with the smoke of itinerant cooking fires. We stared as our train rolled by a soft inferno. A wicked, petty wind made dust devils, flapped paper and billowed under the jellabiyas of the rubbish gatherers.

"What are they looking for?" I whispered, as much to myself as to Mike.

Mike's eyes were moist. He gazed at the children. They scrambled about, laughing, oblivious to the elders, who were stooped, poking at the charnel pits of stinking detritus; coveting fresh dumps of dross.

It was Cairo's last goodbye, a final gauntlet before we escaped perdition and passed into antiquity, where panoramic flat green fields flanked straight ribbons of water. Birds waded along reed banks. Throngs of fellaheen bathed in the canals. Women drubbed clothes under a cloudless sky. Half-naked, honeyed children splashed with water buffalo. Camels and donkeys hung out on sandy banks and goats swiped at blue and white washing spread on thorn scrub to dry.

It was almost dark by the time we reached El Minya. Stepping out from the train station, the scene was the shabby-chic counterfeit of a stage set where Verdi's *Aida* met Victorian

Chapter 9 – El Minya, Upper Egypt

Europe. Soft globes and lanterns hung from Italianate architecture and lit a line of Hansom cabs queued under a row of date palms. Horses fidgeted, and men in long white robes and skullcaps stood and talked.

The coachman nodded when Mike said, "Hotel Lotus?" and the bay mare shifted to take the weight as he loaded our cases. These cabs were no tourist attraction; there was hardly any motorised traffic in the town.

El Minya's fortunes had ridden high when Civil War raged in America and the Union blockade of Confederate ports prevented the export of cotton. Egypt's cotton trade had increased nearly fourfold, and the demand brought enormous prosperity to El Minya Province. Wealthy Armenian and Greek entrepreneurs moved in and engaged Italian architects to build rococo mansions on the Nile. Next to an ageless warren of mud-brick dwellings, a new colonial quarter emerged with fine houses and the broad boulevards so beloved of nineteenth century European town planners, allowing sunset promenades along the Nile.

In the early 1960s, the Hotel Lotus opened its doors, hopeful of a new influx of dollars from tourists attracted by the cluster of antiquities nearby. But the Six-Day War dashed that idea when Israel made a pre-emptive strike, knocking out ninety per cent of the Egyptian Air Force on the ground. President Nasser retaliated, shutting the Suez Canal, scuppering Egypt's golden goose for eight long years. With no income from shipping tolls, and in hock to the Russians for a plethora of out-of-date-weaponry, the whole country suffered.

In Minya, the baroque architecture distressed well. Flaking flamboyance suited the ever-adaptable Egyptians. Telephone wires and washing lines ran riot round architectural detail. Woman beat horse-hair mattresses hung from windows architraved with shell-shaped curves, babbling to their neighbours, showering dust and mites to the streets below.

Looking up at the classical stone edifices, I questioned whether it was a lack of imagination or nostalgia that made men build in the old ways in new places. In Egypt, I would learn, it was neither. The adoption of European style was given deliberate encouragement by Ismail the Magnificent, he who had built the Gezira Palace Hotel where we stayed in Cairo.

"My country," he said, "is no longer in Africa; we are now part of Europe." And with that emphasis in mind, he modelled Parisian suburbs in Cairo, adopted classical European architecture and planted exotic gardens, and El Minya followed suit.

Ismail was a man of huge ambition, a visionary. He poured money into education while investing heavily in cotton and sugar plantations, networks of railways, canals and telegraph lines. El Minya's fertile land became a major centre of cotton production. It didn't come as a surprise to learn Ismail built a palace there, too.

Although cotton prices fell when the American Civil War ended in 1865, El Minya's landowners continued a prosperous lifestyle, for cotton was ninety per cent of Egypt's export trade. Their confidence took a knock when Ismail was forced to abdicate in favour of his son, Tewfik, when Egypt's national debt went through the roof.

Yet, it would not be until after both World Wars that Egyptian nationalism tolled a requiem for Egypt's cosmopolitan elite, who then fled the international quarter of El Minya for other shores.

Our room at the Hotel Lotus was simple and relatively clean. Grubby, but nothing obviously dead or alive, unlike Cairo.

Relieved and happy, Mike and I cradled glasses of tepid date

Chapter 9 – El Minya, Upper Egypt

brandy and sat on our balcony. The lights of minarets hung in the distance and cool air wafted from the Nile, a dim dark line traced by the glow of streetlights.

"Ah..." said Mike, "Just the faintest smell on the breeze... Now, I'm back in Africa."

The company had rented a first-floor apartment near our hotel as a mess for the rest of the team. Its curtains were permanently closed against the heat, rendering the meagre place gloomy and airless. The apartment was office by day and a men's billet by night. Larry, a truculent Irish pilot, and George the engineer, a miserable Pole, were there to do the trials with Mike. Despite, or perhaps because of, a longstanding fraternity, Larry and George were enduringly morose and conversed in curses and grunts.

Project notes and technical journals competed for space with overflowing ashtrays, dirty glasses and half-bitten sandwiches at one end of a long table. Well-thumbed *Playboy* magazines slumped in piles at the other end.

The company's Egyptian entomologists were billeted nearby. Mike endeavoured to make his colleagues feel welcome when they visited the mess, unlike George, who'd grab heavy ashtrays to weigh open a *Playboy* centrefold, pour himself a cold beer and find unwarranted excuses for his few Arabic curses.

Red tape stalled the trials. The tedium was crippling. By mid-morning, it was too hot to do anything other than sit and sweat. We'd soon read everything we collectively owned. There were no English-language newspapers permitted. Incoming mail arrived in batches. As no one could read Dad's handwriting, it was clear the censor's heavy scoring was completely random. We had no playing cards, but I don't remember why; I think it was an Egyptian regulation like the one prohibiting photography, or perhaps it was legislated in company policy, along with the rule banning the use of garlic and chilli in cooking.

Larry would hunker down with a crate of beer and his world radio, the size of a truck battery, balanced on his knee. I sat halfway along the table, my hands over my ears to shut out the creaking of Larry's wicker chair and the fuzzy whine, static and crackle indicative of the success of the Egyptians' deliberate jamming of the BBC World Service.

"We frequent the arseholes of the world," said Larry to me, waving vaguely at George. "Last year it was spraying bodies on lakeside beaches in Burundi with aviation fuel, today it's cotton, next it'll be bloody flies in Saudi."

I wondered if preparing for mass cremations in Burundi following the genocide, had left a deep mark, which was why the two of them were always so gloomy.

"I doubt it," said Mike, "they're just miserable gits."

Larry just wanted to go East to see his girl in Bangladesh. I never once penetrated George's choleric defences to find out what his aspirations were. He had a fixation about 'de fogs'. I was unsure what demons plagued him until Mike told me he meant 'wogs'.

Mohammad, the cook, was Sudanese. As red meat was rationed, he served scraggy poultry and boiled carrots with tomato salad almost every day. The local bread had stones big enough to wreck a tooth, cheese was always gritty, and every beer bottle had to be held to the light to check for dead flies and cockroaches. Mealtimes broke the monotony but weren't convivial. George was particularly oafish and would on occasion pick up his plate of food and throw it at the wall. Mohammad cussed in Arabic while Mike and I rushed to help clear up the mess. One night, George was drinking soda water with dinner and halfway through wrinkled his nose and said it tasted kind of funny. Larry held the green glass bottle up to the light and gave a bellow. An old, bloated lizard spun lazily. George, usually

Chapter 9 – El Minya, Upper Egypt

measured of movement, convulsed and bolted for the bathroom. Mohammad saw providence at work and chuckled in the kitchen, plucking chickens with unusual vigour.

Mohammad and I teamed up. I'd help clear the table and stack dishes for him and he'd beckon me into the kitchen for fresh orange juice and mangoes. As time went on, I'd share his meals of grilled fish, stewed okra and aubergines – with oodles of garlic. The downside was he'd also invite me to check out the squawking chickens, fluttering pigeons and flapping fish before he bluntly silenced them.

Sometimes, the atmosphere in the mess was so oppressive that Mike and I repaired to our hotel room, despite its ferocious midday heat. The proprietor of the Lotus was always welcoming and the staff attentive, too attentive – a boy stood forever outside our room on the fourth floor. We wondered if it was overzealous service, or because El Minya was a restricted area, and foreigners needed to be monitored. Or was the boy a company spy sent by Mr Z to report evidence of Mike's idiosyncrasies? Probably all three.

It became a battle of wits. I'd wrench the door open and catch our minder like a spooked rabbit. Sometimes, he'd fall into our room scrambling madly for his footing.

One sweltering afternoon, I lay dosing fitfully when the door swung open quietly, and an astonished youth stood gaping at my nude body spreadeagled on the bed. I only woke when Mike, coming out of the toilet, bellowed and charged after him. The youth was of course far quicker than Mike, who, stark naked and with a bad case of the trots, made a sudden U-turn and dashed back to the toilet.

Witching hour interruptions were another quirk of the hotel's dedication to service. No matter what time we put the lights out, a knock on the door woke us; laundry delivered, repeat apologies from the management for some broken switch, drain or window which they had not yet fixed and indeed would never fix. Messages that had arrived twelve hours before would be breathlessly delivered at 3 a.m. Explanations about the bed, which regularly collapsed, would arrive at 4 a.m. with the superfluous advice that it had been reassembled the day before. We never stemmed the nocturnal knocking during our stay at the Lotus Hotel and according to George it was simply a characteristic manifested by 'de fogs' throughout the hotel trade in Egypt.

The best thing about the hotel was the little balcony, where we pushed the chairs together and sat close, staring out at the moon and stars. Even our minder could not see us there.

A small boy arrived in the mess as a kitchen assistant; it was Larry's idea because Mohammad didn't like cleaning.

"We'll no sooner get spraying than we'll be dead of food-poisoning."

The small boy was another Mohammad, who became simply known as "Small-Boy", and, within a very short time, "Small-Cheese-Eating-Boy" because cheese disappeared at an extraordinary rate after his arrival.

Small-Cheese-Eating-Boy sported an enormous grin. He gaily emptied ashtrays and wastepaper baskets out whichever window was nearest and carried a begrimed rag over his shoulder with which he wiped the table and God knows what else, but certainly his nose. Small-Cheese-Eating-Boy wore the same filthy jellabiya every day, and there was no noticeable improvement in kitchen hygiene.

Eventually, Larry cracked. He waited until Mohammad was out, rolled up his sleeves and cleaned the kitchen, scrubbing the floor, jettisoning food and accumulated garbage. Next, Larry bought carbolic soap, jeans and T-shirts in the market, then he took Small-Cheese-Eating-Boy to the bathroom drowning out

Chapter 9 – El Minya, Upper Egypt

George's protestations. We changed his name to Shiny-Small-Boy, and he became Larry's shadow. Larry instituted a regular kitchen inspection; Mohammad was unimpressed and got his own back. He told Mr Galaa, the peevish project gofer, who reported to Mr Z, who reported to Switzerland. Eventually, Larry received a disciplinary letter citing unprofessional behaviour, wastage of food and a warning to keep within his job description. Larry set fire to it with his cigarette lighter and dropped the burning missive in the metal wastepaper bin. He was on contract and said he didn't "give a flying fuck".

I asked Mr Galaa for advice on visiting Minya's archaeological sites. Nearby lay the kingdom of Pharaoh Akhenaten, husband of Nefertiti, and founder of a religion worshipping, Aton, the Sun God.

A message arrived from Mr Z. "Tell Mrs Shaddick it is out of the question for her to visit the archaeological remains without a permit, and permits are not available for foreigners."

An invitation came from the provincial governor for a dinner reception. Dressed conservatively, we were preparing to leave when the shifty Mr Galaa delivered another message from Mr Z. "Mrs Shaddick is specifically not invited on social occasions because it is not the custom of our country. Mrs Shaddick can stay in the hotel. She will be quite safe there."

I was of course quite safe. I was also fuming.

By day, I explored the town. I liked to go early before the heat became oppressive. Locals glanced at me sideways, and children shadowed me a little while, giggling and disappearing if I turned around, but I didn't attract beseeching beggars or leery men, as in Cairo. I dodged donkey carts piled high with misshapen tomatoes, and moody camels jostling to avoid the hansom cabs that clip-clopped round the town. Small boys ran errands, their white robes flying while I fastidiously navigated piles of dung and puddles of fetid liquid. Hubble-bubble smokers raised a hand in greeting when I passed close by coffee shops. I skirted the men gathered in groups outside small mosques. Following my nose, I surprised a line of women haggling for flat loaves of bread when I joined their queue. With scarves pulled over their faces, animated and friendly, they pushed me ahead and bargained as I was clearly in danger of paying too much. I pulled at the loaf as I meandered the markets, inspecting untidy pyramids of garlic, watermelons stacked like cannonballs, banks of polished purple and white eggplants and brilliant greens, wilting and revived with sprinkled water. Where possible I avoided the meat sellers purveying their wares, both dead and alive.

The town had a small boatyard beside the river port. Nothing was mechanised; the men used only handsaws and hammers. A flutter of white cotton enlivened the brown of acacia planks and sun-tanned craftsmen. White head rags caught sweat or were raised up to wipe faces and blow noses. White strips were wound on tool handles or used to bind together pieces of wood. White cloths used for mopping up and wiping down, were flung aside to magnet the sawdust. More were dipped in the Nile to cool hot bodies or into oil to smooth chaffed wood or slick a blade.

At the dockside, boats were loaded by hand, and I could hear the cussing, a common language, as men and youths coiled heavy coir ropes while small boys darted between them sweeping rubbish into the Nile.

I moved back to sit on a low wall under the shade of rustling palms to watch the river traffic. Goats picked over the rubbish, looked up, and for a few moments they stared at me, their slit eyes motionless and disconnected from their unfaltering jaws, rhythmically munching. The hum of insects and the chant of human voices, mixing with the clatter and jangle of the port, pulsed uphill and over my head.

Chapter 9 – El Minya, Upper Egypt

I watched great barges packed with grain make lazy journeys downstream with the current. Dhows with lateen sails that picked up the wind mid-stream seemed painted on the surface of the Nile, time-travelling the current. Barques laden with roughly hewn limestone crabbed across the river from a quarry I could just see on the far side. The unloaded blocks were roped to donkeys waiting on the quayside. The poor beasts shuddered and slipped under the strain of the fearful pull up the steep sandy slope to the road, more often on their knees than on their feet, urged on with fearsome belts of the whip.

I was in my element until one day, when I arrived back to the mess hot and happy, with a bag of bread and tomatoes, Mohammad delivered a message from Mr Z, addressed to No one in particular; it read: "Tell Mrs Shaddick she is not permitted to walk alone in the town."

It was never quite clear who was supposed to tell Mrs Shaddick what she could and could not do. Mohammad tried to console me with orange juice. But, by the time Mike returned, I had worked myself into a fury. I raged, threatened to leave, to run naked through the streets.

"I am not going to live my life as a bloody appendix!"

"Do you mean appendage?" Mike suggested.

I wavered and then said coolly, "No, I mean appendix. A useless part."

Mike poured two glasses of syrupy date brandy from the brown bottle that we kept locked in our suitcase so it could less easily be diluted with dirty water.

"You have every right to be angry, with me and with the company."

Of course, he disarmed me. "I'm not angry with you!" I said.

"Then come and have a drink and we will make a plan." He threw his long arm over my shoulders. "There is only one solution," he said. "Join us on the project. You can help with sampling."

"As if I'd be allowed!"

"Steve, if you can't go out alone, you'll have to join me. If anything's said, we'll sort it out later."

Chapter 10 – Egyptian Cotton

At 4 a.m. the next day, I joined Mike for the hour's drive to the trial site. We arrived at sunrise, stunning the Egyptian entomologists and local bureaucrats who stared at me, at each other, and then ignored me, as if I was an apparition that would soon disappear.

When Mike told Dr Sidan, the charming local entomologist in charge of the trial, that I was going to help with sampling, the poor man was lost for words. Mike turned, beckoning me to follow. At the edge of the field, he taught me how to record the age of bollworm larvae, to log sites and sample sizes. When we returned to the shade for a rest, Dr Sidan offered me tea. Then one of the other entomologists shared slices of watermelon, and another pulled bread from his bag. It was awkward through that first day, easier the second, and, on the third, when a local official shyly proffered me a bunch of wildflowers, I wanted to hug him.

From the moment Mike and I had met, there'd been a physical spontaneity between us. We touched each other instinctively. I respected the need to observe local culture and tried to stand well away from Mike, yet our closeness was so natural, it was like breathing. Poor Dr Sidan would discreetly remind us if we stood too close, miming by putting his palms together before moving them apart. When we were too busy to notice, bending over the dry spiky cotton bushes, the touch of our bared arms was never unobserved.

When Mike suggested we would be less noticeable if we worked separately, Dr Sidan's face was a picture. He was about to object until he decided it was the lesser of two evils. So, I was allocated my own fields.

The dykes that irrigated the fields were filled by the Archimedes' Screw, designed two thousand years before, and now remade in polished aluminium. Sounds of water trickling and swathes of vibrant green were a balm that relieved the intensely dry heat. Burrowing past sticky, brittle cotton leaves to pick bolls was hard, grubby, mind-numbing work. Daily, the sun pounded my head, scorched my hands and blasted through my clothes. The inside of my nose was desiccated by the dry heat and bled easily, and my eyes were constantly red and irritated from the dust, yet I never thought of exchanging it for my hotel room.

Dr Sidan worked hard in the fields, yet never looked hot, dishevelled or scruffy afterwards, which we certainly did. Every day, he courteously made a point of thanking me and made sure everyone knew I was working for free.

One day, I was gingerly picking my way along the humped path of an over-irrigated field, trying to avoid getting my feet wet in the Bilharzia-ridden water, when a youth started shouting at me from a perimeter dyke. I used my best Arabic, "tayyarah!", which meant aeroplane. He was to deduce I was with the spray plane operation and authorised to pick cotton bolls. A string of Arabic came in reply. Patiently, I called, "tayyarah" again, stretching out my arms and making engine noises reminiscent of a fighter plane in a death roll. Soon, the youth was right beside me. He observed what I did and then started to pick the cotton bolls with me. Using my few Arabic words, I was able to direct him all over the muddy bits of the field and we finished sampling in record time. He led me along a dry causeway right into his village. I was forbidden to enter any village unless accompanied by a provincial official, so I held back, happy to watch a small and impatient girl tugging ineffectually at a complacent old water buffalo submerged in a canal.

Chapter 10 – Egyptian Cotton

The boy left briefly and reappeared with an old man.

"Tayyarah," said the boy holding out his arms.

"Yes, tayyarah," I said, doing the same.

"Ah, tayyarah," said the old man, smiling broadly and holding his arms out to do a little take-off run.

"Tayyarah!" shouted the little girl.

We all laughed, and I threw rules away and followed them into the village along a sandy alley that ran between low mud-block houses. I carefully sidestepped the slimy, sinister trickle that snaked down the middle of the pathway. Man and boy shouted "tayyarah!" and out of the hovels came children to stare, old women who flapped off like black birds and young women who clustered round, touching my clothes and hair. A young mother was holding a small bundle and, after a few moments, she pushed her tiny baby forward. I gently unwrapped one layer of the many that swaddled it, to find black clay smeared over the infant's eyes. I was still holding the baby when Mike and Dr Sidan turned up. I said, "Dr Sidan, please can we take this baby to the clinic; there is a problem with its eyes."

Dr Sidan looked embarrassed. "There is no clinic here. If we take the child to Minya, it won't make any difference, for afterwards the women will treat it their way."

Each afternoon, back at the mess, we'd tip cotton bolls onto the table and begin hours of monotonous work, counting bollworms and plotting charts so Mike could plan the evening's spray run. George and Larry objected loudly to the dust and pests. Mohammad was scarcely impressed either.

There, in that miserable place, Mike and I toughened our union. The atmosphere was so muted and choleric, it was uncomfortable to speak, so we wrote notes to each other like naughty schoolchildren, sliding them up and down the mess table. I sent one to Mike saying, "Write me a poem."

Mike wrote:

> A stain of mango juice across her lip
> And the stain of ten thousand cotton bolls – on her
> poor bruised thumbs.
> We didn't think it would be like this,
> She and I
> This testing, trying place,
> And who am I to bring her here
> And why?

Shiny-Small-Boy's career came to an ignominious end. Bored, he had thrown lit matches from the kitchen balcony onto the tinder-dry garbage-ridden roof of the house below. He was caught by Mohammad, who erupted in a rage and held Shiny-Small-Boy by the ear. However, Mohammad's incandescence failed to evoke much reaction round the table.

Larry said, "Well, you haven't educated him. He needs to chuck some paraffin down first – or petrol would be better."

"No harm done – small boy, box of matches – rite of passage," said Mike.

Mohammad continued the uproar. The washerwoman arrived, heard of the misdemeanour and started screaming. The commotion raised the neighbours, who began knocking on the back door and the news spread like the wildfire Shiny-Small-Boy had failed to start. Larry went into the kitchen, disengaged Shiny-Small-Boy and sat him with us in the mess. But, the next day, Shiny-Small-Boy disappeared, and we never saw him again.

The still air of evening was the best time for aerial spraying. It lessened insecticide drift. The airstrip was beaten dirt. At one end, a thatched roof on four poles offered hot shade. A windsock hung, mostly limp. A couple of round fuel tanks were posted with safety notices that flapped when planes revved their engines. No one took any notice of what was written on them.

Chapter 10 – Egyptian Cotton

It was far too hot for protective overalls, gloves and goggles. Drums of neat insecticide were hand-mixed in a tank and long hoses hauled to the spray plane hoppers. The workers, stripped to loincloths, were splashed with chemical at every step. And, each morning, the previous day's empty drums had disappeared along with their residual threat, lugged off by the fellaheen to use as water containers and food caches.

The pilots and engineers were contemptuous of the risk. They'd been doing this for years. Blood counts and readings were taken. Larry wanted his to be high so he could get off the goddamn project; whereas George refused to be tested because he knew this hellhole and didn't want to drum his heels waiting for another.

A pink-shirted Swiss residue expert visited the site and added a blue dye to the chemical. The whole load team turned blue.

"A toxicologist would halt the project immediately," muttered the expert.

"And you are not a toxicologist?" asked Mike.

"Not in my role here! I am just to test, to take readings."

Mike suggested a kid goat be brought to the airstrip and fed pesticide. I knew that Mike was thinking back to the airstrip at Kanja when his first Alsatian pup had died of organophosphate poisoning.

The expert looked at Mike in horror. He said the company had invested thousands of dollars promoting the safety of the pesticides, and he could not understand any employee wanting to so graphically illustrate its toxicity. He reminded Mike that the company gave each employee a job description, and the system only worked when everyone did the job they had been assigned. Mike's job was only to direct the pilots on where to spray.

In a loud voice, the residue expert said in English, "From now on everyone must wear safety gear," then asked for a translator to tell the blue-streaked workers. The expert did not go into any details as to why avoiding the pesticide was important. And with that he returned to Switzerland.

I don't know why it took so long for the apoplectic message to arrive that banned me from field operations. We took no notice; our stint in El Minya was nearly over. Mr Z had already turned down Mike's leave application to visit Alexandria before we left Egypt so there was no point in trying to get on his good side.

When Dr Sidan came to the mess to say goodbye, I told him I was strangely looking forward to returning to Cairo, a city one no sooner escaped than missed. Dr Sidan laughed and said he understood. I told him I was sad not to have seen Minya's archaeological sites.

"Oh, but it is easy to apply for a permit," he said. "The provincial governor is very keen to promote tourism in Minya. He would probably have escorted you himself!"

"What a shame I didn't get to meet the governor," I said, as lightly as I could.

Dr Sidan looked confused. "But why didn't you accept his invitation to the reception? I would have introduced you."

"Oh no!" I said looking woebegone at poor Dr Sidan, "Mr Z must have misread the invitation. He didn't think I was meant to go."

On a home run now, I added, with mischievous intent, "I'm so sorry, I would have been honoured to meet him. And I'm going to miss my father's colleague too," I said "he's a professor in Alexandria, but Mr Z says there is no time for us to go there."

"Who is this professor?"

"Professor Toppazada."

"Professor Toppazada! Oh, I know him well. Such an eminent man." He paused. I swear there was a twinkle in his eye, "Does Mr Z know of this connection?"

Chapter 10 – Egyptian Cotton

"I think not," I replied.

The next day, without explanation, an obsequious Mr Galaa turned up with permission for Mike to take four days' leave, train tickets for Alexandria and a booking at the exclusive Cecil Hotel.

Mike said, "Bugger it, Steve, you could have dropped that name a bit earlier!"

Over dinner with Professor and Mrs Toppazada, I asked about the baby with the mud-covered eyes. The professor shook his head. "The children get conjunctivitis from the dry dust, and the traditional remedy is to plaster their eyes with mud. The dirt harbours burrowing parasites that attack the nerves behind the eye. That poor child may grow up completely blind..."

As we flew from Cairo to Khartoum, I stared down and my heart went out to the fellaheen, the backbone of Egypt, toiling away on the banks of the Nile. Time and time again during our time in Egypt, we'd experienced their kindness, shy smiles, slices of watermelon and cups of tea. I recalled the helplessness I'd felt one day when we were returning from the fields. Our car had stopped at a bridge to let a string of camels go by. Loaded with reeds, they were herded by two women who had bundles of green reeds carefully balanced on their heads. Abdul, a young and wealthy Egyptian entomology student, who had been sampling with us, jumped out and, roaring with laughter, grabbed at the women's loads scattering the reeds, which slid across the track and into the canal.

I leapt out to help the women and turned on him in a fury, "Why did you do that?" I shouted.

He shrugged, "Why not? They are only fellaheen."

Chapter 11 – Khartoum and Omdurman

Mike and I were excited to finally be on our way to the Sudan, our home for the next three years. We'd have a permanent flat in Khartoum but live several months of the year in a field house on the cotton project. A car for our personal use had been shipped out from Switzerland.

Dad had flown the length and breadth of Africa during World War II. Once, when his float plane developed engine trouble and made an unscheduled landing on the Nile at Khartoum, he had repaired to the Grand Hotel for a couple of nights. The Grand was one of a string of iconic hotels – Shepheard's in Cairo, Raffles in Singapore and The Peninsula in Hong Kong – that stretched Britain's empire route.

Dad had written to Mum, "The crowd in the hotel is a joy. Old dried-up chaps who just live here. Greeks, Armenians, Egyptians, all sorts and sizes." And, in the next letter, "The hotel is the last word in luxury – fans, iced gin, mango ices." From his bedroom window, he could see feluccas and dhows on the Blue Nile. An evening stroll took him to the confluence of the Niles where two streams of water, white from Lake Victoria and silty blue from Ethiopia, ran parallel before they mingled into one.

Just before we left for the Sudan, Dad had written to me, "Oh, Gill, I wonder if the Grand is still there."

I could feel his grin rising off the notepaper.

Larry joined us on the commercial flight to Khartoum. "Here we go again," he said. "'When Allah made the Sudan, Allah laughed'."

George, Larry's sidekick, had departed for some other fog-

Chapter 11 – Khartoum and Omdurman

ridden hellhole. Larry had cheered up, I said. Mike chuckled and said it was in anticipation of being reunited with the madams of desirable Khartoum brothels.

On the flight, I chatted happily to an elderly Sudanese man. I told him how Mike and I had met in Zambia. He straightened up, "Oh, Zambia… They are Africans. In Sudan, we are Arabs; there is no comparison. None at all."

That lesson again: black skin is not a fraternity, Africa is not one place, but a continent brimming with extraordinary diversity, its peoples as divided as they are in any other landmass by deep ethnic fractures, language and religion.

As we circled to land, my new friend pointed out the twin cities of Omdurman and Khartoum, separated only by the Nile, yet a gulf apart. No one could remember when Omdurman scrambled out of the desert to make an untidy straggle of a town, its street turns and buildings irregular. It was a city that had never bothered with a budget for town planners.

Khartoum was much more recent. It was established as a military base in 1820 when Muhammad Ali Pasha, grandfather of our friend, the palace builder, Ismail the Magnificent, raised a force to annex the territory of Sudan and harvest slaves to train for military service and as labourers.

From Khartoum Airport, we took a taxi to the Grand, dropping Larry off on the way. Mike disappeared to make a phone call and a long-robed waiter in a dark red fez showed me to a table. The wicker of the chair wheezed as I settled beneath an arched portico. For a few moments, Mike's absence allowed me to narrow my eyes and slip away to join a sea of wartime khaki, hazy through the smoke curling from cigarettes, pipes and cigars. Chinks of glasses and bellowed laughter floated out over the Nile, for they were there, and the war was not.

Mike came back grinning from ear to ear. "Love it already!" he said.

Sudan was that kind of place.

Khartoum had been the stuff of my school history lessons. Teachers spun a nostalgic view of empire where Britain ruled sea and land with magnanimous impunity and the help of the Almighty. Perversely, the odd failure was light relief. It was failure that put Khartoum on the map.

Egypt and Sudan had become de facto British colonies in 1882, soon after Ismail the Magnificent was deposed for his overspending. At first, the British paid little attention to wild rumours of the fighting capabilities of a bunch of tribesmen in the Sudan. Yet, unease grew when it became clear that their leader, one Muhammad Ahmad bin Abd Allah, had amassed a sizeable army. When Ahmad proclaimed, "I am the Madhi, the Successor of the Prophet of Allah," and declared a holy war, fierce and courageous fighters flocked to his side. The arrival of the messianic redeemer of the Islamic faith was comparable to the second coming of JC.

An expedition of nearly seven thousand Egyptian troops, led by a reluctant British Ex-Indian Army Colonel, William Hicks, was sent to arrest the Madhi and put an end to the insurrection. (Billy Hicks' preference would have been not to poke the Madhi, but to let him rumble around the desert of which Sudan had plenty, especially as Hicks had not a great deal of faith in his conscripted Egyptian troops, who had little appetite for the fight with a fervent Muslimhood.) Nevertheless, Pasha Hicks struck out across the waterless wastes of Kordofan to the west of the Gezira region where Mike and I were headed. His troops were followed by an immense baggage train of five thousand camels and a thousand donkeys that carted supplies and artillery including the latest in machine guns. While this was the largest force ever assembled in Sudan, it was, in Winston Churchill's account of the conflict in his book *The River War*, "perhaps the worst army that has ever marched to war".

Chapter 11 – Khartoum and Omdurman

Lost or misled, and short on water, the expedition reached a place where the desert gave way to an acacia forest. Hicks was nervous that night, urging his hot and thirsty troops to build barricades of earth. His intuition was right, for after darkness fell, all hell broke out when the expedition was ambushed. Hemmed in, surrounded by dead and dying men and animals, the dervishes pinned down the force, letting it wilt the next day in the blazing sun. Unable to successfully break out, they were eventually overrun by the Madhi's force of 40,000 men. Pasha Hicks and all but three hundred Egyptians were slaughtered, and the artillery plus 7,000 rifles were carted off in what was to go down in history as the Battle of Shaykan.

Next, the Madhi turned his attention to Khartoum. The colonial administration had more pressing problems and would have ignored the threat to the city had it not been that some British nationals, including women and children, and an Egyptian garrison, were holed up there. Looking around for a good chap to manage an evacuation, they thought of General Charles Gordon, who'd served a spell as governor-general of the Sudan a few years earlier. That experience had driven him to a nervous breakdown when his attempts to combat slavery were thwarted at every turn by Sudanese traders, who objected to losing their livelihood.

Recuperation rebuilt Gordon's shattered health. It may also have intensified his religious fervour. Invited to return to Sudan, he became a man on a mission. When he reached Khartoum in February 1884, less than four months after the inglorious demise of Billy Hicks, Gordon duly bailed out the European civilians but then changed the game plan and vowed to hold the city against the mystic Muslim and his army of dervishes.

A month after Gordon's arrival in Khartoum, the Mahdi arrived in Omdurman. Gordon possibly watched the warriors gathering on the opposite bank of the Nile from his Governor's mansion. The Mahdi first sent his men to cut the telegraph wires that ran across the desert to Cairo, isolating Khartoum from the outside world. Then he laid siege. After that, it was just a question of time, idling in Omdurman until the river fell, and there was little fight left in the starved and diseased population on the opposite bank. The Mahdi took no prisoners. The defenders – the hapless Egyptians whom Gordon had failed to evacuate – were, each and every one, put to the sword and Gordon's own head paraded on a spike. Forty-eight hours later when the British relief column arrived, the black flag of the Mahdi was flying over the city. Many of the very stones of Khartoum had gone – carted over the river to Omdurman. With no one to rescue, the relief column withdrew and left the Madhi in control.

Public explanation for Gordon's shock defeat was that he'd fought a madman, and the alliteration worked so well: the 'Mad Madhi'. Privately, members of HM Government knew that the 'mad' epithet was more deservedly Gordon's: he had defied orders and made himself God's champion, mounting a boys' own defence of the doomed city.

Six months later, the Mahdi was dead, bitten by a flea that carried typhus. Despite popular demand to avenge Gordon's saintly sacrifice, it was more than a decade before Britain came back for retribution when Major-General Kitchener defeated the Mahdi's successor in the Battle of Omdurman in 1898. Ten thousand men mowed down with Maxim guns and Martini-Henry artillery for a British loss of only forty-eight. Kitchener desecrated the Madhi's tomb, threw the redeemer's bones in the Nile, and set about Khartoum's reconstruction, insisting it be laid out in the shape of a Union Jack to drive home the point about who was boss. All that for only another half-century of

Chapter 11 – Khartoum and Omdurman

Anglo-Egyptian rule.

Strangely enough, the whole saga had led to Mike and me sipping gin on the terrace of the Grand for, by the time Kitchener had re-imposed rule on the vast and empty Sudan, its strategic value had gone up several notches. Sudan's coastline had to be guarded to secure the Suez route to India. A British presence in Sudan had become imperative, and some kind of earner required to pay for its administration and security. That's when the concept of a huge agricultural project took hold and cotton was just the thing: a bargain supply to bolster declining Lancashire and Yorkshire textile mills. The scheme would also provide lots of jobs, just the thing to keep the rebellious from getting carried away by the next desert prophet.

Planners looked south of Khartoum to the Gezira, a great triangle of fertile alluvial plain between the converging Niles. Gezira farmers grew grain and some cotton while nomadic herdsmen went in search of pasture, mingling with itinerant traders and West African pilgrims making the hajj to Mecca.

The Gezira Cotton Scheme became the largest agricultural project in the world. The government appropriated the land from the owners who, without consultation, became 100,000 tenant farmers beholden to the Sudan Gezira Board, which administered the enormous farm with rigorous discipline. The construction of the Senar Dam in 1925 transformed the Gezira plain into a massive grid of uniform fields split by irrigation canals.

It was, by most measures, a huge financial success, and cotton continued to be Sudan's main export until it was surpassed by oil in the 1990s.

All aspects of the cotton scheme had been managed by the Gezira Board until the early 1970s, when the Board outsourced crop protection to international agrochemical companies. (Given considerable freedom to determine pesticide requirements, there was a predictable increase in usage which would eventually threaten to overtake the value of the crop.) Mike's Swiss employer won over the Gezira Board with an attractive package which included a research unit. A company office was opened in Khartoum with Mr Falla as the requisite local Sudanese partner. My high hopes that Mr Falla might help me find a job or a volunteer position were quickly dashed when I met him; a wily and unlovely man. He was a pudgy sloth. His gibbous eyeballs swivelled like brown and yellow shot balls. When he leaned back in his chair, his white cotton jellabiya strained tight over his enormous belly, and I was mesmerised by his protruding belly-button that jiggled independently.

No one's fool, elbow-deep in grafts, he manipulated everyone for his own advantage.

Falla's string of business enterprises nicely dovetailed. While he worked tirelessly for the Swiss company, arranging the paperwork to import vehicles, radios, telex machines and the like, he shared their exasperation when the equipment mysteriously malfunctioned in the heat, failed from an electrical surge or was depreciated under some local rule and quickly written off. Fortunately, and with uncanny surety, the capable Mr Falla was ever able to lease the identical equipment from his cousin in the hire business. One Swiss manager laughed as he said to us, "Better the devil we know."

Falla insisted Mike and I stay at the company's resthouse declaring that, as the spray season was about to start, we'd soon be leaving for our field house in the Gezira. After the season, we could look at apartments. Mike was disconcerted. And the car? The one sent from Switzerland for our use? Falla looked blank.

When Falla's driver took us to the resthouse, we didn't know that the company forbade the entomologists, pilots and

Chapter 11 – Khartoum and Omdurman

engineers who flew in for the season from bringing along their girlfriends, partners or wives. Thwarting regulations, the men brought them in on tourist visas and rented a separate house, nicknamed the 'Passion Pit'. In response, company regulations were tightened to prohibit any girls setting foot in the resthouse.

Which may have been why Mohammad, the cook and caretaker, after a huddled conversation with the driver, glowered as he showed us around the house. Finding ourselves a room was no simple matter. It was the third year the company had operated in the Sudan, and team members tipped him, 'baksheesh' to keep their rooms allocated for the following year. With each door we opened, he said, "No, not that one, that is Mr Noel's," and, "No, that one is for Mr Jim." Eventually, we dumped our bags in a small windowless room that led off the main living space. Larry rolled in later in the day and took up his old room – one with a balcony.

A day or so later, Russell, a delightful white Kenyan entomologist, arrived. And so did Tim, who was from the UK and acted as general gofer and factotum. He must have been nearing sixty, small and puppyish. Tim treated me as if I was the most junior member of the team, streaming gratuitous advice as if I had never set a foot out of the home counties. With each arrival, there was astonishment that I was in the house and legitimately so. Once, when I arrived back at the mess, a disembodied voice shouted, "Bloody hell, there's a white sheila in the driveway!"

A pause, before a peevish reply from Tim. "Nah… that's not a sheila, it's just Mike's wife."

"What the hell's she doing here?"

The words did give me pause for thought. Did being a wife rule me out as a sheila? I'd have preferred the thrill of illicit love in the Passion Pit to this wife business. Larry explained the others thought I cramped their style. Mike said it meant they couldn't discuss what was new at the brothel. I heard it anyway, when Mike spent a night or so away, and they'd forget I was in the windowless room directly off the living area.

These minor tensions broke quickly for Sudan had, without notice, insisted that foreigners held international driving licences. Mike and I had them, but no one else did. Mike was busy checking that aviation fuel was getting up the one-track rail line from the Red Sea and securing permits for the pilots, so Falla asked me to drive the team round the town. There was student unrest and minor rioting, and we'd often be stopped by the army or police. Held up in the hot stuffy vehicle, watching scuffles with demonstrators and driving the Land-Rover through back streets, with the occasional bottle or stone thrown at our vehicle, changed my standing overnight, and even Tim piped down.

I took time out to start exploring on my own. Just walking the dusty streets was a delight, for the Sudanese people were confident, handsome and tall, the men's inherent grace enhanced by long white robes, prayer caps and turbans.

I went to the Omdurman markets, where I asked men sipping coffee for directions to where silversmiths plied their trade. Laughing at my Arabic, they waved me on. Dad had bought two silver dishes in the markets in 1944. Each had a Maria Teresa Dollar, or 'thaler' in the centre. These coins, of pure silver, had fuelled Europe's trade with the Middle East and Africa for centuries. I found the same dishes, not with thalers, but using other large silver coins. I think, had I had more time, I could have found a thaler.

Next to the silversmiths were the bone and ivory carvers and potters turning out water jugs and bowls. I moved on to watch the farriers shoeing horses and thought a decade back to my lovely Mrs Mops. The smell of singeing hooves mingled

Chapter 11 – Khartoum and Omdurman

with the dust-thickened acrid, earthy odour blowing over from an enormous livestock market. Brightly painted souk trucks were lined up, belching diesel fumes while waiting to take fresh produce to provincial towns.

My olfactory nerves rebelled, so I headed to the spice markets for some light relief where I saw clay bowls and flat baskets filled with mounds of colour and texture: whole chilli, ground chilli, poppy seeds, golden turmeric, carob. I leaned over, my bare ankles brushing hessian bags of cumin seeds and black pepper, to exchange my piastres for plump folded scraps of paper. A whole enclave was devoted to garlic – strangely showy beneath wispy green trees. Men and boys, white-robed, blended behind the piles of ivory bulbs, animatedly chatted while their fingers nimbly broke the pungent bulbs into individual cloves to sell by weight.

In Omdurman, the dusty bones of ten thousand dervishes had not quite settled. I visited the Mahdi's empty tomb and nodded self-consciously to the pilgrims gathered outside. Opposite, in the little museum, jellabiyas splashed with antique blood from the Madhi's fallen warriors were displayed in glass cases as grubby and dusty as the relics. Spears and shields made of hide were poignant reminders of the unequal battle. Gordon's tin trunk and jingoistic depictions of his last stand brought a disquiet. I shivered a little, and it wasn't cold.

Outside the sunshine made me blink, and I stuck to the shade of the mud-brick walls as I wandered back to the Nile. I saw Omdurman as vigilant still, its elders reproachful that intemperate Khartoum so easily laid itself bare for the newest wave of foreigners.

Chapter 12 – Wad Adam in the Gezira

Desert flanks the narrow road from Khartoum to Wad Medani, Gezira's capital. We set off mid-morning and drove into the arid wilderness that started just outside the city limits. The fuzzy zigzags of yellow dirt that snaked across the road at the start of the journey soon built up to shifting billows of sand that completely blotted out the tarred surface. I felt as if our Land-Rover took-off and flew over long stretches of desert.

We made a detour to visit a local official. Jim, the spray season manager, was nervous; it was an important connection. He lectured me on local manners: I was to eat whatever was offered. I jumped out of the Land-Rover and swept into the house ahead of Mike and Jim on a tide of irritation. I did know how to be charming and was delightfully gracious in declining the raw camel lung dripping with slime. And while the raw liver and tripe soused with lemon juice set out in enamel bowls looked wonderful, if you don't mind, I might just pass on that, too. While Jim and Mike washed down raw offal with warm Coca-Cola, I joined the women cooking liver on a charcoal brazier. It was delicious, wrapped in warm flatbread and served with sweet black tea.

We arrived in Wad Medani late in the afternoon and were introduced to Taj, the local entomologist, and to Sayed Nur El Huda. Both were immediately likable. Sayed Nur was a local legend. He had worked his way up from counting boy to become a respected member of the Gezira Board and the director of a leading bank. We were also reunited with Mabrouk, one of the Egyptian entomologists visiting for the season. He spoke contemptuously of Sudan whenever the local entomologists

Chapter 12 – Wad Adam in the Gezira

were out of earshot, while the Sudanese gently mocked the Egyptian when he wasn't listening.

We spent a few nights at the company's Medani resthouse before we moved to our field house, one of many bungalows built in the 1920s for British agriculturists and inspectors. They were easy to spot in the flat, sandy landscape for each bungalow was surrounded by a ring of mature greenery, while a whole village often had just one solitary tree.

The journey to our field house took an hour on a rare day without diversions and breakdowns. Head office, puzzled that the car shipped for us had been requisitioned for some other use, said it would take six months to ship another. Meanwhile, they combed the asset list and offered me a motorbike. Mike was doubtful, but I liked the idea and saw myself with some old-fashioned goggles and a leather helmet flying through the billowing sand like Biggles. But, like much else on the asset list, the motorbike could not be found.

Mabrouk drove us to the house, warning that it was not ideal. We turned off the Wad Adam canal road between two listing stone gateposts and followed the long drive to the bungalow. It had a flat roof and an all-round veranda screened with mosquito wire.

When Mabrouk told us to watch for scorpions under the steps to the veranda, I leapt in one bound while Mike was deliberately pedantic. The glaze of the floor tiles had worn through with the passage of feet over time, leaving them soft, warm and uneven underfoot. The Wad Adam house was quite empty, neglected, stripped bare. It felt as if some young colonial had raced off to catch a dhow sailing downstream, and never returned.

We knew immediately we were the next keepers before white ants or a haboob, a dust storm, carried it away altogether. It just felt right. We stood and grinned at each other.

Tall trees shaded a lush garden filled with birdsong and tended by Abdulla, the watchman. There was a stable block, outhouses and servants' quarters. Mike prowled round the grounds making plans to resurrect the overgrown tennis court, fringed by an orchard of gnarled citrus trees: orange, lime and grapefruit.

"And this space is lawn," Mike laughed. "I can just see us playing croquet."

Taj chose our servants. Abdul, a truly grand old man, was to cook and clean. He had a resolute yet cavalier energy about him, underscored by his turban, which always had an end flying wild. His face was twisted. I presumed he'd been hauled from the womb with makeshift forceps, but his missing teeth suggested the violence came later. Abdul had an on-off friendship with Abdulla. And there was Mohammad-the-Bucket, so named to distinguish him from Mohammad-the-Driver.

Falla sent out a truck with our entitlement of company furniture; two single stretcher beds, some wicker chairs, one table, a paraffin fridge and a gas ring to supplement the charcoal stove.

The first night we hauled the stretchers onto the veranda to escape the stifling old air in the bedroom. An hour later, we were driven in again by the mosquitoes. Our mosquito wire proved a trifling obstacle for insects; it simply framed our space and there was a comfort in that. After I waved Mike off to work at 4 a.m., I would enjoy a quiet cool hiatus until the dawn light gathered enough lustre to filter through the trees and Abdul started to sweep the veranda, piling up the grit and dead insects we took on board every night. The house had a kitchen sink and a bathroom but no running water. Once upon a time, water had been gravity-fed from the village tank that stood high on metal stilts. Abdulla puffed out his cheeks and swirled his arms

Chapter 12 – Wad Adam in the Gezira

like a windmill, then dropped his arms and looked dejected. We understood, for we'd passed the village and seen the windmill with its broken vanes. Even a strong wind didn't fill the tank. The village standpipe worked in a desultory sort of way. At the village, we could fill jerrycans, load them into the Land-Rover and cart the water to our house. Mike, Abdul and Abdulla then hauled buckets up to our roof tank for us to have a shower. Drinking water was brought by jerrycan from Wad Medani. On no account, said Taj, were Mike and I to accept the canal water, which was riddled with bilharzia and God knows what else.

Electricity was courtesy of an old diesel generator we named 'The Beast'. It should have been bolted to the ground, but the concrete floor of the shed was too thin, so the generator threw itself around alarmingly until, wedged in a corner, it grumbled for days before setting off again on another crazy perambulation. Its switch got damaged in one of these adventures and thereafter the only way to stop it was to wrench out the fuel pipe while it was still running, which sprayed diesel in all directions. Occasionally, The Beast roared into overdrive and we madly turned everything off, or on, unsure how best to appease it. In my dreams, it got free and came past the scorpions to gobble us up.

I'd arrived in Sudan with an electric typewriter so sometimes I asked Mike to start the generator before he left for work. But once the switch broke off, neither Abdul nor I dared go near The Beast, and it roared on until it ran out of diesel or Mike returned. The nights that Mike left for a meeting in Khartoum or stayed over in the Board's resthouse at Senar, Abdul and I made do with oil lamps and candles.

The toilet was a small outhouse with a bum-sized hole cut in a wooden shelf over a galvanised pail. It was serviced by Mohammad-the-Bucket. He was, as Taj put it bluntly, "a simpleton". Mohammad-the-Bucket accessed the pail from a hatch set low down into the back wall of the shed. He was diligent in his duties but without a timetable, so we could never be sure when Mohammad would take the bucket. All you could do was to clench your sphincter when you heard the rasp of the catch. A draft of air followed the squeak of the hatch-door swinging free. I squirmed at the thought of my buttocks presented thus, so I made sure I knew Mohammad was otherwise engaged before I paid a quick visit. Mike, on the other hand, would take his book and spend hours in contemplation until there was a holler, and Abdul and I knew immediately what had happened. We would rush onto the veranda to watch Mohammad-the-Driver and Abdulla in pursuit of a terrified Mohammad-the-Bucket fleeing down the lane.

After the shouting died down, Mohammad could be coaxed out of the bushes and the bucket returned to its rightful place. I tried to intervene and say that I thought that it would be as quick to let Mohammad do his job and empty the pail, but I never got traction for the idea. Mike always bellowed and the quest was far too much fun. When a stray dog attached itself to Mohammad-the-Bucket, I never knew whose side it took when the chase ensued.

The dog howled mournfully after dark until Mike, Abdul or Abdulla sent it screaming off into the night with a well-aimed stone or tin can. Its yelp set off all the dogs and donkeys for miles around. Mike, concerned about rabies, said the dog had to go. A day later, Mike arrived home with a live duck, handed it to Abdul, who lost his grip, and the duck flew off and settled on top of the generator shed to gather its wits before it took to the air. The two Mohammads, Abdul, Abdulla and Mike raced after it. The duck was last sighted flying low along Wad Adam canal, pursued by the dog. Neither was ever seen again.

Another wing-in was a kid goat. I heard him bleating in the garden and bleated back. He emerged from the shrubbery and pressed his nose against the wire of the veranda. He was

Chapter 12 – Wad Adam in the Gezira

black with very long ears and surprisingly large feet. From the moment I let him in, he was at home and followed me around the house. Abdulla made enquiries and said none of the locals were missing a goat. Mike named him Horatio.

Each night Abdulla locked Horatio in an outhouse. Released at dawn, Horatio would fly to the house, paw open the door handle and bound onto our bed. My devoted companion during the day, Horatio changed his allegiance when he heard Mike come home in the afternoon. The pair of them would race around the garden together, Horatio's ears flying out like sidewinders.

Abdul took a dim view of Horatio. Abdul washed our clothes in a tin bath in the garden. He used the Hindi word, 'dobhi' for laundry, which must have come over with the British colonials. He warmed the water on a charcoal fire and added soap powder, stirring it in vigorously until the bathtub overflowed with bubbles. At this point, Horatio would tear across the grass and with a great leap, land right in the tub and jump out again, suds flying, heading for my protection on the veranda, pursued by Abdul screaming invectives.

When we went out, Horatio would scamper up the concrete steps to the flat roof of the house and keep watch. On our return, he'd leap in the air, land with a shattering smash on the sloping tiled roof of the veranda, and skid down to drop on all-fours right in front of us. He grew quickly into a fine young goat, and I was suspicious when an old woman arrived to claim him. Mike offered to buy him for me but did add that he foresaw the day when Horatio, matured to a huge billy goat, would crash through the veranda roof and squash us.

It wasn't only Abdul who was happy to see Horatio's departure. Abdulla was pleased, too; he complained that Horatio drank too much milk and ate the feed of his bony cows.

Abdulla's cows were the colour of soft toffee. We named

them Buttercup and Daisy. We should have realised Daisy was a bullock. The animal was chained up, except for the days he ripped his chain out with the stump and tore off down the drive pursued by Abdulla and, in the early days, most gleefully by Mohammad-the-Bucket. Buttercup's calf was penned up at night. The trick was for Abdul to milk Buttercup first thing before Abdulla let the calf loose. The two men seldom synchronised and, when the dawn broke to Arabic swearing, I knew I'd get no milk. On silent days, there was a share to scald. I hated to see milk wasted so, with Abdul's help, bought muslin in the markets and sewed little bags that I hung up to make cottage cheese.

We settled into a routine. Mike left each morning in the dark to meet Russell. After sweeping and milking, Abdul took hot charcoal from the previous night's oven and tipped it into the iron to start smoothing the dhobi, and I'd walk to the village along the canal bank, happy to reach the shade of a date palm, greeting boys in jellabiyas with lopsided skull caps carrying mattocks and adzes. Sometimes, a man would greet me as he passed on a donkey, or I'd smile at a little girl herding a few goats or avoid a bullock, heavy-browed and heavy-eyed, led by a bored boy kicking stones. When I reached the village, the women crowded round pulling me towards their little cloths laid out with tomatoes and eggs. Each woman had a little bowl of water for me to float the eggs and make sure they were fresh. I suspected the water came from the canal, so I didn't bother.

As I had no transport, the cook at the company's Medani resthouse was instructed to shop for me. What he sent never remotely matched what I'd asked for. And was the haunch of meat goat, camel or mutton? Mike said that whatever it was would be fine if we tenderised it first by marinating it in the local date sherry. That idea was not successful because we could not stomach every meal tasting so strongly of dates. Mike's next idea was mincing everything which worked rather better.

Bread, if it arrived at all, hosted little beetles which fascinated Mike – *Cryptolestes ferrugineus*: the subject of his undergraduate thesis. I started to make bread, kneading the dough and setting it to rise by the charcoal fire. Abdul waged a constant war on the weevils that came with the flour from the market. He decanted the flour into deep tin trays that he put in the sun, forcing the critters to burrow down to escape the heat. After a while, he'd scoop off the top layer leaving the weevils behind. I don't know that Abdul's strategy was particularly effective, but somehow the dead bugs in the bread I made never worried me as much as the ones in the bread I bought. Some days, Abdul and I would sit together on the veranda with a great round sieve balanced between us, and we'd pick bugs and grit out of dried lentils and beans.

We'd wrap-up our housework mid-morning when it got hot and Mike would return, muddy and exhausted, to throw himself down on a stretcher on the veranda. Sometimes, I thought he looked too thin, too buggered. He insisted it was only the heat. The pesky migraines that ran up the back of his head came less frequently, he said, as the cotton grew, and he did not need to stoop over it.

It was impossible to do anything except rest fitfully during the daytime heat. Our servants disappeared. We had no fans, no cool escape. Everything metal, the table, the hinges on our stretcher beds, knives and forks, door handles and enamel cups, became too hot to touch. Relief came mid-afternoon with a flutter of air; the signal to stir ourselves, towel off the sweat and drive to the airstrip. I liked catching up with Larry and the other pilots. Those guys always had so many tall tales to tell.

We'd try to get home before dark. Then Mike poured us a warm beer or the local date brandy called Konyak and we'd pull our chairs to the edge of the veranda listening to the night sounds emerging from the punishing heat of the day.

We were so goddamned happy with each other. We'd share the day or make plans, conjure up where we would live in Khartoum, brainstorm a shopping list for the next year's stint at Wad Adam, or fantasise about the holidays we'd have when we got our company car: trips to the Dinder National Park, to the pyramids of Meroe and to Port Sudan to dive in the Red Sea.

Some nights we were content simply to sit quietly by the light of the oil lamps; on others, Mike got the generator going so we could use our record-player. The speakers belted Beethoven, the Rolling Stones or Glen Miller into the velvet dark to The Beast's unique accompaniment. On days when the heat refused to leave and hung about the veranda, we'd take our sundowners and walk up to the canal to find a breeze. Horatio liked to come, too. There was a spot on the sloping canal bank that gave us ringside seats to a big sky theatre of romantic sunsets, wondrous cloud shapes and brewing storms.

We learned the hard way that distant storms could bolt straight for Wad Adam. If we lingered too long, the temperature dropped like a stone and, holding hands, we'd dash up the long drive after Horatio, trying to reach the house before a dust-devil of scummy mustard wind caught us to whip grit against our bare legs and arms. Those nights we slept inside, stuffing towels under the doors. In the morning, the light on the veranda was dull and yellow until Abdul brushed off the sand clogging the mosquito netting.

One night we woke with the rain drumming on the roof and a huge storm overhead. In the morning, the garden was flooded. I watched Abdul wade very slowly through the water with his jellabiya hitched up around his knees. He emerged with black mud clumped around his ankles, making them look like the fetlocks of an English carthorse. The mud was so heavy, he could

Chapter 12 – Wad Adam in the Gezira

hardly climb the steps to the veranda.

Gezira was famous for its muddy black clay. It was ideal for canals, sealing the sides so well that there was no need to line them with concrete.

Chapter 13 – Bollworms, Birds and Borders

Whenever there was a lull in the spraying, we'd grab our spongebags and head to the Medani resthouse. There was no particular road to town; we started along canals and navigated by the sun and in the direction of the Wad Medani communications pylon, breaking out across country over fallow fields, hitting canals and finding crossings that changed with the irrigation cycle. Sometimes we had to abandon the car because of punctures or breakdowns. We took water and fly-spray with us wherever we went as we never knew where we might end up. Once we got bogged in mud and walked for two hours back to Wad Adam. In the morning, Mike put a sign up at the canal that read 'SHADDICK IS STUCK'. It was three days before anyone came to the rescue.

The team grumbled about Medani being a dump of a town, but, for us, after Wad Adam, the bright lights and running water were sensational. There'd usually be an impromptu party when we made it to the mess. The crop-dusters were a wild bunch with an endless supply of anecdotes. They'd built a barbecue in the garden. Larry found a gum tree and loved to throw eucalyptus leaves on the fire and talk about his childhood in Australia, a country that he was far too eccentric ever to return to.

One day Abdul hitched a lift with us to see a dentist in Medani. I'd given him money, and he brought back a horrible yellow molar as proof he'd not short-changed me. Next day, he had a fever, but Mike had had two punctures and was waiting for spare tyres. Falla had refused Mike's pleas for extra tyres quoting some company regulation so the ancient Land-Rover was often out of commission. I had no way of getting Abdul to the doctor,

Chapter 13 – Bollworms, Birds and Borders

and Mike didn't think his temperature was high enough for malaria, so I dug broad-spectrum antibiotics out of our medical kit. Abdul curled up in the foetal position and next day said he was better but stayed supine.

Keeping the house on an even keel without Abdul and with no transport was challenging. At the end of his long day, Mike used a huge knife to scrape the black clay off his legs but there was not enough water to wash off the last traces or to do any washing because there had been no wind to drive the broken windmill. We ran out of gas and were cooking on charcoal.

It was at this point, one of the pilots came to collect Abdul as the Medani mess cook had walked out, and a Swiss visitor was expected. Mike said Abdul was sick, and, in any case, our needs came first.

A written instruction came the next day. Mrs Shaddick could cope on her own for a few days and Abdul was a company employee who was needed in Medani. Mike scribbled a rude message and sent back the missive.

Fortunately, the argument reached the ears of Sayed Nur. He was a diplomat, something Mike was not. He found another cook and suggested a small grant to fix the borehole windmill would not go unnoticed by the Gezira Board, and restoring piped water to Wad Adam would help Mrs Shaddick to be more independent.

We joined the villagers gathered to watch the workmen erect the new windmill. We all stared up as the vanes began to turn and clapped as we heard water sloshing into the tank. And we all heeded the warning crack over the noise of the ongoing celebration and had time to scatter before the rusted legs of the tank buckled, a barrage of water cascaded out and the whole twisted metal rig thudded into the mud. The children were delighted, chasing rivulets of water to the canal. The company's generosity did not extend to a new tank for the villagers, so we never did get piped water to Wad Adam.

One positive did come out of the Swiss visitor's visit. He questioned why we had no radio. One soon arrived, as clapped out as the Land-Rover. We could not call anyone specific, but, with it, we could reach random operators and ask them to pass on messages.

We made our own small improvements: patching the mosquito wire and, after Abdulla cut himself badly struggling to fill the tank on the roof, Mike devised a bucket shower so no one had to go on the roof again. We struggled with only one table. I wanted it for my typewriter, Abdul needed to serve us meals, Mike had it covered in graphs and, twice a day, the counting boys used it to dump paper bags full of sprayed caterpillars and leaves speckled with bollworm eggs. I felt quite ridiculously pleased when Mike arrived home with a rare find in the Sudan, some planks of wood and a few bricks to cobble into an extra table.

I made table lights from big green glass carboys I'd found in the street markets of Medani. Next, I fashioned lampshade frames out of wire and bought crochet prayer caps to cover them. In my mind's eye, light would stipple through the crochet, casting mesmeric shadows on the old walls, delighting us and the myriad geckos and small electric blue lizards that shared our house. I dyed the prayer caps with black tea to take an edge off their puritanical whiteness. The concept was good, but the wire had been too thick to bend neatly. Even if the occasional visitor laughed, I could conjure the vision. The crochet holes gradually filled up with sand and the bodies of dead insects drawn to the light.

I'd taken on the job of collating counts, plotting graphs and ratios. Results came in from all over Mike's huge territory. I developed a card system to keep tally of the field-blocks. Mike

Chapter 13 – Bollworms, Birds and Borders

and Russell told me it was bloody marvellous and then drove me nuts by scattering the cards for me to file again.

Insecticide resistance was building in the cotton pests, yet Mike and Russell had a hard job getting the seriousness of the situation across as their reports were reframed by Falla before being passed on to a Swiss Head Office that did not like bad news.

One afternoon, I heard footsteps on the veranda and a voice yelled, "Hello!" followed by, "Holy Christ."

It was Jim, the spray season manager. I found him staring at the larvae of the cotton pest *Heliothis* swarming out of the paper bags the counting boys had dropped in an hour earlier. Jim sat down, wiping the sweat from his forehead.

"Where are these from?"

I enjoyed filling him in. And letting him know I was used to exploring larvae. They twined the legs of furniture and climbed to the roof beams to drop on us without warning. At first Mike said that was a good sign, the insecticide had made them woozy. But they were just convalescing. I hated it when they landed in my hair or onto my bare skin where they could give a good nip.

The sight of newly sprayed bollworms alive and well was a graphic warning that increasing insecticide application – the go-to solution – was not solving the problem. Jim would have to reframe his next report.

'Spin' was ubiquitous in the company from minions to management. Mike's scepticism included the company's research project, which was the pride and joy of a funny old codger who'd spent much of his working life trundling around Africa following desert locusts which he hypothesised were swept before inter-tropical fronts. If it could be proved that the same was true for *Heliothis*, chemicals could be sprayed with pin-point accuracy.

An air-conditioned trailer-caravan fitted out as a mobile laboratory trundled out each night. Inside, technicians scanned for insects on the wing using radar and infrared night-vision cameras. The enchantment of African night captured on clunky cathode-ray tube screens was abridged to hazy green frizz. The flickers of insect wings were the night's excitement. Dials, screens, switches and blinking lights filled the chilled, muted blue-light interior of the trailer. A surround-sound of hushed voices, blips and techno-purr made us whisper until someone would talk normally and we'd remember the surveillance was of insects and not of human malcontents.

Mike and I stepped from the surreal atmosphere of the caravan onto soft warm sand in the moonlight as a man with two camels walked past.

"As-salamu alaykum."

"Wa alaykumu as-salam."

Mike took my hand to walk back to the Land-Rover, looked up at the stars, sighed and said, "That, in my opinion, was all hogwash, if the research had any likelihood of success, it would be directly at odds with the company goal of maximum sales. It's a good yarn to spin for the Gezira board, though."

The next job for the spin doctors came when birds fell out of the sky. Not quite dead, they fluttered to the ground, weak and disorientated before succumbing to the heat. Mike collected some and found that they revived after he fed them water with a dropper.

Word spread and villagers brought us baskets and bags of birds. We lined up rows of cardboard boxes on the veranda and developed a recovery program. After their rehydration and rest, we let the small birds fly around for a day before we let them go. We pored over a bird book to identify them and kept a log. We had one mouse eater with talons and a tail feather quite out of proportion to its small body. It had a red beak and matching red rings around its eyes. There were finches and skylarks with cute crests; bonny little brown quails with no tails who instinctively froze, before rising up moments later with such a start, they blew the covers clean off the boxes. They'd land in a heap, shuffle off to hide and later unnerve me as small explosions bursting from dark corners of the veranda. We didn't save all the birds we nursed. I cried when a beautiful bee-eater died in my hands. Its teal feathers reminded me of soft Scottish cashmere.

The first bird of prey was a Peregrine falcon. Abdulla trailed it up the drive by one wing. Once it could stand again, the falcon assumed a terribly indignant air, hunched and furious. Mike consigned him to an outhouse with a flyscreen door, and soon we had filled all the outhouses and old stables with kites, owls and hawks. They'd ingested the spray from their prey as well as getting caught in the drift. Their stages of recovery were from the floor to a perch. Once they were perched, we could get a good look at them. Mike wrapped his hands in leather and fed them slivers of raw meat with long tongs. Hooked beaks and curved claws affirmed the rage in their hearts. Our good deeds did not win them over, yet we were always thrilled when we released them. We prayed they would survive the season.

As the season progressed and the cotton grew, it was harder for the counting boys to find the birds. We hoped more shade would help them recover naturally. Mike was very distressed. He stood all day in the fields on dead birds, their small bones crunching, their feathers stilled in the black mud.

The carnage was horrific. The agrochemical firms insisted it was just normal die-off from the heat but everyone knew it was the insecticide. Eventually, the Gezira Board spoke out, stressed the region's role as a resting place for migratory birds and began to ask difficult questions. A confusing response of statistics, blame, denial and rebuttal worked wonders to smooth over the concerns of the Board. The company spin seemed blindingly effective.

Mike's outrage at the duplicity was another nail in his company coffin.

Our driver was poached by a rival company and Belo, the replacement, was a tall guy from the Cameroons. He'd run out of funds on his way to hajj in Mecca and had been marooned in the Gazira for years. Belo pleaded fasting for Ramadan made him too weak to drive. Mike preferred to drive anyway. Belo was also too weak to change a tyre, to dig anyone out of the sticky black mud that mired vehicles several times a day or to load water or supplies.

Left with very little to do, he fermented trouble, finding fault with the way other drivers conducted their prayers. Then he turned his attention to Abdul.

"Abdul is a gypsy!"

"What are you talking about?" Mike asked.

"He's a gypsy; he believes in Jesus Christ."

"You mean he is a Catholic? A Christian?"

"He's a gypsy, Catholics, gypsies – all gypsies."

Mohammad-the-Bucket had developed a slavish and creepy relationship with Belo. He spent a lot of time with the older man and sadly changed from affable idiot to sullen goon. He began to question Abdul's authority and took to shouting "gypsy, gypsy" as he danced around Abdul, unnerving us all.

The bush telegraph was surprisingly swift and not our doing. Mabrouk and Taj arrived unannounced, dismissed Belo and Mohammad-the-Bucket, packed up their possessions and drove them away. That was the last we saw of them.

I don't remember who emptied the bucket after Mohammad; it was never an issue again.

Chapter 13 – Bollworms, Birds and Borders

As the long hot season wore on, I began to feel hemmed in. I could only go as far as my feet would take me. I either turned right to the village or up the canal to the shady tree. I wanted Mike to take a few days off, but he thought his reputation with the company was too fraught to ask for leave. So, I asked Sarah, Russell's girlfriend, to come on an expedition to Kassala on the Ethiopian border, a place where Hadendoa warriors, proud and tall tribesmen, strode around the town with swords strapped across their chests and huge heads of curly hair. These were the famous 'Fuzzy-Wuzzy' fighters, immortalised in a poem by Rudyard Kipling. The Hadendoa had fought fiercely for the Mahdi and, in 1885, made history as one of the few indigenous forces to ever break a British infantry square.

A few days bumping across endless desert in old trucks and lorries, past camel markets and isolated settlements, did wonders for me, although Sarah was not as convinced. The small township of Kassala sat clustered below great humps of bare rounded rock that rose out of the flat desert plain. These dramatic landmarks were unlike any others for hundreds of miles around. Once the outcrop of rocks appeared on the horizon, it was impossible not to fixate and watch the boulders grow bigger and bigger as we neared the town. I likened them to a giant's pebbles collected on some far shore and discarded. The sun and moon played with them, casting dramatic shadows, delighted to have something more to work with than endless waves of sand. Baboons and birds hugged as close to them as to lifeboats in a sandy sea. We spent a couple of days in the town then bumped back by lorry and the luxury of an ancient bus.

I returned revitalised and determined that Mike and I were going to take such journeys at every opportunity.

Mike had a present for me. He'd bought me a donkey, a very small one. I rode bareback, and my feet just about touched the ground. Mike had fed him lots of durra (sorghum) to fatten him up.

Abdul was agitated, "No good for donkey. Too much difficult for Madam."

Abdul was right. I only ever got Mr Moody to go any distance twice. The women of a village along the canal made a great fuss of me and gave me tea. When I waved goodbye, Mr Moody set off for Wad Adam at a great rate, the vertebrae of his bony backbone pistoning into my soft English bum. I could not sit down for days and lay on my tummy feeling fragile and foolish until the enormous blisters subsided. The next time I rode Mr Moody, he fell over his own feet in the excitement of turning for home and dumped me very hard on the ground. We never really made a team. Mr Moody was sold back to his owner at a substantial markdown.

Chapter 14 – A Mighty Miscarriage

Mike and I were happy in the Sudan and looked forward to the next season. We congratulated ourselves for being a good team in such a ridiculous situation. Mike's wicked and irreverent sense of humour helped with perspective. We developed a great affection for Sudan. A grainy canvass of sand stretching level in the distance, corrugated and patchy close up, with thornbush, cotton bolls, wing-horned cattle, flowing jellabiyas – all bleached by an incandescent sun. It made the blackness, ebony skin, shadow, night – startling, substantial and comforting.

I don't know if it was the spray that drifted over our house, bumping to Kassala, falling off Mr Moody, or just the fates. I had a miscarriage before I even realised I was pregnant. I was admitted to a private Khartoum clinic for a D&C: dilation and curettage, a routine procedure after an incomplete miscarriage to scrape the uterus free of tissues. Serious complications are rare, unless, like me, you get an infection in the operating theatre. An infection that antibiotics couldn't shift.

As long as I lay still, I was OK, wan and losing weight, but not in discomfort. However, when I got up, I started to bleed and was in pain. I was admitted back to the clinic and a Professor at Khartoum University, a Scottish gynaecologist, was summoned. He arrived with the air of a great consultant and performed another D&C. Still my malady continued. He did a third D&C. The problem remained. The eminent professor declared there was nothing physically wrong with me. The disorder was psychological. Was I a needy person? Did I seek attention? Mike told him he was talking bullshit. The professor recommended a holiday, adding, if I said sex was painful, Mike should press on for it was all part of my mental disturbance. Mike was incensed.

We decided that a holiday was a good idea anyway. We'd spend Christmas in Ethiopia. Asmara had been the capital of the Italian colony of Eritrea and, before World War II, it was tagged Piccola Roma (Little Rome) so much did its ambiance reflect the culture of the Italian settlers. It was a gentrified holiday, as I could not walk any distance so we pottered about, enjoying Italian cafés. I was slow on the stairs and Mike went ahead and covered the mirrors in our bedroom, writing in lipstick, "I love you so much," over and over again.

We flew back into Khartoum and that evening joined the team for dinner at the German Club. When I went to the loo, I started to haemorrhage. I steadied myself against the walls of the cubicle as blood streamed from me, flowing out and away under the door. So much blood. Then my liver went, slithering off out of sight, and I stared helpless expecting other organs to follow. Mike asked one of the girls to check on me. Then he was there, wrapping me in his white jacket and carrying me out past all the diners. There was consternation at the clinic. I was dizzy, I needed them to know I had lost my liver. They quieted me and explained it would have been a huge blood clot and not an organ. So, my whole body was not disintegrating? That made me giggle, as they begged me to lie still. Maybe I was mad. The professor appeared at midnight and announced the diagnosis was now clear. I had a grumbling appendix which needed to be removed, and he would check his operating list in the morning.

Norah, an Irish nurse, had been a constant during my clinic stays. As she fussed with my sheets that night, she whispered, "If you repeat this conversation to anyone, I will lose my job. You must go back to England immediately."

I said, "My appendix..."

Chapter 14 – A Mighty Miscarriage

"Go home, get out, go as soon as you can." And her eyes filled with tears. "When I leave the room," she said, "ask one of the other nurses to wheel in the telephone and call Mike, but don't let anyone hear you."

I made the call, and the next morning Mike arrived with a ticket for the afternoon flight to Heathrow and an exchange of telegrams with Dad's colleague, Sir John, a distinguished gynaecologist, asking me to bring my medical notes.

When the professor arrived at the clinic, I gave him Sir John's telegram. He glared at me, his expression strangely vehement. It was, he said, a quite ridiculous overreaction. He certainly had no time to write up my notes. He had genuinely ill patients to attend to. He would send my file by mail.

Within twenty-four hours I was in Oxford, sitting at Sir John's desk, explaining that my medical notes were on the way. Sir John gave a half-smile, and said, "There will be no notes in the mail."

"Oh yes," I said, "the professor just needed time to write them up."

"Your father and I go back a long way, so I will tell you why there will be no notes in the mail. I sat on the disciplinary board that examined your professor. I voted for him to be struck off, but the medical profession is soft on their own. Instead, he was forbidden to practice in Britain ever again. I had heard he was in the Sudan. You have had the equivalent of a botched back-street abortion. The infection is so severe that you are lucky to be as well as you are, but removing your appendix would most likely have finished you off."

I had to rest for a few days before Sir John operated again and removed the remains of the dead foetus, the focus of the infection. Back home my parents nursed me as the little girl they loved and every couple of days drove me into the Radcliffe

Infirmary for injections followed by heat treatments to reduce the inflammation. After a while, I was able to take short slow walks. As the weeks passed, I pushed myself to walk further and faster until one day I could run again. I flew home and burst into the kitchen, "I ran… I can run!"

Mum and I danced together, and I bawled my eyes out. I think that was the first time in the whole kit and caboodle of that disastrous pregnancy that I fully wept. I had, of course, cried with Mike, the shallow tears of the scared and sick, the bereft and brave. These tears flooded for recovery, relief and joy. I was normal again. Dad came into the kitchen to see what the noise was about. Then of course he did the Dad thing and said that called for a bottle of wine with dinner, even if it was only Tuesday.

Letters arrived from Mike almost every day. He said that living at Wad Adam without me made him too sad. He'd moved into the mess at Medani, calling in at the old bungalow whenever his route took him along the Wad Adam canal, until only Abdulla was there to greet him. With the change in season, a fierce biting wind whistled around the veranda, lifting the occasional feather and dead bollworm.

Mike wrote about the project and quirky little things about the team. At the Medani mess, he'd put on a record of Tchaikovsky's *Nutcracker Suite*. Tim, the plump little old woman of a man who so got on my nerves, danced the 'Sugar Plum Fairy' on the moonlit lawn, holding out the sides of his baggy shorts and pirouetting so fast down the slope that Larry and Mike thought he would end up in the Nile. I read the letter thinking that Tim would never have been able to do that with a woman around, even with me, who wasn't a sheila.

After a month, Mike wrote that he had resigned. "I'm sorry I

Chapter 14 – A Mighty Miscarriage

didn't do it sooner."

I felt sad that I would not see Wad Adam again. All the small trials and tribulations of our time in Egypt and Sudan were incidental to the warmth we held for our time spent there.

Larry told Mike that he too was resigning. He didn't want to fly crop-dusters anymore; he was leaving to hang-out with his girl in Dacca. He made Mike promise that we'd visit them there. He said, "Tell Gill, no more hellholes."

We didn't meet Larry in any more hellholes. He was killed in the Sudan a couple of months later when he clipped power lines across a cotton field, one he had sprayed many times before. It was his final spray run before he finished the season.

Larry's sister asked for his ashes to be sent to Australia. There were no cremation facilities in Sudan, so Jim had Larry cremated on a pyre built at the edge of the Nile, surrounded by his hellholes mates. I hope they added eucalyptus leaves.

A year later, Russell was dead, taken out by a drunk driver in England. I wrote to Sarah. She was devastated and alone. She'd had no one to grieve with. Girlfriends didn't have much standing with family unless they had a ring on their finger.

Although I missed Mike badly, I was so lucky to be at home to heal my body. Mum delighted in feeding me for I had lost nearly fifteen kilos. Sir John said I had sustained permanent damage, and that it was unlikely I would get pregnant again, though not impossible. And he added that if we were going to try for a family, it had to be somewhere with world-class medical facilities as there were a number of complications that could develop. I kept the news to myself until I could speak to Mike.

Time hung on my hands. One day, I went up to the loft where we'd stored our wedding presents. A wooden box lay gutted, wood shavings spilling out. When we were in France during the autumn after our wedding, we had bought wine, Kriter Brut Mousseux, to celebrate the birth of the children we'd have. Mike had wanted half-a-dozen bottles, I'd insisted we only bought two, consoling him that we could always restock the cellar. Workmen brought in to mend the roof had helped themselves. I cried, spooked; reading meaning into a random pilfering.

The dynamic consciousness that points out affinities and connections is fiendish in a woman who has been told she may not conceive. Everywhere I went, women popped, pushed and polished babies. Giant brands like Mothercare advertised on buses and billboards, turning procreation into an industry opportunity. In every magazine I picked up, breast was best, natural birthing and to dummy or not to dummy were the hot topics.

My relationship with my body was in question. I had a secret that shared felt awkward, yet withheld, raised a question. Mike and I had been married for two years, so friends asked me. Asked if I was 'trying'. Was anything wrong? They did not ask Mike if his dick worked, or what his sperm count was.

And then I had the other problem. On hearing that Mike had resigned, Mum piped up, "He said he'd never leave a job again without another one lined up, so presumably he has something in mind?"

I thought of the late-night conversations in Sudan at the company mess. The plans for new companies operating out of New Zealand, Canada or somewhere in Africa. Mike uncertain whether to join them as an entomologist or retrain to be a pilot or an engineer. Possum trapping in New Zealand, wild agricultural schemes, running live goats to Mecca for hajj. Cowboys, big money and hellholes. I had no idea what he had in mind.

I was sensitive about Mike, and dogged in my support. He

Chapter 14 – A Mighty Miscarriage

deserved that, he was uniquely mine, utterly loyal and I could not imagine loving anyone else. My answer, "I haven't a clue," was truthful and discouraged more questions.

At last, Mike arrived, scooped me up, dispersed my worries and made me whole again. Nothing mattered, as long as we had each other, he said. Yes, he wanted a family, but he could not live without me, so it was academic if I couldn't have kids. As for the first-world country, he'd just accepted a six-month assignment in Iran on a cotton project. After that, we'd find somewhere sensible to settle.

Chapter 15 – The Shah's Iran, 1974

I wasn't overjoyed at the thought of more cotton, but I was excited about Iran. The Biatian project was said to share the site of the oldest farm in the world. True or false, the phrase was a cryptically beautiful scene-setter. Much nicer, I thought, than placing it in oil-rich Khuzestan Province, which was more factual.

Persia was going through a pretty grim patch before oil was discovered in 1908. Subsistence agriculture had been the lot of many, with droughts, famines and locust plagues adding extra hardship to peasant life. Opium and carpets formed the bulk of the country's exports.

Change came swiftly. By the 1920s, Persia was the Middle East's first oil-producing country. The British Government was the major shareholder in the Anglo-Persian Oil Company that developed the oilfields and took both shareholders' dividends and a profit-share. The double dipping left not a great deal for Persia.

In 1925, Reza Khan, a military officer, came to power in Iran. He altered his name to Reza Shah and founded the Pahlavi Dynasty to rule the Imperial State. He changed the country's name to Iran and set about reform. Men were compelled to wear European suits and women encouraged to discard the hijab and mix freely with men. Fitzroy MacLean, in his book *Eastern Approaches*, wrote, "The Persians were being modernised, whether they liked it or not," after he'd witnessed a policeman rip the veil from a woman's face.

Reza Shah wanted capital to build infrastructure to push his country forward. Frustration with Britain over the unequal split of oil revenues dragged on allowing Germany to step forward and offer a more equitable economic partnership than Britain ever had. Unfortunately, in World War II, those German connections gave Britain an excuse to ignore Iran's neutrality to secure the oilfields for the allies. With the Russians, Britain invaded Iran in 1941. There was no declaration of war; Iranian cities were bombed without warning. Reza Shah's military advisers urged him to destroy Iran's fledgling road and rail networks to repel the invasion, but he refused such wanton destruction. He was forced into exile in South Africa, where he died a couple of years later.

After the war, Britain withdrew from Iran. Stalin wanted to hang in there until, under intense UN pressure, the Soviets too packed their bags. (Iran never received reparations for the damage inflicted by the Allies.)

Mohammad Reza Shah, son of the exiled Reza Shah, became the new Shah, with Mohammad Mossadegh, a champion of secular democracy, elected as Prime Minister. Mossadegh continued Iran's reforms and checked the powers of the new Shah. Still, the old grudge about Britain's share of the country's oil wealth remained. When refused an audit of oil revenues, Mossadegh got fed up with Britain's intransigence, nationalised the Anglo-Iranian Oil company and ejected British business from Iran. He alienated not just the British but the US and the Soviet bloc.

In retaliation, the British organised a world boycott of Iranian oil. When sanctions bit hard, Mossadegh's own people got fed up and saw him as increasingly autocratic. It was relatively easy for the British Government, with help from America's CIA, to incite operatives to foment unrest within Iran's conservative religious community and orchestrate a coup in 1953, which led to the overthrow of the country's democratic government. The consequences of this intervention reverberate to the present day.

Mossadegh spent the rest of his life under house arrest. In 2000, the US Secretary of State, Madeline Albright, conceded that the West's intervention had been unwise. The coup, and ongoing US support, made the young Shah all-powerful. It also made him deeply suspicious of virtually everyone, including his new friends. Which was perhaps why he kept his finger in every pie. He continued aggressive reform, billed as Iran's White Revolution. He moved to eradicate feudalism, remodel land ownership, give voting rights to women and support religious minorities. He also pulled back Islamic religious education.

The Shah's reforms outraged Iran's conservatives who found a voice in Ayatollah Khomeini, who knew how to simmer discontent. The Shah, quite sure everyone would come round when they saw improved health care and experienced new freedoms, made quick work of any opposition through his secret police SAVAK, an organisation he'd established with the help of the CIA and Mossad. The Ayatollah, after a year in prison in 1963, thought it was best to remove himself and eventually settled in Paris. From there he built a network that would settle his grudge with the Shah once and for all.

Whatever the Shah heard from SAVAK of growing discontent and the Ayatollah's popularity, he did not share it with Western intelligence. Instead, the Shah scratched the back of his US advisers who, lulled into a false sense of security, didn't even question the Shah's extravagant lifestyle and his enormous wealth.

When Mike and I arrived in 1974, Iran was the world's second-largest oil producer and had achieved sovereignty over its own oil. The country was heralded as an economic miracle with development at a speed only oil could fuel. The ambitious Biatian agricultural project was a joint venture between an Iranian quasi-government body that included the Shah's family and two

Chapter 15 – The Shah's Iran, 1974

Western partners. The young Iranians we met, the educated elite of the emerging technocracy, were hugely optimistic. They saw corruption as an inevitable by-product of the wash of money and rate of change and strangely, did not begrudge the Shah his wealth.

Biatian was a four-hour drive from the airport along a straight strip of tar road flanked by a single railway track and power lines. No company staff or dependants could drive in Iran, a decision made after the first three British general managers had been killed in car accidents in the same number of years. Huge trucks and buses hurtled the highways, their drivers notorious for falling asleep at the wheel. The quick-witted avoided head-on collisions by sheering off the tar strip onto the desert and, with hardly a backward glance, shifted gear and bumped back onto the tar strip again. We left the road twice that day on the trip from the airport.

The living conditions on the farm could not have been more different to Sudan though the desert terrain and cotton fields were common to both. The project's eccentric German engineer had chosen a small hill to site a clubhouse with a pool. He'd then scattered ten houses for expats, each private and unique although within walking distance of each other. They were airconditioned, fitted with every mod-con and finished with imported English soft furnishings. I thought Sanderson's pale blown roses looked strangely uncomfortable in a country famous for growing them. Tiled floors were lavishly covered with gorgeous Persian carpets that the expats bought to take home. The company's logic was that such comforts would keep the wives happy. Only Mike and I found it incongruous.

There were eight couples on the station, plus Dougal, the spray pilot. An ageing Biggles character with a bristly moustache and a rolling gait, he was self-effacing, liked to sit quietly and chip in occasionally with a one-liner. He didn't drink as much as everyone else. It didn't mix with flying, he said. Most of the expats were ex-East Africa. "When we" were in Nairobi, Mombasa or up Kilimanjaro. "When we" enjoyed the best days of our lives, which yours will never touch.

Each night the whole station turned up at the club at 6 p.m., drank copiously and usually finished up at someone's house for dinner.

The main watering-hole was the Hamiltons' house. David Hamilton was Mike's boss. His wife, Jean, was a talented artist and one of the most beautiful women I had ever met. I was magnetised by her musky, posh, come-hither voice. She was a little over forty; curvaceous, warm and witty. Once the toast of Nairobi, Jean boasted three daughters by three different men. She'd killed snakes, faced lions, evaded Mau Mau and outfought a violent husband. She was a warrior. Jean was also brazen, promiscuous and a high-functioning alcoholic. When she wasn't being bloody funny, she was a pain in the neck. After a couple of drinks, she challenged us not be lily-livered, boring poms and to drink more, eat more, and stay up late. For men, there was always the extra challenge of, "Are you man enough to sleep with me?"

David was Jean's second husband and ten years her senior. Everyone loved David. He was a man big enough to love Jean; he was her rock, her redeemer. In his own right, he was a tall, handsome man with a shock of white hair, wickedly funny and delightfully philosophical.

Jean organised shopping expeditions where she and I never got further than the first hotel bar in town. Each sortie, Jean would start the third-degree, dragging me into uncomfortable conversations, which all led to why Mike and I had no children. She said, licking her lips, that Mike deserved them, he was

Chapter 15 – The Shah's Iran, 1974

such a gorgeous man. I guarded myself carefully from this extraordinarily inquisitive woman whose real aim was to share her Karma Sutra knowledge and was, more interested in my preferred positions and Mike's techniques than in any yield. Yet there was a part of her that never ceased to amuse and captivate. She was a singular human, part succubus, part bosom buddy. Mike knew she unnerved me, and never fuelled the fire. Decades later, when her voluptuous beauty was over, she was left tipsy, funny and generous. Her beauty may have been an albatross; she was genuinely loveable without it. Or maybe I softened because she stopped trying to sleep with Mike.

Mike was happy in Iran, his time was valued, and the farm was state-of-the-art, with huge mechanical cotton-pickers and a new Grumman Ag-Cat spray plane. His days were not wasted trying to find spares to keep a worn-out Land-Rover on the road as they had been in the Sudan. And there was no pressure to use more pesticide than needed.

Yet Mike's routine hadn't altered. Up before dawn and returning mid-morning to rest until the 45-degree heat abated in the afternoon. Except this time there was air-conditioning and fridges and water in the taps. We partied hard, and Mike was clearly tired, but I wasn't. As there was no niche for me to help Mike, I got itchy feet and wanted to explore. The collective view went: not now, it is too hot.

I only had the now.

Whenever we went to Dezful, the local town, Mike and I visited the old part near an iconic bridge across the River Dez built by 70,000 Roman prisoners of war in 300 CE. I was intrigued by the classic archways and carved timber doors that dignified the mud-brick jumble of houses. No one hustled us; there was just polite interest and curiosity – a mutual trade.

Vegetable sellers formed a market gateway of hubbub and colour. Stacks of watermelons, aubergines and tomatoes contrasted wonderfully with the dazzling white robes of a scribe sitting attentively listening to his client before writing. Next were men working on goatskin water carriers, shaving the hair off the hide in concentric circles to make intricate patterns.

A small boy sat cross-legged plucking thorns and dirt from a grubby wool fleece. Curious, we squinted into the darkness of the open-fronted room behind him. There, two men with long-handled combs, like enormous back-scratchers, moved around shaking and spreading tufts of wool evenly to make a fluffy marshmallow of the entire square of floorspace. Next, they sprinkled boiling water before starting another layer. In the adjoining room, we saw the next stage with two sinewy old men clad only in loin cloths, who stamped in unison from one side of the room to the other, balanced on a long sausage of felt that was almost ready to make nomad tents, blankets and warm winter coats.

I didn't appreciate at the time that making felt by hand was a dying art and how precious an insight we had had.

I didn't take photos. Dezful's back streets were so archaic, I felt a camera would introduce a virus into a healthy host. Maybe I regret that now. We followed our ears up a lane past the tin fraternity fabricating coffee pots, hubble-bubbles and trays to reach the heavy industrial area, where a myriad of small furnaces glowed red hot. Incandescent metal shapes were extracted on long tongs to be beaten: short sharp taps on pots and pans, heavy booms on implements. We watched a foursome make a plough share, an old man holding the white-hot metal on the anvil with huge pliers while three men pounded away with sledgehammers. We held our ears and moved on to the quieter end of clinks and chinks. A stooped and wizened man was making chain from short lengths of wire. A few expert bangs of a small hammer, another link, his stall festooned with chains. Next came cowbells, and I bought some. In the woodwork section, I bought a rolling

Chapter 15 – The Shah's Iran, 1974

pin. Mike questioned something so prosaic.

"Every time I roll pastry, I'll think of Dezful," I replied.

Everything was useful: shoes were made from old car tyres, shovels, buckets and cooking pots from oil drums, knives and scythes fashioned from car springs.

That night at the club, someone said it was sad to hear that artisans were using materials like car tyres. But I felt it must always have been thus, making use with initiative of anything new that came along.

Out of the market on the main streets, bright shopfronts spilt out plastic wares and transistor radios. Mike and I were on our best behaviour in Iran, careful when walking down the street not to link arms or hold hands. So, when I glanced at Mike to say, "Not in the street darling", and realised it was not his hand fondling my neck, I reacted with a ninja pivot and slapped the face behind me with extraordinary accuracy. The sound was phenomenal, a reverberating crack. It was an entirely instinctive reaction. The whole street stopped to stare at the young man backing away, doubled over, his hand to his face. His friends fell back laughing. An old man clapped, and women giggled shyly. Mike was terribly impressed. And so was I, for I'd not acted, some inner defender had taken control.

When we got to the Club that evening, word had travelled fast. The story already changing. I had not only slapped the youth but bashed him with my handbag. I felt that embellishment detracted from the purity of my delivery.

Chapter 16 – Exploring Khuzestan

The incestuous atmosphere of our little enclave at Biatian was mercifully broken by visiting expats and young Iranians. One night, it was the staff from a nearby paper mill managed by Americans. Jean organised pool games – swimming in pyjamas and egg-and-spoon races. There was nothing I liked less, while the lovely Iranians happily and wholeheartedly joined in, not blinking an eye as the night degenerated into drunken dunkings.

One morning, quite early, there was a knock on our door. Ours was the first house on the station. It was ten US Air Force guys.

America supplied Iran with reconnaissance aircraft and had air force bases in Iran, convenient for spy missions over Russia. The Shah, a former military pilot, loved planes. Two years previously, in 1972, President Nixon had visited Tehran and invited Iran to buy anything it wanted, overriding US weapons export policies. The Shah wanted F-14s that could fly fast enough and shoot far enough to confront Soviet MiG fighters. He ordered eighty. It made Iran the only country outside the US to operate what some called the most powerful interceptor jet ever built: the Grumman F-14 Tomcat, swing-wing carrier fighter with sophisticated radar and long-range missiles.

The Air Force contingent, on our doorstep were from the Vahdati base at Andimeshk on the other side of Dezful.

"We just heard there were British people out here, and we'd like to invite you to a whoopee party on base," said their spokesperson.

We accepted and passed on the message. None of us were at all clear what a whoopee party was. It turned out the name

Chapter 16 – Exploring Khuzestan

came from a Mickey Mouse cartoon made in the 1930s. We girls donned long dresses and piled into two Land-Rovers for a very hot, dusty hour-long drive to the base. We danced all evening and feasted on delicacies – lettuce, chicory, and mussels – flown in from the US.

We got home at 4 a.m. Mike and I were up early to go for a swim before it got too hot. We were walking to the Club when our Air Force friends rolled up in a bus bringing a gallon of Bloody Marys in a cooler and several crates of cold Schlitz beer: 'The beer that made Milwaukee famous'.

The social life was unrelenting, and I despaired of getting off the station. When I started to voice my frustration, Dougal sat up, delighted. He was in. With three of us, we could more easily get company transport. So started a series of adventures, often hot, often uncomfortable and quite frankly not everyone's cup of tea.

At first, we'd snatch an hour or so to explore close to the plantation where ancient tepes rose as huge, long mounds of sun-parched mud, upstaging the sequestered squares of green irrigated cotton. We soon understood why David said, "They must have had a smashing time pottering about."

Each mound *was* made up of broken potshards, which crunched under foot into still smaller fragments. Deep eroded gullies gashed the hillsides laying bare layer upon layer of clay pottery. We first explored in the late afternoons when the sun rested on the horizon like a huge golden orb. During the day, the sun's glare flattened Iran's monochrome landscape, ironing everything level. As the light changed in the afternoon, villages and ruins rose up out of the earth in relief. One day, we'd arrived early and, sitting on the top of the tepe, watched in awe as the distance unfurled in the changing light. A village took shape. A gate opened in its high mud walls to let in a sparse herd of sheep and goats driven off the desert by a shepherd boy.

We followed bumpy tracks no more than scars in the sand. Monotonous dried ridges of sand repeated and repeated, broken only by a play of light, the odd bird or an encounter with a shepherd.

It was high summer, so no archaeological digs were taking place. What we did see made me marvel at the skill it took to excavate mud-made artefacts buried in thousands-year-old dried mud from mud, mud and more dried mud.

Sometimes on a Friday, the Islamic day of rest and worship, we had a whole day to explore. Settlements in Iran have been traced back to 7,000 BCE. The Persian Empire had once stretched from Central Asia to North Africa. Despite a series of devastating reversals, including a visit from Alexander the Great in 334 BCE and the Arab-Muslim conquest in 633 CE, the tenacious Persians retained their distinctive language and culture and each time cleverly adapted the art and ideas foisted upon them by their conquerors. Bending their culture like a willow, Persians, lively and enquiring, were not defeated. Although they abandoned their own Zoroastrian religion to adopt Islam, it would be their own interpretation, thus creating an unending schism with their Arab invaders.

In the thirteenth century, the Mongol armies of Genghis Khan arrived, threatening to snuff out the enlightenment of the Islamic Golden Age, where literature, philosophy, science and medicine flourished ahead of the rest of the world. Fortunately, the Mongols, too, fell under the Persian spell, slowly converting to Islam.

All that history left Iran with a marvellous breadth of sites for us to explore despite our confined radius. Shifting clouds threw dramatic shadows behind the huge structure of the temple complex of Choga Zanbil. The desolate sand-blown landscape was so theatrical, I imagined us actors in some spooky film

Chapter 16 – Exploring Khuzestan

classic, startled discoverers of an acropolis deposited from outer space. Although only the bottom of the ziggurat survives, the windowless mud brick walls are extraordinarily well preserved. The regimented facades with alternate panels set back and proud of each other looked almost new, the corners so sharp it was hard to believe it had withstood the ferocity of the desert climate for over three thousand years. I felt strangely minimised. When Mike and Dougal left my sight, it was easy to imagine they'd been hijacked or found a way into another dimension.

We'd read up about Choga Zanbil's archaeological pedigree, but, on the impossibly hot day we arrived in Shushtar, it was no more than a name on a map. Whoosh… water catapulted through the air, lunging out of cockeyed cliff face tunnels, tearing in streams through the town and tumbling into dams and basins to rest briefly in blue-green pools marbled with sand. The cliffs, walls, roofs, pathways were all the colour of sand. Dashed through the rushing hydrants of wild water were shrieking, tumbling small bodies, a rout of flying sand-coloured kids mimicking bits of the town spun free.

It was hard to make any sense of it until we picked out the ruins of an elaborate system of canals, dams, tunnels and mills. No guides lined up to tell us stories.

Years later would I learn that the town was built on an island in the Karun River in the third century CE with labour provided by the captured Roman soldiers who'd built the bridge in Dezful.

It was a remarkable engineering feat and included underground cisterns where hydraulics channelled water to secure a supply for the town, a great irrigation network for their crops and storage for times of drought.

One archaeologist has described Shushtar as the largest industrial complex built prior to the West's Industrial Revolution.

I've travelled a lot since my spell in Iran in 1974, yet half-a-century later, the memory of its discovery still delights me. It's hard to visit anywhere now without some concept of what lies ahead. Travel guides, documentaries, film settings and articles see to that.

There were other expeditions to hot cities at the end of long drives through lunar landscapes on hair-raising roads. And there were days up in the mountains, paddling in icy waters where we picnicked in peaceful forest.

I wanted to see more, Isfahan, Persepolis and Shiraz, but the tourist office in Tehran was adamant that local buses were not for single female tourists. David heaved a sigh of relief and said those were also company guidelines.

Mike was enjoying the job so much that I grew nervous about his enthusiasm. It wasn't a real surprise when he was offered a permanent role. After Iran, there'd be other opportunities in Ethiopia, Kenya or back in Sudan.

But I couldn't say yes.

"Death by cirrhosis of the liver? I'm sorry, I can't live in a bubble, and I want a job."

"I did think of all that," said my poor Mike.

We had a grand send-off with a roasted sheep. The American airmen bought over the hindquarters of a wild pig they had shot, and David organised a separate spit so as not to upset our lovely Persian friends.

Mike and I did get to Isfahan. The essential Persia was also the tourist Persia. Extraordinary and beautiful, of course. Still, my vote for the loveliest place in Iran will always go to Shushtar. I discovered it, after all.

Two years after we left, the Biatian project folded. The costs were too high and returns too low. Pilot studies on small plots where every variable was controlled simply didn't equate to

Chapter 16 – Exploring Khuzestan

thousands of hectares under cultivation. Other problems hit the company and six months later everyone we knew found themselves unemployed. That salved my conscience.

Four years after we left, the Shah and the Pahlavi Dynasty were gone, too, swept away by the revolution.

It appeared to be sudden, but support for the Shah had been crumbling for some time. Voluble clashes in the American Congress over the supply of fighter planes to Iran started a critical overview. Next came reports of human rights abuses in Iran. The Shah was already dying of cancer, another piece of information he'd not shared with his American friends. Anti-Pahlavi riots in Qom, a holy city near Tehran, were brutally put down, strengthening resistance to the feared SAVAK. The Shah, remote from his people, had underestimated the strength of the clergy.

The US administration cooled in their support. Inflammatory speeches by the Ayatollah-in-exile had been recorded and smuggled into Iran in diplomatic bags, sustaining and expanding his significant following. It didn't help that the commodity price of oil was dropping. The American administration added it all up: the Shah had to go. In January 1979, US officials put him on a plane out (or was it under a bus) and a month later joined the welcoming committee for Ayatollah Khomeini.

And those Grumman F-14 Tomcats? They got delivered in 1978, a year before the revolution. Iran's new regime inherited the Tomcats and subsequently became one of the USA's most vociferous enemies.

Mike and I returned to England and, considering our options for accessing world-class medical services, chose New Zealand. We were temping again, waiting for the emigration paperwork, when Mike woke up with double vision.

The doctor in the London emergency department was young, tall and good looking, the whiteness of his coat intensifying the blackness of his skin. He was from Lagos, he said. Naturally, we talked of Africa. But the Central Africa that we had left behind was not his Africa. They, he said, were Bantu. We told him about our time in Sudan. Neither were the people of the Horn of Africa his familiars. He was West African; different. We chatted easily. He said Mike's vision would sort itself out in a week or so, adding, "Too much stress, man," and waved us on our way to 'The Land of the Long White Cloud' or 'Aeoteroa' as Maori navigators had named the land.

Chapter 17 – New Zealand, 1975

Mike decided to switch to marine biology and found a job with Fisheries Research in Wellington, New Zealand's capital.

We didn't make too many jokes about the climate, the weekends where nothing opened, the men-only pubs. Food was plain, cheese was cheddar, mild or strong. At first, we lived in a down-market motel. From the tiny kitchen, we crawled through a doorway onto the end of a double bed that took up the whole of an adjacent cubicle. It was a miserable beginning, and I became way too familiar with white port, which we bought on tap, filling our flagons by the gallon. Neither of us was too sure about what we had done.

I decided camping was the thing. A spot of country air would fix our doldrums. I hustled Mike downtown to buy a tent, backpacks, sleeping bags, boots and a billy can. From the bus stop outside the camping shop, we aimed for a dot on the map, where we got off the bus for a pub lunch. We had no idea.

The name on the map was not a place at all, just the name given to a rural area without any shops let alone a pub. My new boots gave me blisters long before we reached the national park. The Waihone was a shallow river running fast through wide tracts of shingle. At a bend where grassy banks brushed deep pools of water and fir trees rubbed shoulders with tree ferns, we made a big fire, christened our billy and chargrilled lamb chops.

Early the next morning, I came face to face with cows chewing the new wool socks I'd draped on a bush and realised we were at the bottom of a farmer's field. We hadn't quite made it to the national park. Mike said no one would notice we were there, went off and came back with his hat piled full of mushrooms and blackberries. We caught the train back from Mataarawa Station, a tiny concrete platform enveloped by weeds. The guard scratched his head and said he didn't know the right fare as the train hadn't been flagged down from there in living memory.

When Mike started his job, I joined a PR agency. My boss, Dai, once a journalist, was the son of a Welsh coal miner and a dyed-in-the-wool unionist. He had a marvellous wit and eyes that twinkled – a shade too lecherously.

We went house-hunting and fell for one by the sea. The basement filled at every high tide and you could fish from the windows. The wall-creeping damp had an oddly picaresque salty crust and the constant wash of waves undermining the foundations had us in raptures. The other option was a dilapidated house on a windswept promontory with beautiful views. When I told Dai, he groaned and told us we would need lead-weighted boots to do the gardening. When the bank did not approve our first choices, we looked at a new townhouse until the agent said that the estate would be full of young families, and all the children could play together. We looked at each other. That might not be the go. We were not townsfolk at all, we said, and moved to the Wairarapa where Mike's eel research project was based, up in mountain country. Our big house sat on Bell Street in the small, sleepy town of Featherston.

Mike dubbed the house Gormenghast after a sprawling decaying castle from Mervyn Peake's fantasy series.

I bagged a wood-panelled octagonal room at the south end for my office and sewing room. I had only to go through the door to feel inspired, custodian of legacies and comforted by the muse. I swear the company of faeries joined me there; it was a beautiful room. Cold as charity, though.

We loved Gormenghast, which was not the same as doing the

Chapter 17 – New Zealand, 1975

right thing by the dignified old house. We tore the place apart. Mike built a magnificent brick fireplace without considering the need to underpin the joists, until the floor gently caved. I gave a poky bathroom with a high roof dramatic treatment. Out went the classic bath with its lion feet, which Mike had the temerity to say had character. I painted the roof gold to match my choice of white and gold striped wallpaper, which made the space look even taller and smaller. It was my worst decorating faux pas, my Versailles moment. Mike built kitchen units without kickboards, and it took us days to work out why we had backache.

We conjured memorable meals, with Mike writing the recipes on the kitchen's wooden walls: Rognons Wairarapa and Cape Palliser Hotpot. When I said I had always wanted a stable door, Mike sawed the kitchen door in half there and then as I cooked dinner. Toby, our red Labrador, loved it as he could stand on his hind legs and drop his slobbery ball into the kitchen.

We'd emptied the pound when we acquired Toby. The ugly bull-terrier-cross had no name, so we called her Jug. And the two kittens just had to come, too.

Mike's eel project suited him. He met quirky characters and extracted a bit of science on the way. In a wild, isolated spot he waded about the river designing traps and tagging eels. "Haven't been able to work bare-arsed since Zambia," he said, reminding me how his pure white dick had amazed me when I had first met it. He'd explained back then, "Oh, I put a sock over that when I sunbathe."

We collected mushrooms the size of dinner plates and Mike brought home eels, sliced them up and threw them into sizzling oil. The pieces leapt around demented, and I was so spooked, I could not stomach them.

I made crab apple jelly so clear and pink it seemed mystical and made me ridiculously happy. I thought of Abdul when

I hung the outhouse with cheese in muslin bags above the second-hand cream separator we had bought on a whim at an auction. Mike nicked neat alcohol from his lab and lined up vintages infused with various herbs, and I was terrified we would wake up blind. He built a hen coup and one morning with my Saturday breakfast-in-bed tray, there was a tiny black and gold striped fluffy chick in my teacup. We were adding a new brood of fighting hens to the more plebeian chooks in the hen house.

We bartered, acquiring a rip saw for a year's supply of fresh eggs, and had our concrete posts dug out and taken away by a local as a thank you for Mike's letters to the newspapers about ratepayers' rights.

On one side of us lived an old lady with thirty cats and on the other a local businessman of German extraction whom we unkindly named the Bumptious Burger of Bell Street or Triple B for short.

Mike took evening classes and swimming lessons and started to build a Sunburst sailing dinghy. He got a bee in his bonnet about backyard-built ferro-concrete yachts. We'd sail the world.

"Maybe you could learn navigation, too," I said. A little bit of me was beginning to understand Mike. Nothing was impossible, but, as long as he was on ideas, self-preservation eluded him. His reply was, of course, that he already knew a bit about the stars. Enough, he said, to get by.

Next, came a particularly New Zealand way of fishing, by Kon Tiki, a homemade miniature wooden raft with a sail. A piece of barley sugar drilled with a hole was threaded with fishing line. The raft floated out to sea and the barley sugar dissolved, letting the weighted line drop to the bottom with a string of baited hooks. Once Mike had his raft, it was easy for me to get him out camping, and we bought a clapped-out long-wheel-base Land-Rover.

Chapter 17 – New Zealand, 1975

On grey days, on long, lonely, stony beaches, I tied a rope round Mike's waist to drag him from the huge breakers if he fell launching his raft. And then we'd sit huddled together, watching the brave little craft bob out, dancing and rocking through squalls, and set sail for the horizon. Once, when it started to pour with rain, an old jeep drove down to rescue us.

We squeezed in the back beside three youngsters clutching rifles, piles of dead possums and rabbits, a pail of crayfish and several dogs. We ground up the steep track to their bach. The place smelt of damp salty air, tobacco, wet socks, fish and dogs. The two men were old friends, Dutchmen from Indonesia who'd moved to NZ after World War II. One stoked the wood fire while another fixed up great enamel plates of indeterminate stew. We played poker with matchsticks and rolled back to our tent in the moonlight. That night, gale-force winds and rain swept over our camp, and, in the morning, the Dutchmen arrived, laughing and joking, with fresh fish and dry firewood.

There were camps near glow-worm caves, a night when a huge possum climbed in the back of our Land-Rover and frightened the bejesus out of me. Once, we misjudged a tidal river and had to swim home. A late arrival at Cape Palliser found us struggling to find a site in the fog as evening mists rolled in – it was the southernmost point of the North Island and said to be its bleakest spot – shipwrecks littered its grey volcanic sand. And romantic camps where Mike gathered branches and leaves to cushion the ground, where we sat by the fire, drank wine and dreamed of lucrative short-term contracts and long sea voyages on our ferro-concrete boat.

My work in PR went well right from the start. After I'd pulled together an event linking North and South Island using homing pigeons and had enormous fun talking to wonderful old men in their pigeon lofts, Dai took me to lunch and said I might become a partner in his firm after a few more coups like that. He also wanted to be a partner in my bed, but swore the two offers were not related.

I refocused: babies were no longer everywhere I looked. I loved my job and had it not been that Mike, mindful that we were in New Zealand for one main reason, reminded me, I might well have let the whole procreation thing slide. Mike was puzzled. Poor man. He might have been a wild one, but he wanted a family, a tribe of his own.

The gynaecologist we consulted was an old student of Sir John's. He agreed to try a small operation on my fallopian tubes but suggested we explore adoption as it was at least a five-year process. Dai gave us character references while at the same time promising me a fantastic career ahead without children.

A month or so later I was to be found flat on my back, legs up in stirrups and surrounded by spotty youths (it was a major teaching hospital) for a pre-operation assessment. Just as we started, a nurse beckoned my consultant away. He came back and said, "This is all a bit superfluous – you're pregnant. Up you get." Everyone clapped and cheered. I was horrified. I was pointlessly naked and exposed on a stainless-steel gurney, and the sky was falling in.

At home, Mike was totally confused as I lurched, in floods of tears, from fury to the pits of despond without pause for any celebration. I'd worked hard to build a new future, and it didn't include a baby!

Of course, I came round to the idea. Mum wrote suggesting I not over-prepare, that small babies were perfectly happy sleeping in a drawer for the first few weeks.

"Presumably, you don't shut it?" said Mike.

Winter came. The wind howled round Gormenghast, the fire smoked, and it snowed. "Worst winter in quarter of a century," said the locals. We'd pictured New Zealand as a warm Pacific island, so the climate came as a profound shock.

Summer came. We read our books lying on a tartan rug in the garden. Mike suddenly said, "The heat, the flies and will the sound of lawnmowers never cease?"

"What?"

"Oh, nothing. I think it was a quote from a film, or maybe Nick and I made it up in Africa: 'The heat, the flies and will those drums never cease'."

Kim was born following a short, intense labour at the tiny cottage hospital.

The sight of Mike's face mask disintegrating in tears will never leave me. He was ecstatic to have a baby girl.

A week later, Mike welcomed me home with a bottle of Kriter Brut Mousseux, the wine that had been stolen from the loft in Oxford. He'd tracked it down in Christchurch and collected it on a research trip.

Although I had absolutely no idea about babies, I was good at following instructions. Babies in New Zealand were fed by the clock, went to bed on schedule and put on weight according to charts. Mike threw all that out the window, which left me with nothing to hold onto. He took everything in his stride and worried about nothing, which left me to worry about everything. I went quite batty after Kim was born. I saw huge red germs crawling up our newly painted walls – and I mean huge – big enough to carry Kim clean out the window, or was it up the chimney? There were no mothers' groups, I knew no one in Featherston, and we'd never heard of post-partum blues.

Mike's solution came in the form of an infinitely extended relative-by-marriage who, of all places she could have lived in New Zealand, had been found in Bell Street. She was after all a grandmother who would know about these things. Daily, as

Mike left for work, she turned up on the doorstep with two of her friends and spent an inordinate amount of time sitting by the roaring fire. I'd serve them tea and biscuits, stoke the grate, make sandwiches and do the washing while they bounced Kim and warmed their stockinged toes. Every time I took Kim, they would admonish me for not holding her right or not burping her correctly and take her back. I named them The Crones. I hadn't done *Macbeth* at school for nothing. It wasn't long before Kim and I got it together, and I had the gumption to send the witches packing to their coven.

To this day, I'll not pick up a newborn or offer to soothe a tiny baby. That's their mum's job. I won't be a baby-snatcher crone.

I was besotted with Kim, while Mike, equally besotted, was also listening for lawnmowers, bored with eels, fantasizing about soft cheese and terrified that his life was heading towards a normal, suburban existence.

Parallel events far from us would ensure his fears never had a chance of eventuating. A letter arrived. Someone, we never knew who, had highly recommended Mike to manage an aerial spraying project. No more details until he flew to London for an interview.

A week later, in the company boardroom, the first question he had to answer was, "Is there anywhere in the world you will not work, Mr Shaddick?"

"Saudi Arabia."

End of interview.

That was that. The project was in Saudi and all the tea in China was not getting Mike there. He knew all about that hellhole from Larry.

On his way home Mike made a stopover in Botswana to look at a fish farm project. He didn't really want to return to New Zealand, and an announcement from the wings meant he never did.

Chapter 18 – Casablanca Moment, 1976

Mike's favourite film is *Casablanca*. And his favourite line comes when Rick, played by Humphrey Bogart, looks up to see his old flame, Ilsa, played by Ingrid Bergman, walk unwittingly into his bar in Morocco:

"Of all the gin joints in all the towns in all the world, she walks into mine."

Of all the weeks in all the places in all the world, Mike walked back into Central Africa on a Friday at the end of September 1976, just as Ian Smith announced his acceptance of a two-year plan which would lead Rhodesia to black majority rule. Dick and Marilyn, Mike's friends from Zambia, lived in Salisbury, Rhodesia's capital. Mike phoned them from Gaborone. They were euphoric and their enthusiasm was infectious: peaceful settlement, majority rule, a dream come true. With the races working together, Rhodesia would well and truly be God's own country.

Dick said, "Come celebrate this weekend."

Once there, Mike was caught up in the jubilation. He rang me. This was a huge opportunity, he said, "Just come and see! Walk down First Street once more, and I promise I will not try persuasion if you are set against it."

I said, "Yes," for the second time because anything else was really out of the question.

But, this time, as Mike celebrated in Rhodesia, I cried my eyes out, because the world seemed suddenly small, as if there was nowhere else for us to go. I had signed up for a place beside Mike because I just adored the man. A man who loved Africa.

Ian Smith, Rhodesia's white Prime Minister, had presided over a population where only five per cent shared his skin colour. Britain's refusal to grant the colony independence in the 1960s had been because Rhodesia's Cabinet would not sanction universal suffrage. Smith argued that any route to black rule would lead to tribal violence, rampant corruption and a black leader looting the country's national wealth.

When negotiations with Britain stalled, Smith expeditiously removed Rhodesia's assets from the reach of the Bank of England before declaring UDI, a Unilateral Declaration of Independence, on 11 November 1965. The date, Armistice Day, was chosen to highlight the sacrifice of Rhodesians in two world wars. The move stunned everyone, even Rhodesians. The hyperbole was excruciating, the Almighty onside to defend civilisation's last bulwark in Africa.

At the same time, Smith cleverly pledged ongoing allegiance to the Queen. Britain, unable to justify fighting loyal kith and kin, could only impose economic sanctions. Other countries followed suit, while others seized the opportunity to make lots of money aiding and abetting sanction-busting.

UDI gave Smith's regime another ten years, with an economy that grew despite sanctions. And Rhodesia boasted impressive statistics around black health, housing and education, though only when compared with a pitifully low base in other African countries.

What Smith failed to do was anything that would make the future other than as he had predicted. Those years were a huge vacuum of missed opportunity. But the shift needed was as momentous as a socialist revolution: re-allocation of land, mass education and power-sharing with a concrete pathway to majority rule, all an anathema to Smith's tiny white, and comfortable, electorate. They preferred a fool's paradise. For Smith, a sense of cultural entitlement would be his enduring

Chapter 18 – Casablanca Moment, 1976

legacy – one that future black President Mugabe and his friends adopted wholeheartedly.

When African nationalists became militant and reached out to the communist bloc – Soviet Russia, China and Cuba – Smith thought the West would wake up and applaud his country's plucky stand against communism. There were precedents, of course; the West had no qualms overturning elected black governments in Africa when it was necessary to protect their mining and industrial interests. Unfortunately for Smithy, Rhodesia had no exciting assets to extract, and propping up white governments was not nearly so easy to explain as deposing black ones.

The game-changer was a peaceful revolution in Portugal in 1974, when people flooded the streets to place carnations in the gun barrels of the armed forces. With the fall of the country's fascist dictatorship, all military intervention in Africa was halted and their colonies made independent. Overnight, Mozambique, on Rhodesia's long eastern border, once a colonial comrade-in-arms, changed to malignant neighbour, hosting basecamps from which guerrilla fighters could make hit-and-run incursions to attack isolated missions and farms in Rhodesia.

The South African Government rightly saw that Portugal's Carnation Revolution was Rhodesia's death knell and withdrew their support, even entering into talks with the Zambian Government, hoping to force Ian Smith's hand. It took the weight of the USA, finally heeding the communist influence rolling down the continent, to bring Ian Smith to make his momentous radio broadcast accepting a two-year path to black majority rule.

At five-months, Kim was a good listener as I packed up in New Zealand. It helped me to talk out loud explaining how the bungee cord that attached Mike to Africa had just snapped back.

Mike met us in Rhodesia holding an enormous bunch of flowers with tears of joy running down his face. So gorgeous, so proud, so happy. He wrapped his long arms around us, and it was enough.

We drove to Dick and Marilyn's house where their maid, Eunice, in her red and white uniform, served tea on the lawn. Kim gurgled on a rug while Dick juggled bottles of gin and vodka turned mauve by the sun filtering through the jacaranda. I watched an eddy run through the vodka like oil and I uncoiled with the swirl, distilling, sloughing off my old skin of uncertainty and weariness. They all watched me. I knew it was too late for a chat on First Street.

On Mike's first celebratory weekend in Rhodesia, he'd been casually browsing the weekend papers. The notice was not large, yet, Mike said, it carried such a punch, he almost dropped his beer. The Lake Kariba Fisheries Institute was asking for expressions of interest in a limited number of kapenta-fishing licences soon to be released. Mike could not resist.

Lake Kariba, the world's largest man-made lake, was a colonial hydro-electric scheme to power industrial growth in the three British colonies of Central Africa. The border between Zambia and Rhodesia (Then called Northern and Southern Rhodesia) was the Zambezi River and the dam was built where the river funnelled into a narrow gorge.

Building the Kariba Dam had been a monumental exercise. There was no road to the remote site, yet huge turbines and tons of building material had to be transported over the torturous hill ranges of the Zambesi escarpment. Surveyors head-scratching the expense of heavy-duty bridges, hit on a brilliant solution so prosaic it seemed in jest. Elephants heading for the river traversed the ravines and tributaries at the shallowest crossing places. What if they followed the herd and made concrete fords instead of bridges? And that was how it was done. The engineers called it the Elephant Road.

The township of temporary pre-fabs built high up on hills above the gorge was for management and expatriates, while below, much larger townships were built for ten thousand African labourers.

Tenders went out for electrical and mechanical engineering contracts, for generators, switch gear, floodgates and valves. The largest contract of all, the building of the power station and dam itself, was won by an Italian engineering consortium called Impresit. Italy's construction industry had plenty of experience building hydro-electric schemes in the Alps, the Italians, recovering from World War II, were willing to go abroad and work long hours for low wages.

A British consortium protested loudly to Westminster that Britain was funding "a wartime enemy", while there was widespread disbelief in white Rhodesia, too. They'd fought the 'Itie' bastards in the war and had no faith in their expertise. A deep-rooted paranoia took hold. Would the buggers go home when their time was up or stay and share Utopia? Would the wogs erode white standards? Would the Mafia come too?

In his terrific account, *The Shadow of the Dam*, David Howarth, paints a vivid picture:

> When the first Italian artisans arrived, they were eyed with grave suspicion. Mistrust appears to have centred on their shorts, which were extremely short, and rather tight, and sometimes even coloured, quite unlike the stately, voluminous white or khaki garments in which Anglo-Saxons conduct their colonial affairs.

The Italians surprised their detractors with their enormous skill and resilience. They worked with thousands of African labourers in hot and dangerous conditions. Authorities had

had the foresight to recruit labour from far away Nyasaland (Malawi) for the dangerous work in the tunnels of the turbine powerhouse. Too far away for families to make trouble if there was a fatality. And there were fatalities of African and Italian workers. The dam was completed within budget and ten months ahead of schedule in 1959 and officially opened in 1960. Five years later both Zambia and Rhodesia were independent.

It was the Zambian government that initiated a series of airlifts to transport tens of thousands of kapenta, a small freshwater sardine, from Lake Tanganyika for release into Lake Kariba. The Zambians did not tell the rogue Rhodesian government that the lake was being stocked with fish. However, the Lake Kariba Fisheries Institute on the Rhodesian side soon guessed! Paradoxically, it was the Rhodesians that first swung into action and invited a South African company, Irvin & Johnson, to kick off Kariba's fishing industry with a purse-seiner that used a net to encircle schools of fish. Much to the chagrin of the Zambians, the kapenta showed no loyalty at all, and the fishing on the Rhodesian side of the lake was a great success.

The new licences were geared to small entrepreneurs who'd fish at night using mercury-vapour lights to attract the kapenta to shoal above a lift net. The catch would be salted on board, landed at dawn and dried in the sun.

Bob Cameron of the Fisheries Institute put Mike onto an expert, a Portuguese guy who seemed as excited as Mike... perhaps because he had equipment to sell from his own venture on Lake Tanganyika. The two of them had sketched out the rig before I arrived and even before Mike had the licence.

Yet, despite the promise of a settlement, Rhodesia was still embroiled in a nasty civil war and every able-bodied European had to do regular reserve duty with the police or army.

That was a step too far. If Mike took up arms, I told him

Chapter 18 – Casablanca Moment, 1976

that Kim and I were out of there. Mike had that covered. As a new immigrant, he had a two-year exemption from call-up. The concession didn't sit comfortably with everyone.

"Well, you can always volunteer," some said.

Later, I knew that just by being there, we had taken a side. Ironically, the side of the white minority was being defended by a Rhodesian armed force where black African soldiers significantly outnumbered their white counterparts. Yet, I still could not have countenanced Mike volunteering or being called up. Patriotism has never been high on my radar. It was a shit situation, and I could relate to most sides *and* find them incomprehensible, all in one thought bubble.

Mike used a quaint term to promise. He said he would not 'bear arms' and in the end *he* didn't.

Another concession allowed new immigrants to import a luxury car duty-free and sell it for a great many Rhodesian dollars. Mike planned to fund the business that way and since the proceeds would be invested in a fishing boat, we'd simply tow the boat out if the Rhodesian situation turned completely pear-shaped.

Mike's enthusiasm was so infectious, it was spine-tingling, and the decision was a foregone conclusion.

International sanctions were responsible for a chronic lack of new machinery. Mike thought outside the box, ferreting around for second-hand parts, improvising and, despite many frustrations and low days when the task seemed too enormous for us, the whole enterprise started to take shape.

A reminder of the war came halfway through Mike's visit to the Public Health Department to discuss standards for dried fish, when officials dashed off to a suspected smallpox outbreak on the Mozambique border.

"The Portuguese were slack about rabies and immunisation. Now terrs are flooding in from Mozambique with diseases that we got rid of years ago!"

When I visited the engineering workshop with Mike, I found his pride and joy was an ungainly contraption of huge oil drums joined by a great deal of angle iron together with numerous pulleys and winches. I could only think of the eccentric Heath Robinson, an English cartoonist, who drew fantastical machines from improbable components. The vessel bore no relation to the transferable asset I had envisaged. This was no fishing trawler we could tow down a highway to launch at Cape Town or Beira. Not wanting to deflate Mike, I spoke to Kim about it. Perhaps we'd add wings? She gurgled in agreement.

Finally, it was time to leave Salisbury for Kariba. We'd bought a Toyota ute, locally made of unmarked parts to beat sanctions, and packed it with tools and luggage.

Dick said, "You're cutting it fine."

"Why?" I said.

He looked strained. "Oh… tsotsis. You shouldn't drive after dusk."

Tsotsis are basically African thugs, random muggers. So that was comforting. Not guerrillas armed to the teeth and out to get us. We took Dick's advice and stopped halfway at the Elephant's Walk, a small pub with pretty gardens. The guest rooms were conical thatched huts, whitewashed inside and out. It was a brief respite after all the packing up. We toasted our future, bouncing Kim between us in the golden afternoon sun.

The next day, on the road to Kariba, I asked Mike, "What about the security situation? I can't help feeling nervous."

The settlement talks that had brought us to Rhodesia had already faltered, although optimism remained that a settlement would be reached.

"Oh," said Mike, "the trouble is only round the borders."

Kariba *was* on the border.

That was the thing about Mike. He delivered answers with such confidence and dash, I just acquiesced.

Chapter 19 – Commissioning *Hu Hu*, 1977

We drove straight up to the dam lookout to give Kim a bird's eye view, holding her aloft to see the massive cement wall that arched its back upriver making a lake that stretched west for 280 kilometres. It was high summer, and no sluice gates were open so the massive concave wall stood dry and exposed. It looked utilitarian – like a huge, stained pissoir.

Mike had friends in Kariba. He'd known Mervyn and Lesley in Zambia. They'd organised a house for us a few doors from their own on a road that overlooked Kariba Gorge to the Zambian hills. Elephants sometimes came from the gorge to dip their trunks into rainwater collected in Mervyn's parked speedboat.

We moved into the house by torchlight as all the light fittings had been stripped of their bulbs. Kim slept between us on a makeshift bed with moonlight streaming through the windows. The next morning, I discovered the decor ranged from pale grey to lemon to dirty pink.

My creative journey has been a bumpy path. While I thought my Versailles moment with gold and white stripes in the boxy bathroom in New Zealand was the worst, my efforts to banish mediocrity in Kariba came a close second. I painted our bedroom chocolate brown with white woodwork, imagining the greenery of pot-plants would look fantastic. Perhaps the single bulb that had sufficed for the Italian contractors was the problem. Kim's room became fire-engine red before I read that red made children hyperactive. Kim was already a wild child. None of it suited the little house in Africa and would later give our landlords a fit.

Kim was ten months old and beetled around the house stirring up geckos and giant millipedes called shongololos. Their party trick was to walk up walls and kamikaze off ceilings. Their thousand legs scrabbling for traction on naked skin was bad enough, but the ruddy things squirted liquid crap when they were upset, which they always were after their forestalled suicide. Each evening when Mike came home from work, he and Kim did a gecko hunt because he so loved the way she said the word, with a guttural hiss that she'd picked up from Mary, our African maid. Kim's favourite part of the day was washing the floor with Mary. It was so hot that the two of them could swamp it with impunity.

During the weeks we waited in Kariba for the pontoon, rumours were rife. Ambushes on lonely roads at night had increased and so had attacks on isolated church missions and farms. Our young neighbour was in a wheelchair, a victim of the conflict. On reserve duty, when his armoured troop-carrier came to a halt, he'd unbuckled his seat belt just as the vehicle rolled forward a fraction onto a landmine. No one else had unstrapped. He was the sole casualty.

We met the other licence holders, all white Rhodesians. Mike was the odd man out. He wasn't Rhodesian, he was a bit of a boffin, a bit broke and bloody funny. We also found we were the only ones who had no other income stream and would have to be first on the water through sheer necessity. We talked endlessly about what we all knew nothing about: what it would be like fishing on Lake Kariba. There was competition, jocularity, camaraderie. Bob Cameron at Fisheries Research championed Mike.

"The others have the money, Gill, but he's got the brains."

We formed an association to urge the Rhodesian Government to ban the import of poor quality kapenta from Malawi. We were

Chapter 19 – Commissioning *Hu Hu*, 1977

all very naïve since Malawi was helping bust sanctions by selling Rhodesian tobacco on the world market and the authorities would do nothing that might damage the relationship.

Our first job was to prepare our land site. It was overcast when Kim and I joined Mike and his crew erecting drying racks that undulated over every ridge and hump. Small fires dotted the site. Thick smoke billowed out from under metal drums set over the flames to liquify lumps of solid wax so we could wax-coat the hessian overlay for the racking. At dusk, the scene was starkly desolate, creepy and gothic.

The other kapenta fishers took one look at our handiwork, landscaped their sites first and bought expensive bright orange plastic mesh to roll out onto their serried rows of even racking.

The big day came when our pontoon arrived on a wide loader. It took a whole day and over twenty labourers to unload using borrowed shear legs with a block and tackle. That no one got maimed and injured was testament to the agility of the Africans who, shouting to each other continuously, ignored protestations from Mike and Mervyn.

The rig had to be welded together: decking, masts, booms, winches and a wheelhouse. By mid-morning the metal was too hot to touch and jokes about frying eggs were running thin. Kim delighted in pouring water over Mike and Mervyn each time they took a break.

The engineering firm had modified the design of the booms, forgetting the weight of the fish. The rig was unworkable. The firm's owner was terribly embarrassed, arrived in Kariba, said he'd sleep on the problem and disappeared. When Lesley went looking for him, he was slumped over the bar at Lake View Hotel, blind drunk.

Mervyn, a bush mechanic well used to improvisiation, modified the rig. But some problems were beyond solving. The engineering firm had used mild steel for the propeller shaft instead of hard steel, fitted a brush instead of a bearing, and we had a left-handed propeller instead of a right-hand one. The whole shaft had to go back to Salisbury. Mike and Mervyn stoically carried on welding, wiring and painting until the shaft was returned.

I told Mervyn I felt embarrassed at his unstinting free help. He looked up, perspiration hostile to the oil and dirt on his face. "Gill, 'ow come Mike didn't tell you? He helped me in Zambia. I couldn't return the favour, and he said to think nothing of it. Neither of us ever imagined our paths would cross again. I was paid, long ago."

I'd never seen Mike so wound-up. Our dwindling savings, rumours of atrocities far from Kariba yet not far enough, and fishing theories, kept him from sleeping. I would wake at night to find him, poring over blueprints or staring at the moon.

Finally came what Mike grandly called "sea trials". The nets had to be installed with the pontoon afloat, so using a borrowed Seagull outboard, Mike and Geoff, the netmaker, set off together with a crate of cold beers, just in case they had a problem, said Geoff mysteriously.

They did indeed have a problem. After they had drifted out with the wind behind them, they discovered the outboard steerage took them only in circles. The sun shone, the lake was calm, the net got fitted, the beer drunk, and the two of them laughed their heads off until someone with a speedboat towed them in.

The night before the marine surveyor arrived to register the pontoon, Mike fashioned navigation lights from two of Kim's baby bottles daubed with red and green paint, while I painted the name and registration numbers onto wooden boards and on the life jackets. The surveyor scratched his head; it was the first

Chapter 19 – Commissioning *Hu Hu*, 1977

pontoon he'd surveyed. He ticked the box. The last hurdle was insurance. No company would touch it.

Friends gathered at the harbour for the pontoon's formal commissioning. Lesley asked Nyami-Nyami, the Tonga snake spirit of the Zambezi River, to protect all who sailed in her. I broke a bottle of beer over the hull and Mike named our rig *Hu Hu*, the Tongan word for hippo.

Just the three of us went on *Hu Hu*'s maiden voyage. We immobilised Kim in one of the deep-sided blue plastic salting-boxes. The ancient Lister engine throbbed comfortingly, the rig shook and rattled, ropes crisscrossed to nets, winches and booms, it stank of diesel and fish from the net trials and Mike, tanned and fit, sat perched on the handrail with the tiller in his hand, smiling at us, at himself, at life.

On Mike's first night's fishing, it was my turn for insomnia. When he rang at 5 a.m., he was over the moon. He'd netted a third of a ton of kapenta. I scooped up Kim, and we raced down to the harbour where the other fishermen had already gathered. Mike's success was good news for all of them.

When we got home, we danced around the house. Mike whooping for sheer joy made Kim cry, and Mary scooped her up and took her for bread and jam while we opened cheap champagne.

It wasn't quite that perfect, though. That first night, the engine spewed oil, and the net frame broke and had to be welded back together.

The next night, *Hu Hu* took another third of a ton before the generator belts snapped, leaving them without lights. On the third night, Mike caught three quarters of a ton, and we ran out of drying racks. That day it was a jammed pulley to rectify.

The fourth night, the catch was over a ton. But the weather turned humid without a breath of air, and the fish didn't dry.

Mike arrived home, barely coherent, his eyes bloodshot. He asked me to go and help his men. I protested that I had no idea what to do.

"Anything, just do something… anything," he said and lurched off to bed as the shongololos started off up the walls.

Sorotiah, our site boss, and the men, were trying their very best, waving branches at all manner of flies descending on the fishy corpses. Sorotiah and I drove to the township store to buy rakes. While the men were turning over the fish, I headed home to check on Kim.

Mervyn met me on the first bend and shouted, "The public health inspector is in town. Says he'll be visiting you this afternoon."

I turned back to the township to buy pots of fly bait.

Sorotiah was distraught at the news of an inspection.

"It's no good, Madam," he said, "we must get rid of it."

He was right. The men piled the rotting fish into 55-gallon drums, loaded *Hu Hu*, and Abisha, the pontoon captain, took out a ton of fish to be re-consigned to the deep.

The health inspector never came on that occasion, although we had many future interactions. The man had a toilet fixation. Flies, rotting fish, mould on racks, all were incidental, toilets and latrines were his thing. Thys, one of the other fishermen, had constructed a pristine toilet that was only unlocked on inspection days. Neither he nor his staff used it, his men shuffled off with our guys to the public latrines. I muttered to Mike that I doubted the loo was even connected to the sewer. Desperately short of cash, we acquired a second-hand camp toilet and a tent.

The inspector was not impressed and said he would insist on progress next time. Each next time was next time. "Why don't you take a leaf out of Thys's book," he said. "Look at the facilities he has built for his staff, and always spotless."

Chapter 19 – Commissioning *Hu Hu*, 1977

Every day brought something that had to be mended, welded, fixed, ordered or borrowed. The drying had to be supervised, the fish graded and packed. By night, brushes stuck, motors surged, lights blew, and if the equipment worked, some vital part would fall, break off or disappear from the rig. When the auxiliary motor was thrust into reverse by mistake and sheared off its mountings, Mike was delighted that he'd had the forethought to attach a safety chain, so it was easily retrieved, but when the anchor was thrown out a few nights later and disappeared, he was apoplectic. No one owned up to unshackling it, but the shackle turned up later holding a primus stove to the railing.

The crew worked hard, yet were all chronically fatigued from worms, bilharzia and malaria.

The men slept on the pontoon, while Mike stayed awake to rouse them every hour for net lifts. At dawn, when the men went home, Mike always had more work at the site and so could only snatch a few hours' sleep each afternoon.

Yet Mike was one happy man. He joked that he sailed the *Marie Celeste*, generator hammering, lamps flaring eerily under the water throwing odd shadows on the black bodies sprawled on deck.

And I was pregnant again. A second miracle baby. There was no doctor in Kariba but the formidable hospital Matron – she needed to be formidable in that role – said she'd try to organise one. She gave not the hint of a smile when Mike said not to worry, he'd seen Kim's birth and knew what to do. Matron had first met Mike when sinister red streaks spread from a scratch on his ankle. She told him that dead men couldn't catch fish and threatened to have him certified if he did not keep the wound dry, clean and elevated for a few days. Mike stayed home but rose like a ghost each night to drive to a vantage point overlooking the lake and check for the lights of *Hu Hu*'s rig. If he could not spot the rig, he drove down to the site to see if they had returned to the dock. It was easier to dig Kim out of her cot and go with Mike than be left behind in limbo. Sometimes, I just wanted to go back to bed, but, other nights, we'd sit in the cab of the ute and stare over the water that twinkled with the lights of fishing rigs, mirroring the mantle of stars above.

While Mike was on the lake, I weighed and sealed kapenta into plastic bags for retail sales. Our house smelt permanently of dried fish.

Down at our lakeside site, African storekeepers left scribbled notes, which I deciphered with Sorotiah. The white farmers were poor payers, whereas the African businessmen paid immediately and cheerfully.

Being first on the water had given us an advantage, and we secured two big contracts. Dried kapenta was popular with mining companies, which provided workers with food rations. Kapenta kept well and had a high protein content. There were advantages to Rhodesia's old-fashioned propriety, for some months later when one of the other licensees tried to undercut us, the company buyer said, "I told him… that's not the way to do business. Cutting throats will sink you all."

We kept the contract and built the business, yet every cent we earned disappeared into endless repairs and improvements to the rig. We were able to buy a small speedboat, though, which made a big difference, allowing Mike the option of visiting the rig instead of staying out all night.

Fishing was governed by the moon and the weather. When the lake was rough, catches were poor, and Mike and the crew spent considerable time retching over the side. We were all shaken when another pontoon turned turtle, even though no one was hurt and it was back on the water within days.

Chapter 19 – Commissioning *Hu Hu*, 1977

A full moon outshone any lamps, and, for five nights a month, we got an enforced rest when fish swarmed the lake surface and would not congregate.

Chapter 20 – Kariba

Our lives developed a highly strung rhythm and a day without a challenge felt quite flat. It was smug euphoria on mornings when we had the biggest catch and desperate despondency the next when we had the lowest.

Being part of a community helped enormously. Fisheries gave us a replacement anchor after ours went overboard. When *Hu Hu*'s engine disappeared to Salisbury to be rebored or something that sounded painful, someone towed the pontoon out each evening. When the generator died, we were lent one.

When the crew came in with the net badly ripped, saying they had caught a croc, Mike pointed to petrified wood entangled in the net, and Abisha conceded *Hu Hu* had drifted onshore while they were all asleep. On the day Abisha took a forbidden short cut and ran aground, bending the prop, Mike's patience was finished, and Abisha was put off. Mike paced the floor all night and at dawn drove down to the township and put him back on the payroll.

There were many absurdly happy moments. The lake's backdrop was idyllic. We celebrated at the site when the catches were good, making the crew happy with bonus payments. Mike and I picnicked in secluded inlets with wine and blue cheese while Kim splashed and laughed at glittering mica sparkling the lake water. We shared dinners with Mervyn and Lesley and made new friendships. Kariba township was a vibrant and self-sufficient place. An amateur dramatic group put on plays at a little open-air theatre. Visiting bands and comedians came to the hotels. The Cutty Sark Hotel held regular dinner dances – and gave us a room in which to erect Kim's camping cot, for everyone took their kids with them wherever they went because of the security situation.

I loved the opportunity to get dressed up and escape the smell of fish, but we could never go too far. A tap on the shoulder as Mike and I danced was a message to say *Hu Hu* was in the harbour. We arrived at the site in our finery to find out they'd just dropped off one of the crew who was sick. We stood, incongruous in evening dress, which made all the crew laugh. Mike put his arm around my waist, and we waved them back out before we took the crew member home.

Although Kariba was an unlikely target, the armed struggle had become a constant background note. Rhodesia had no friends left. Mervyn, on duty with the police reserve, spent his stints at the far end of Lake Kariba and told us insurgents based in Zambia were crossing the lake under cover of darkness and heading for African Tribal Trust Lands (TTLs). About forty-five per cent of Rhodesia was made up of TTLs reserved for rural Africans, living under the autonomy of a local chief.

The sound of Casevac helicopters, ferrying badly injured troops to hospital in Salisbury, unnerved me. At night, I woke and worried about what lay ahead.

It was a shock when, in mid-May 1977, Zambia's president, Kenneth Kaunda, declared war on Rhodesia. We could see the more-blue-than-green hills of Zambia from our house, out past the acacia trees. Mike and I had met in Zambia. Were we really at war?

Kim came out in spots on the day of our fifth wedding anniversary. Matron said, "It's measles. There is no measles up on the hill, it's because she plays with the African children."

Mike took the night off and at dusk we were playing with Kim who, despite the measles, was in fine fettle. We sat on our little patio overlooking the gorge, enjoying sundowners and were about to put kebabs on a charcoal grill, when an unfamiliar sound disturbed the evening. I'd never heard a mortar. Never been in conflict. Yet I knew. There was no doubt about what it was, no doubt at all.

We flew inside, turned off all the lights and huddled together, clutching Kim between us, backs against the wall, listening to shells whirring overhead. There was an almighty crash nearby. When the shelling stopped, Mike jumped up saying he had to check on *Hu Hu*.

We'd just arrived at the vantage point when an army Land-Rover pulled up. "What the bloody hell are you doing?" said an officer. "Get down the hill now – and no headlights."

"I need to get nappies for my baby."

"No way!" shouted the officer. "Get down the bloody hill!"

He shouted to his African driver, and they roared off, a spray of small stones rattling against the door of our ute. We hightailed it after them. Unlit cars shot out of side roads, army Land-Rovers tore by, filled with black and white troops, their weapons in rows pointing skywards. The whole township was being evacuated.

At the bottom, the army mustered us, and we were directed to the Lake View Hotel. The hotel's lights were dimmed, and the big lobby was crammed with people. There had been a wedding reception that afternoon, and the bride and groom greeted us like late arrivals, inviting everyone to help themselves from their buffet. Lesley burst in the door, very shaken. She'd been on the way home after tennis with her eight-year-old son Paul in tow and was carrying her little girl, also named Kim, when a mortar exploded in the carpark, the flying fragments of tarmac and dust briefly blotting out Paul. She screamed to him to run for the car. Down came another mortar. She drove to the main road where soldiers were frantically waving the traffic down the hill. Her car coughed and stalled. Panicked drivers overtook her, hooting loudly, so she coasted down in neutral. Mervyn was far away, up the lake on reserve duty.

The hotel spread mattresses on the floor in the public areas and dished out blankets. Kim in soaking wet nappies and covered in spots was causing havoc, poking sleeping children and tripping up adults until someone found us a baby bottle and formula, and we took her to the quiet, familiar surroundings of our ute where she fell asleep. We took it in turns to sit with her.

At midnight an army spokesman arrived. He confirmed the mortars had been fired from the Zambian side. It was initially thought the attack was a distraction to allow insurgents to cross the river and target Kariba township. The army had cleared the area and the bangs and thumps throughout the night would be Rhodesian forces at work. It was safe to return home. Lesley's car would not start, so the six of us crammed into the ute and drove to our house where we put the three children to sleep. We sat cradling brandies, listening to muted explosions and shellfire, jumping at the occasional bright flash in the gorge below.

The next day everyone exchanged their stories. The *Hu Hu* crew had seen the rockets and been visited by a police patrol boat. The crash we'd heard was a shell going through the roof of the empty house next door. And Lesley discovered her car radiator had been punctured by shrapnel.

A flurry of activity began. In every backyard, a bomb shelter took shape. Ours was made of railway sleepers, sandbags and reinforced concrete. It had baffle walls after we were told at a security meeting that "phosphorous grenades are the worry". They sounded worrisome to me. We whitewashed the inside of our shelter, and I hung a batik from the Sudan, a reproduction of an early Christian painting found in an underground cave north of Khartoum. I'd always wanted a place to hang it, and the shelter and circumstances seemed ideal. Quickly, things went back to normal but not quite. Everyone was more united, black and white. Bombing does that. Even just a little one.

The attack had taken everyone by surprise. Kariba was not a hot spot in the Rhodesian war. We did not live the life of the white Rhodesians who spent every night surrounded by sandbags with elaborate trip wires and call signs, ready to respond to a threat so real it was often deadly. Nor did we have the inescapable terror of Africans in the Tribal areas. They were caught between the devil incarnate black and the devil incarnate white without the luxury of taking sides. Ordinary Africans were the greatest sufferers in the Rhodesian war and died in far greater numbers than white Rhodesians whose murders dominated all the news coverage.

While Robert Mugabe was the revolutionary leader of the Shona, his base was far away in Mozambique, and the Shona Tribal Trust Lands around Kariba faced insurgents from ZIPRA (Zimbabwe People's Revolutionary Army). These fighters were Joshua Nkomo's men, his Matabele tribe, traditional enemy of the Shona. Scores went way back. When ZIPRA men arrived in a village, the smallest affiliation with Rhodesian authorities could be fatal. Dipping cattle at government corrals, having a relative in the Rhodesian police, or just paying tax, could label villagers sell-outs, targets for symbolic grandstanding. Their punishment was staged for maximum shock and awe; the reckonings unbelievably cruel. And, once ZIPRA forces had pulled out, the Rhodesian Security Forces moved in to accuse the villagers of enemy-collaboration and initiate another round of terror.

On the political front, Prime Minister Smith tried to bypass Mugabe and Nkomo, the two exiled revolutionaries, by making last-ditch attempts to cobble together an internal settlement with Bishop Abel Muzorewa and other moderate Nationalists, which the international community might accept.

Lesley and Mervyn and their kids had joined us for a beer on the day of the second mortar attack. Our shelter wasn't finished so when the shells first flew overhead, exploding behind the house, we all huddled together in the corridor again. It was comforting to have Mervyn, his FN upright between his knees, for we knew the underlying threat was an incursion of CTs – short for Communist Terrorists. This time, the township was not evacuated. Once the mortar-fire stopped, we moved outside and sat in the moonlight watching the tracers of Rhodesian fire going over the gorge to flare briefly in the Zambian bush.

Duggie, a doctor, that Matron had summoned, arrived in the township the next day, a month before I was due. Matron thought him wet-behind-the-ears, and he didn't like her much either. And Mike was alarmed to see Duggie clutching a large tome on the complications of childbirth. Mike took him for a drink, and Duggie confessed he hadn't much experience in obstetrics.

When I was well past my due date, Duggie said I had to be induced, because his stint was almost over. Matron declared her hospital did not have the necessary drugs and was not equipped for complications. Nature should take its time. Duggie pulled rank. Their arguments continued as a marginal distraction from the excruciating pain of having my waters broken with a spike, the likes of which would have delighted any medieval pikeman. Despite Mike's entreaties that my first labour had been very quick, everyone disappeared once I started contractions leaving Mike and I to swelter as war-measure power restrictions prohibited us using air-conditioning. I was left alone when Mike disappeared to get help. I think they had time to scrub up before Dale arrived, but I couldn't be sure.

Afterwards, the relief was palpable. Mike was over the moon, produced a bottle of local champagne, wet Dale's head with a drop, and even Matron clinked glasses with Duggie.

Dale was beautiful, long and thin, weighing in at 9.5 pounds.

Mike took time off and made Kim his constant companion so she would not feel abandoned. A baby basket, hand-made by an African weaver, was waiting at home together with a doll-sized replica for Kim. Kim was vaguely interested for a day or two, before she pointed at Dale and said, "You take her back now."

Duggie disappeared, and a succession of locums were quite unable to explain why I had not stopped bleeding until a German physician wanted to do a D&C. This felt like Sudan all over again. I needed to get to Salisbury and see a gynaecologist. Lesley had a dentist appointment there, too, so we decided to go together. Mike had no qualms about being left with a toddler and an eight-week-old baby, although we did have discussions about the wisdom of driving. Although there had not been any incidents on the Elephant Road, Mervyn knew army intelligence thought a hit on the road to be only a matter of time. He said we must be armed. Mike bought a locally-made gun.

Mervyn had a spare FN for Lesley. He gave us a briefing at the local rifle range. Ambushing traffic was a simple terror tactic. We were to stop for absolutely no one.

"If anyone stands in the road, accelerate straight for them," said Mervyn.

"You mean run them over!" Lesley and I said in unison.

"They'll jump."

And on no account were we ever to pull off the tar strip onto the dirt. The dirt would likely be mined. "It's easy to make a roadblock," Mervyn said, "a few boulders rolled across the road."

We were sure as hell not to stop or get out and investigate

Chapter 20 – Kariba

anything. I remember thinking Mervyn told us what not to do. I didn't ask the obvious: what to do if the road was blocked. A U-turn would be clumsy, and a shoot-out seemed out of our league.

Next, came weapons practice. Neither Lesley nor I were prepared for the noise and kick of firing a gun. We were woeful on aim, but surely to God the bang would scare anyone. Mervyn flicked Lesley's FN to automatic to get us used to the violence of rapid fire, but when Lesley screamed, "How do I stop?" and swung round still firing, the three of us hit the ground. I got up spitting red earth. We walked back to the car, shaken and sombre.

"I thought we were going to die," I whispered to Mike.

"Me, too."

The next day we left with me riding shotgun, while Les drove with the butt of Mervyn's FN between her thighs and the barrel out the window. Crazy. Stupid stuff. Scared and sober, we drove like drunks, hurtling along the lonely tar strip with stuff-all chance of stopping in time for anything in our path. Fortunately, in the heat of the day, most game was dozing rather than crossing the road.

Les and I were euphoric when we checked into our hotel in Salisbury.

I didn't need a D&C. I can't remember now what I *did* need, but it worked. After we drove back, I never wanted to do that trip again.

Mum and Dad arrived to visit in January 1978. Mum came everywhere with me on my errands doing the rounds of African stores.

Dad loved the sound of the drums that drifted up from the townships and evoked memories of his time in West Africa. The ten days went all too fast.

On their last night, we went to the Cutty Sark Hotel for dinner. We left the girls with Mervyn and Lesley – the first time I had ever left them at night.

It was still light, and Mum and I took a swim in the hotel pool before we joined Mike and Dad on the terrace for cocktails to watch the sunset over the lake. We had just started dinner when I heard the now familiar whirr and whoosh of mortars. My eyes locked with Mike's. The other diners stiffened. I looked at my parents and said, "I'm sorry, it's a mortar attack."

Then the lights went out.

Waiters shepherded us into corridors. As before, the attack did not last long. Once we could hear the distant crumps, we knew the Rhodesians had pinpointed the launch site. I insisted Mike get the girls. Mike protested that Mervyn and Lesley would look after ours as their own, and they'd be in their shelter, but I wasn't rational. The drivers of troop carriers yelled at Mike as he doggedly drove up the hill. Lesley was reading stories to the children in the shelter while Mervyn stood by with his FN. He told Mike he was a bloody idiot to take them, but I was more fearsome than Mervyn, so Mike collected the girls.

The hotel set up cots and Kim and Dale were soon fast asleep. When the all-clear came, we sat down to resume our dinner. The mood in the dining room was elated. The band struck up some rousing number, and Dad called the waiter over and said, "The very best red you have in the cellar, please."

Mum had an enormous grin. When the wine was poured, she raised her glass and gave the old Scottish toast. "Here's tae us; wha's like us?" Then she laughed and said, "I know I shouldn't… I know it's wrong of me. But, my God, I haven't felt like this since the war." Mum took a sip of wine and put her glass down firmly. "I'd never have known… couldn't have imagined… I've missed it."

What Mum articulated was that élan, that untapped verve, the vanity of conflict. Just enough to stiffen the sinews, summon up the blood. Enough undoing to bond with the stranger, enough relief to fill the void.

It mattered not that the risk of danger was not very great; there was a coming through, a flow of confidence, of renewed appreciation of life, of people, of self. Surviving on a minor key is a very under-acknowledged accomplishment.

Chapter 21 – Bumi River

The political mood had lifted a little. The internal settlement with Bishop Muzorewa was still on the table, and our African customers believed the deal had grassroots support. One said that if the settlement held, he wanted to buy shares in our company.

Mike's biggest concern was that we couldn't dry catches in wet weather, so he contacted Liebig's, an international food company with a Rhodesian office, and suggested a cannery at Kariba. A fortnight later, Loris Zucchini and his two colleagues arrived, and we showed them around. They were very enthusiastic and took samples for their food technologists.

The next problem came a month into the season when catches dropped off for all the rigs. A rumour that at the mouth of the Bumi River, south of Kariba, kapenta lay in carpets so thick you could walk on them, was too intriguing for Mike to resist. He calculated the journey would take a day, and he'd need to stay there a week. I made it clear I was not going to be left behind.

The pontoon was loaded with racks, fuel, spare parts and rations and *Siesta*, the small speedboat we had acquired, with Kim, Dale and me on board, was roped to the pontoon. We left the harbour in the calm of dawn. The girls slept easily rocked by the motion of the boat. It was late afternoon when we reached the old Masampa fishing camp, erected drying racks, and *Hu Hu* was prepared for the night ahead. The security situation was a little problematical. Insurgents who crossed the lake at night favoured such remoteness, and, by daybreak, they disappeared into the TTLs, away from the lakeside. There was no question of staying on shore at night, so the girls and I slept with *Siesta*

Chapter 21 – Bumi River

tethered to *Hu Hu* while Mike fished with his crew.

By day, Mike joined us on *Siesta*, and we beached at strips of sand on the shore to stretch our legs and unload an incongruous neon-blue baby bath to scrub the children and do our washing. The spots were so quiet and deserted, it seemed impossible that anyone knew we were there, yet I was always glad when Mike announced we should pack up and get back on the boat.

On the fourth night, lightning flashed at the edges of thunder clouds in the sky. Grey masses scudded past the moon. *Hu Hu* had two good lifts. I watched the light storm play out in the distance as the boat rocked gently and voices drifted over from the pontoon. I dozed off and woke with a start when the temperature dropped, and the swing of the boat changed. Mike pulled *Siesta* close to the pontoon and called out, "I think the storm's veering in. There's a swell coming upriver, and the bloody wind is coming down. We may get buffeted around. We don't know this water well. Put lifejackets on the girls. We're putting ours on."

Within minutes, while I was fitting the girls into their jackets, *Siesta* started to snap and tug at the holding rope. Through growling thunder, I heard a strange drumming and looked out of the cabin to see a curtain of rain moving in, huge drops hitting the lake like steel pistons, sending spurts of water flying up from the surface. The shoreline was obliterated. The pontoon was gone too – the towrope erased halfway in a ricocheting spray backlit by the blurred lights of the rig. The crew pulled *Siesta* through the maelstrom to the fenders of the pontoon. I thought thankfully that we could get on board the much bigger vessel. Mike was shouting to me, but the wind flew off with his words. Abisha leaned over, holding the rope, patting the air with his hand, signalling 'stay put'. Then, without warning, Mike jumped onto *Siesta*, losing his footing and skidding into the cabin.

"Abisha says we can't risk a transfer, and I agree."

Already, Abisha was playing out the long towrope, and we were sliding back into the flurry of spray. Mike started the engine to give us way. We rose and fell on a huge broken swell. As the storm raged, flashes of lightning illuminated the hull of *Hu Hu*. One moment the pontoon threatened us from above and the next found us surfing towards *Hu Hu* below.

In one flash, we saw Abisha, pointing and shouting, but we could not hear him, and Mike told me to pull the rope closer. Kim had woken and was steadying herself with her hands on each side of the cabin doorway. She didn't cry, just stared out wide-eyed. Dale slept through it all, her basket wedged firmly in the cabin.

"Baas, baas… camp!" shouted Abisha, pointing to the shore. "Look up, baas."

Mike waved and whistled.

"Look up, Steve, see the roofline. It's a building." The shore was lost in waves and spume, only the hilltop was visible. Mike dropped the line to the pontoon and opened the throttle. "Hold on tight."

We vaulted the swell. The prop screamed in the air before waves swept the cockpit, streaming over Mike who was navigating by flashes of lightning. Suddenly, the lake steadied beneath us, and *Siesta* ran almost smoothly along a headland until Mike piloted her between trees onto a bed of reeds. He scrambled ashore with our only torch. I turned to Kim, but she was ahead of me, jumping off the bows into Mike's arms. Mike started up a steep slope, crashing through thornbush and scrub, with Kim right behind him, as I grabbed some milk formula and clothes and followed with Dale.

We emerged into a clearing at the top of the hill. It was a lawn of sorts, in front of two thatched chalets. Everything was deserted. The deluge lashed us, and the wind howled. We jumped under the eaves to shelter and stood panting behind the falling water.

Mike said, "Try the door."

I turned the handle and with quite extraordinary timing as the door swung open, a flash lit up the room. Deliverance. Three beds, all immaculately made up with clean sheets. By torchlight, we found candles and matches laid on a long sideboard. I pulled the curtains and lit the candles. Mike stripped Kim of her wet clothes and remarkably, she simply hopped into one of the beds and curled up in a ball, and I tucked Dale in beside her.

Mike had to get back to *Hu Hu*, and we stood in the doorway waiting for a flash of lightning to pick out the pontoon. He said I was to stand on the hill and start flashing in fifteen minutes to give him and Abisha a bearing so he could guide the rig into the inlet. Then he kissed me and left. Kim sat bolt upright and said, "Daddy gone. Daddy gone."

My heart missed a beat. "*Not* gone, darling, Daddy coming back with Abisha."

And come back they did. The small white hull of *Siesta* loomed out of the rain as it reached calmer waters, guiding *Hu Hu*. They all came up the hill together. Abisha greeted me, laughing, pumping my hands, rain pouring off his shoulders, his teeth flashing in the night.

"We are alive, madam, we are OK."

The other building was a large recreation chalet, and the crew settled in there.

We were up at 5 a.m. All the men were keen to get off the shore. Who knew who might have seen lights on land? All was still. The storm was gone leaving a misty landscape, delicately pastel and freshly washed. The thatch still dripped and big puddles settled across the uneven flagstones.

We left a note but never heard from the camp operators. In those troubled times, it might have been many months before a ranger went by. Soon, the sun came out, sucking away the mist, and *Hu Hu* and *Siesta* gently steamed as we dried all our gear, emptied bilges and mopped up.

Although we watched more storms advance and retreat, no more gales came close. Nevertheless, the water was too rough for us to get back to Kariba, so we stayed. The catches were not great; no carpets of kapenta. Each night, it rained, and we would potter ahead of the pontoon in *Siesta*, using an echo-sounder to trace depth and forge a path up the river between the dead trees.

Mike and I ran short of food, so the crew shared their rations with us. At first, I longed to be safe and dry and have a shower. We were all sunburnt, grubby and tired of the mopane flies that buzzed constantly around our eyes. It is strange, though, how quickly we adjusted to our new existence – cat-napping through broken days and broken nights. By day, we drifted into wooded bays, brushing *Siesta*'s hull along reedbeds, disturbing fish eagles and dragon flies. We watched hippo families in the water and herds of small buck on the shore. They stared at us, flicking their ears. We were shaded by Dale's lake-rinsed nappies festooned around *Siesta* to dry. Mike and Kim fished together, and Dale lay in her basket, mesmerised by cloud patterns and sun shadows shifting in the sky. In the afternoon, we'd push off from shore and anchor, sip warm gin and watch elephants come down to drink. Sometimes they bathed, their trunks turned up as periscopes. Kim, indifferent to the elephants, was fascinated by the white egrets with yellow beaks and black legs that stalked the jumbo.

At dusk, *Hu Hu* towed *Siesta* for the night's fishing. I loved to hear Mike laughing with the crew and watch the raising of the net dancing with silver sardines. At smoko time, their

Chapter 21 – Bumi River

faces shone blue in the glow of a primus stove, and the smell of cigarette smoke mingled in the night air with the smelly evolution of fresh, decomposing and dried fish.

Somehow, after the night of the tempest, I stopped worrying about bumping into terrorists; I felt we rested in the eye of a storm. Brushes with danger slow us down. After the thumping heart and adrenalin rush, the body takes stock and for a while we still ourselves before we crave adventure all over again. So, for the rest of the time up the river mouth, I marvelled at the moonshine on the water, clouds rolling above us, at banks of mist each cool dawn before they were chased away by the rising sun, and evenings when the rain just held off, now and then splattering the roof of the cabin. After sunset, darkness fell like a black-out blind, and I sat silent, inviting the sounds of the night for company.

Sometimes it was easy to think the lake had been there forever, so hauntingly beautiful and quiet. Yet all around were petrified and sun-bleached forests of dead Mopane trees as a reminder that this land was flooded. This land was hijacked and flooded.

When construction of the dam began, preparations were made to move the valley's settlements. First, the menfolk were led away from their homes and livelihoods, their lifelong connections and extended families. No area big enough for the whole tribe could be spared, so resettlement was to scattered enclaves of land on both sides of the river. The new land was different to any they had ever farmed. It was far from the lake shore, which was to be reserved for tourism and fisheries. Each man was given enough material for a hut. It was important, said the colonial overseers, not to 'spoil' these men who needed to be industrious in rebuilding their lives and livelihoods.

Baboons and monkeys shrieked from the trees, and smoke from cooking fires drifted up with the morning mist to meet lorries grinding down hundreds of newly slashed roads into the valley to collect the men's families and their possessions. Household goods, stocks of corn and seed, whatever could be salvaged – a hut door, a canoe, baskets, tools, goats and chickens. It was the old people who felt it most. The children least. The women balancing the two. The debris left behind, reed mats, an empty gourd, made puny fodder for the biggest tractors ever built, waiting to roar down the muddy tracks to the valley and fell the trees that might snag the fishing nets to come.

The human tragedy of the Gwembe Valley was overshadowed by the rescue of the animals when Lake Kariba's Dunkirk moment stole the show. Again, I quote David Howarth:

> The fate of fifty thousand Tonga had hardly caused a ripple in the world's newspapers, the fate of a few thousand animals was to cause a storm.

It had been anticipated that most animals would escape to higher ground as the waters rose. A cull was not unwelcome as the mass migration of game out of the valley would overstock other areas.

Curious, game rangers took out boats and picked their way between trees full of snakes and all manner of slithery life seeking refuge. While most big game had escaped the rising water, plenty of warthog, porcupines and buck, bush pigs and baboons were stranded on diminishing islands. Instinctively, the rangers rescued some of the wildlife. When the story got out, well-meaning individuals towed their boats to the lake and joined in. The international press descended, a journalist dubbed it "Operation Noah", money poured in and a legend was born.

At best, the animals were released into national parks. At worst, they were decanted into areas where hunters were being paid to clear wildlife for the new settlements or where tsetse

Chapter 21 – Bumi River

officers were practising game reduction. Africans were mystified to see rescued baboons. Their colonial masters had previously declared them vermin and had put a price on their heads.

A prosaic block of concrete with a plaque stands at a vantage point overlooking the Lake to commemorate Operation Noah. The silent, petrified trees remain as enduring and haunting monuments to the displaced tribes of Tonga.

Chapter 22 – The Chicken Run

Holidays that year were brief camping weekends with Mervyn and Lesley when the moon was full and catches were low. We went by boat to Tashinga in the Mutsadona National Park. Kim, at eighteen months, needed her first pair of shoes for the thorny ground. She found the concept strange and sat down every few steps to pull out the thorns from the rubber soles of her little blue tackies. (Sand shoes were called 'tackies' in Rhodesia and car tyres were 'fat tackies'.)

The Tashinga game wardens were raising a herd of disease-free buffalo. The hand-reared calves were more friendly than their pet mongoose, Goosey, who nipped every child that visited.

Mike and I spent a happy morning paddling with the girls in a quiet bay. The next morning the warden wandered over. He said, "By the way, make sure you don't go near that bay over there; it's full of crocs. And keep the children well back from the shore."

Mervyn looked up and said, "None of us are that stupid."

Holidays were fun, but we could not escape the worsening security situation. Farmers were leaving. Others battled on. One gave me news of our best farm-store customer, "Oh, they've gone – store burnt out. Made us get ready," and then told me how her husband had shot a hole in the bath practising loading his gun at speed. Roaring with laughter, she carried on, "So we opened a bottle of wine, drank it and plugged the hole with the cork."

A convoy under military escort had started along the Elephant Road. A friend of Mervyn's showed me the custom-made armour plating around his son's child-seat and the brackets for machine guns he'd welded to the car doors. He bragged, "Just let 'em try it!"

Chapter 22 – The Chicken Run

One morning, I was leaving the library when I saw Lesley sitting on the grass, talking with her friends. Her eyes were downcast, and her hand was plucking pieces of grass. Their voices were hushed, but I heard the conversation. Leaving. Leaving Rhodesia. Getting out. A girl was speaking. Her husband had been on a night-time raid on an African village. Children running, women screaming. A firefight. Flushing out insurgents. The chaos of the flaming dark. Firing. Weapons jamming. Great fear. Terror. Dust rising. Bodies. A torched village. A pyre. Her husband distraught. Hadn't meant to. Would never again. They were leaving immediately. Getting out.

I wanted to shout, "But it's too late. It's done!"

Right enough, but not my call, with Mike excused from reserve duty. I got up quietly and went home to wait for Mike.

Mike's call-up papers would soon arrive. I didn't tell him my fears as he would simply deny that he'd ever take part in slaughter. Mike had a strong moral compass, yet I knew from listening that a compass swings from true near high voltage. None of us know ourselves in all seasons, in all circumstances. Few of us are prepared for the confusion of hell on earth.

As he walked through the door, I blurted out, "We can't stay. There is not going to be any peace."

Mike didn't answer immediately. He sat down heavily, pulling me onto his lap.

"I know," he whispered, "I know."

We cried, rocking each other in our tears.

It was called 'the chicken run'. All Europeans who left Rhodesia were chicken. Once we made the decision, everything changed. I wanted us out. I felt we were already on borrowed time.

Mike said he never wanted to be anyone's employee again and left for a month in the UK to find a new business. The day he left, the Elephant's Walk, the guest house where we'd stayed half-way to Kariba was 'revved'. Burnt to the ground.

While Mike was gone, I saw *Hu Hu* off each evening. Every morning, Mary, our maid, met us at the site and took over Mike's circuit with the girls visiting a family of ducks that lived by the mooring, feasting on stray kapenta. Each morning, Abisha would report small grievances. He refused to have Amos as crew because he had hollow teeth and cried like a baby. I took Amos to the hospital dentist. And there were always repairs to supervise. I felt I was managing, until the catches started falling off.

Thys offered to check up on *Hu Hu* and was as good as his word. He had drifted his speedboat up to our rig and found the crew fast asleep while the water around the lights was seething with kapenta. They were not bothering to lift the nets. Thys climbed on board and kicked and cursed our crew. And when Abisha challenged him, Thys said he was acting on my behalf.

I knew nothing about what had happened as I hadn't seen Thys before I got to the dock. When he saw me, Abisha grew apoplectic with rage. Sorotiah ran to stand beside me. The crew joined Abisha, shouting at me and at each other. All I could make out was that they were walking off the job. They would come back when boss Mike returned. The men began gathering their belongings. When the story came out, I apologised, and I should have known better. But my apologies sounded flimsy, and I stood side-lined while Sorotiah and Abisha harangued each other in Shona. Then Melo came forward and took my hand. Melo was a lovely old man from Malawi who had been with us from the first day. When he started speaking, the men quietened. Sorotiah whispered, "Melo's saying they can't leave you in 'big mess'."

At last, Sorotiah gave me a sign and said softly, "It's OK,

Chapter 22 – The Chicken Run

everyone agrees. Wait for Abisha to speak."

Abisha said they would go back to work, but if boss Thys set foot on *Hu Hu* again, he would kill him.

Mervyn advised me to take Abisha's threat seriously. He did not doubt him capable of murder, especially in these times. There had recently been a strange incident on the lake when an unpopular DC – a European District Commissioner – had inexplicably drowned.

Mervyn offered to check up on *Hu Hu*, but only if I forewarned the crew.

When I asked Thys not to visit *Hu Hu* again, he said, "Ach… you pommy bastards… Mike's too soft. He'll never learn."

In the midst of all this, Liebig's executives made their third visit to Kariba, this time bringing their wives. I spent all day with them. They were staying at Caribbea Bay Hotel, a resort on the lake. I had a drink with them at the end of the day but could not stay for a meal as I had to get back to my little ones.

I wrote to Mike:

> Loris has left test cans of kapenta, tiger and bream for us to try. He says the taste is not bad but suggests a candlelit dinner until they do more work on the appearance.

I drove the Liebig men and their wives to Kariba Airport the next morning. The Air Rhodesia Viscounts took off climbing steeply over the lake as a precaution against ground fire from insurgents. Kariba Airport was small and picturesque. Quite often, the runway had to be cleared of game, and the army drivers guarding the airstrip enjoyed that extra responsibility, racing their Land-Rovers round the perimeter.

A security meeting was called for kapenta fishers. The army spokesman said they were wasting too many man-hours fooling about with kapenta boats, and things had to change or we'd be ordered off the water. From that day, on we had to give the location where we'd be fishing and could not visit our rigs by speedboat without calling security first.

"And don't fish off Mica Point. No need to give ZIPRA sitting targets that might be close enough for them to actually hit."

Each of us got a dressing down.

"*Hu Hu*: your crew is always fast asleep. If they drift off-location, we are liable to blow you up – that's if some CTs haven't boarded you first."

A Rhodesian patrol boat had reported it had nearly sunk a rig when it drifted towards them on a dark night.

"We had our cannons cocked; it was a close shave," said the spokesman.

Another rig had almost been mistaken for a Zambian patrol boat.

The day before Mike arrived back, the Elephant Road convoy was ambushed forty kilometres south of Kariba, killing four – an elderly African bus driver and three young girls. Mervyn's friend was in the convoy. All his bluster was gone. Still in shock, he told how when the convoy halted unexpectedly, out of the bush appeared a tall CT who stood with his legs apart, laughing, swinging his AK47 from side to side raking the cars. "I'd no time to return fire, just pulled out of the line and put my foot down."

We sold Sea Farmers to a Danish guy called Hans Hansen. He thought Kariba would be a good place to "await the outcome of the Rhodesian dilemma". That had a familiar ring. Hans paid us partly in US dollars. I would smuggle them out the country in Dale's dirty nappies, the rest in Rhodesian dollars couldn't be transferred, and we knew our bank account would be frozen when we left the country.

We had one month left in Rhodesia and Mike and I flew weekly to Salisbury to settle our affairs. We felt safer flying than

Chapter 22 – The Chicken Run

risking the convoy. And we took a last holiday, flying to Victoria Falls. A day spent beside the Elephant Hills Hotel was surreal. The resort had burned down after a CT attack, and only the swimming pool and golf-course had survived. We had the pool to ourselves. The resort sat high up on a kopje, with a grand view of golfers on the course below trailed by security forces in mufti. It was the same on the Zambezi booze cruise, where security forces pretended to be casual fishermen on the banks. We also took 'The Flight of Angels', a joy flight over the Victoria Falls.

Leaving, I was happy. I wanted to feel safe again. I knew Mike had a heavy heart, yet he did not voice his regrets and was a wonderful enthusiast for our next venture – rabbit farming.

Our families were delighted to have us back. It was only Mum who understood what we had left behind and despite her relief, she cried with me, and I loved her so much for that. We were so fortunate to be able to walk away from our adventures unscathed. So many people, black and white, in Rhodesia would have liked to have had our options.

The Rhodesian conflict had faded from British newspapers. No one wanted to hear how the conflict had exacerbated old divisions so that while black majority rule was legitimate, it was no panacea, the bloodshed was unstoppable. The weight of wasted lives haunted us. Enjoying security felt reprehensible. Our prosperity made us queasy. A week home, and we needed time by ourselves.

Mike's auntie offered her caravan in a park near Bristol. It was late autumn; the place was deserted, and it rained for days.

Mike finally said, "Enough of this, I'm going to the pub to get a bottle of wine."

When he returned, rivulets coursed down his face, and it wasn't just the rain.

On the pub's television, Hans Hansen, who had bought our business, had appeared. How surreal, Mike thought, struggling to comprehend the newsreader. A heat-seeking missile had brought down a passenger plane leaving Kariba Airport. Hans, a man clearly traumatised, had survived the crash together with Diana, his wife. It would be some time before we knew the full story.

Lesley worked as a Kariba tourist guide and, on the third of September 1978, ten days after we had left, she delivered her tour group to the airport. Lesley waved to Hans and Diana and other friends, checking in for the daily Flight 825 to Salisbury. The plane was a four-engine Viscount named *Hunyani*. Barely five minutes after take-off, a SAM 7 surface-to-air missile struck, lodged in the plane's starboard wheel-bay, and exploded with an almighty bang. The strike from a Soviet-built shoulder rocket launcher took out the controls and ruptured fuel lines, cutting out starboard engines and igniting the wing. The pilot sent out his last call.

"Mayday, Mayday, Mayday. This is 825. We have lost both engines and are going in."

With virtually all control lost, the pilot nearly made a perfect touchdown in the Urungwe Tribal Trust Land, except the wing caught a tree and a great ditch did the rest. The tail section sheared off as the plane careered on in a ball of flame.

Eighteen passengers from the rear of the aircraft survived including a baby and toddlers. Dazed, some badly injured, they congregated at a distance from the burning debris of the crash. Hans and Diana were uninjured and went to search the scattered luggage for clothes to make bandages for the wounded. As they returned, the sound of new voices was followed by a burst of machine-gun fire. They dropped to the ground and in the dusk through the haze of drifting smoke watched in horror as the survivors were rounded up and shot dead at point blank range by a bunch of African insurgents.

With darkness falling, Hans and Diana crawled to a shallow ditch with long grass that offered better cover. The gunmen searching the crash site, came so close that Hans and Diana could see their boots go by. There were six other survivors. One, hiding in the same culvert as Hans and Diana, had gone to the bush to relieve himself. Five had gone to find water at a nearby village. Walking back, they too saw the massacre, were spotted and ran to hide. One was a four-year-old girl. Had she whimpered, it would have been all over for them. A new moon made it dark, and the insurgents pursuit was cursory, presumably expecting the Rhodesian security forces to arrive at any moment.

Joshua Nkomo's ZIPRA forces were responsible. Nkomo boasted of the coup. There was no international condemnation.

The Very Revd. John Da Costa, Anglican Dean of Salisbury, preached five days after the crash, castigating the Western world:

"One listens and the silence is deafening."

Bishop Desmond Tutu, General Secretary of the South African Council of Churches, was one African leader who stood up and joined Da Costa's recriminations.

Mervyn wrote that a terrible gloom descended over Kariba. A few days later Mervyn flew to Salisbury with Paul. He said he'd had a beautiful flight and was so drunk by the time he got on the plane, he was past caring. Lesley took the Kariba float plane. The pilot hedge-hopped all the way to Salisbury believing he had better odds against groundfire than heat-seeking missiles.

Four months later, on the twelfth of February 1979, another Viscount, *Umniati*, Flight 827, was shot down by ZIPRA as it left Kariba. All 59 passengers and crew were killed. On board that flight were three Liebig's executives, including Loris Zucchini, who had been so enthusiastic about Mike's idea of a canning project.

Rhodesian intelligence knew the capability of the insurgents but kept it from the public so as not to undermine white morale. And Air Rhodesia, advised to coat the underside of its Viscounts with low-radiation paint to make them virtually invisible from the ground and to shroud the exhaust pipes to deflect missiles, did not get around to implementing the measures.

From the time Dale was born, the ZIPRA strategy had targeted passenger-carrying aircraft with SAM 7 heat-seeking missiles in the proximity of Lake Kariba. At least four unsuccessful attempts had been made to shoot down planes, including a missile launched at The Flight of Angels – the tourist flight we had taken over the Victoria Falls. That missile missed its target and honed in on heat from the ventilation system of the Elephant Hills Hotel where we'd spent a relaxing day. It was not a ground attack as broadcast at the time. All governments have excuses for their lies and deception. The white Rhodesian Government was no exception to that.

Why did Nkomo, who was preferred by Ian Smith over Mugabe, take the drastic strategy of downing passenger aircraft? Nkomo had a problem. The Matabele, his people, comprised less than a quarter of the population. He could never win power through the ballot box, as elections would follow tribal dictates. Nkomo had to shock his opponents black and white and take the country by force.

Kariba has never quite let us go. Every full moon, we imagine the fish on the lake swimming free, diving and dancing in the silver light, unmolested and out of harm's way.

The Liebig's cannery went ahead, and the first product was on the market by mid-1979, less than a year after we left. About the same time Hans wrote to tell us he was selling the business again. We understood.

Chapter 23 – Galloway, 1978

It's hard to explain how we ended up in Galloway. Mike says it was to please me, my Scottish blood and all that. I think when he headed for Scotland and got over the border, he got cold feet, turned left and kept going until he hit the sea. That's the best explanation I can come up with.

Green, white and gold lichen colour the grey granite of standing stones, forts and boulders. Lichens, barometers of air pollution, do well in Galloway, left in peace to ponderously devour stone and rock. There are clusters of simple houses with small windows and isolated mansions grand with turrets. Salt winds flow over brackish marsh, curl through dry-stone walls and whisper along ancient hedgerows. Rivers forge past forest and moor to slow in muddy tidal estuaries that break a coastline of sea-caves, flawless beaches and sandy dunes rimmed with couch grass dotted with sea-pinks. It is sea and sky country, home to sea trout, seals and basking sharks, cloud-shadows, seagulls, shags and shearwaters.

It's famous for an old Celtic breed of long-bodied, short-legged cattle. The barrel-chested Galloway – hardy, black and hornless – and Belted-Galloways, much the same, with a broad white band around their middles.

I couldn't decide whether Galloway was hard or soft country. The gentle rolling landscape had an austere side. You could seldom walk the same walk twice for Galloway's sidekick was weather in all seasons. Sun blinked luminous or burnt disconcertingly, winds howled and whipped, rains sluiced from a claustrophobic sky, or the drizzle of a monkey's wedding made my wool jumper dance with rhinestone. Either a chill grasped the very marrow of my bones, or a charitable sun soothed my soul. Galloway was all of that.

I wasn't naturally a rabbit-farming enthusiast, but since I'd wrenched Mike away from Kariba, he deserved my wholehearted support. And I was nervous since the capital to invest in the venture was my inheritance, once planned for the Orkney guesthouse.

Mike rented a disused chicken shed at Whauphill in the Machars, a peninsula famed for its dairy farms. The farm was owned by Ross and Carol Evans. Pointedly, Ross only spoke to Mike on the doorstep of his large modern farmhouse, set proud on a hill circled by stunning views – and often by howling gales. Ross was not overly keen. He had a prime dairy herd and worried about contagion. Mike assured him that rabbits didn't really have diseases.

Next, Mike sourced equipment and an initial stock of six-month-old does and bucks from a well-known rabbit breeder in the south of England who recommended pedigrees for Galloway's damp, mild climate. Mike named our company 'Coney Garth', the old English name for a rabbit yard.

At first, we rented Low Drumraye, an isolated farmhouse on a hillock surrounded by rough land and grazing cattle. The old croft was spartan. We washed our clothes in the bath and hung them on a line that stretched from the croft to the adjoining byre. Dale mooed authentically when she spotted cows, which was most of the time. Kim was a more specific early-warning siren: "Mum, the cows are coming!" My signal to rush out and whip everything off the line before it was pulled off and trampled into the mud churn outside the byre by curious cows. When I remonstrated with them, they raised their tails in mock salute and dropped enormous cow pats that splattered up, speckling any washing still on the line.

Chapter 23 – Galloway, 1978

We bought an ancient Renault with a driver's door too stiff to open, along with an old caravan to serve as office and warm bolthole. I set about painting the caravan and making curtains and cushions. The girls slept there, while Mike and I worked late clearing out the shed's accumulated rubbish. We disturbed generations of mice, which then invaded the caravan.

The locals were most kind, although their accents made them almost incomprehensible. Introductions by name were often given associations: "Oh, you need Do-It-All-Digby for that job." And there was much repetition. When the farmhand and I struggled to lift a wooden gate over the muddy rutted path, he'd say, "This gate don't work, like Jimmy." Jimmy was Ross's dairyman and the butt of a great many jokes. The dairyman lived across the road from the dairy. He'd been born in the house and worked on Ross's farm all his life. Not long after we left, he was killed crossing the road to the dairy. We were incredulous when we heard. His father, the previous dairyman, had been killed by the dairy bull he had tended for years, so perhaps over-familiarity was a family trait.

A dairy bull stalked his stockade at the beginning of the lane to our rabbit shed, growling when we went past, a menacing start and end to every day. Ross said it wasn't the beast that had killed his old dairyman and then added, "Might as well have been, though, he's a mean machine."

The farm lane soon churned into whorls of chocolate-brown mud, soft some days, crusty on dry days and frozen in winter. The lane was so slippery I often needed a good-natured farmhand to help push the little Renault back onto it when I slid off-piste.

I adjusted fast to a life lived in wellington boots, as did the girls. Kim called, "Mind the cow pats, Mummy," whenever I got out to untie gates, move livestock off the track or chase escaped rabbits. The caravan was a perfect naturalist's hide. Birds came looking for stray rabbit pellets and hay for their nests. One afternoon a fox came sniffing around the shed, standing paw poised in the air with the late winter sun catching its magnificent brush tail.

Our nearest useful town was Newton Stewart, an hour's drive away. There, the ironmonger sold nails by the pound. Some tools on sale were second-hand, and beneath the counter were boxes of bits that you could rummage through and find absolutely everything or nothing depending on what side of bed you got out of that morning. It had some nice grocers' shops and a library. "You'll be wanting to join?" a Scottish voice called as soon as I put my head in the door.

As always, Mike worked incredibly hard preparing the shed for our first lot of rabbits. Cages constructed, lines of water pipes stapled in place, hoppers mounted and fire extinguishers secured. We ordered straw and sawdust.

"No truck driver in his right mind's going down there," said the first guy with the straw. So, offloaded next to the grumbling bull, it was for us to pile bales into the ute that had arrived by ship from Rhodesia, and do circuits, often with the girls on top bouncing on the straw until they came out in strange rashes which the doctor diagnosed as harvester mites:

"Most unusual for this time of year."

Africa receded. I felt peaceful and settled. We explored.

Garliston, with its tiny harbour full of little fishing boats, had a gripping claim to fame. Its beach and seabed profile were similar to the French beaches pinpointed for Operation Overlord, the World War II D-Day landings. Relics remained along the Solway shoreline from the secretive testing of prototypes of Mulberry harbours, the name for the artificial pierheads, that were crucial to landing Allied troops on Europe's mainland.

Chapter 23 – Galloway, 1978

Another day we went to Monreith Beach. Beneath cliff faces rent with layers of rock, stacked upright like sandwiches by a tectonic hand, the girls collected shells, while Mike and I lay on the warm sand and joked that maybe the Solway Firth's reputation of being the Scottish Riviera, was conceivable after all. Closer to our home, our favourite walk led to a stony beach and a cave said to be the retreat of St Ninian, famed for bringing Christianity to Scotland in 397 CE.

Mike combed local beaches collecting laver – edible seaweed – a Devon speciality, and an acquired taste, eaten boiled and doused with vinegar. I preferred to pick sloes and blackberries for making jam and jelly.

The rabbits finally arrived on a cold, wet night. Kim and Dale peered out from the caravan as we worked in the car headlights, sliding and slipping on the mud while trying to shelter the stock from the rain.

At first, we thought the rabbits listless from their long journey. We were worried when they went off their feed and then appalled as their eyes turned pink and their heads grew puffy. Mike and I had both grown up in country England and had seen it before. Myxomatosis, a deadly virus, was not native to Europe. It had been intentionally introduced from the Americas to France and unintentionally crossed the English Channel in the 1950s.

"It can't be," said Mike, looking at the rabbits, knowing that was exactly what it was. "I asked about it. The guy told me, 'You never see Myxomatosis in a commercial rabbitry'."

The vet took one look and confirmed the outbreak:

"They came infected, haven't had time to incubate the virus here."

It did not escape Ross's notice that the vets were on his farm, and we'd only been in the business a week. The disease is limited to rabbits, so his herd was not at risk although he wasn't impressed when we had the distinction of being the first commercial rabbit unit in Scotland with the virus.

The supplier paid for the vaccination of the remaining rabbits, all our vet bills and replaced the losses.

Yet the rabbits continued to turn up their toes and the pride I'd taken in setting up a card system to record matings, mortality and marketing was diminishing as the death-toll mounted.

Vets visited week after week and said stress, pneumonia, mucoid enteritis, and then scratched their heads and said it was difficult to tell. Perhaps staph?

They left us with syringes and a concoction of drugs to inoculate the stock against every known rabbit disease.

Then, when nothing had died for two days, we congratulated each other and swore a corner had been turned. But it hadn't.

"Rabbits are just like sheep," the vet said gloomily, "once they make up their minds to die, whatever you do, they go right ahead on plan."

He decided to trial a new drug, but when the rabbits fell down dead, he swore at his assistant. "How much did you give them? Christ! That dose would have killed a horse." The veterinary practice paid for the rabbits they'd murdered by a reduction in their substantial monthly invoice.

Mike performed amateur autopsies and would turn up at the door of the caravan with a dissected rabbit on a steel tray to ask, "What do you reckon…"

I declined to help him out; I've always been squeamish.

There were other problems. The combination of widespread labour unrest, the greatest since the nation's general strike in 1926, and the harsh winter, saw 1978 dubbed as Britain's 'Winter of Discontent'. Stoppages disrupted manufacturing and delivery; chicken farmers in Galloway gassed their chickens

Chapter 23 – Galloway, 1978

because they had no feed. We put the rabbits on half-rations, and they would have starved to death if Mike hadn't hired a truck and driven to Liverpool to run the picket lines of strikers. The experience of driving through the spitting, kicking and swearing mob was sobering for the left-leaner that he was.

Mike arrived back at 2 a.m. with an overloaded truck, worried that he had damaged its suspension. We hurriedly hauled off the sacks of feed to avoid paying for another day's hire. Mike tore off into the night to return the truck, and, when he came home, he found me on my hands and knees wincing with pain.

"Did we damage your suspension too?" he said, before taking me off to the local quack, who said I'd slipped a disc.

That winter was the sixth worst in Britain ever recorded, and in some places it was the worst ever. One of those places was Galloway. The Galloway peninsula was swept by snow blizzards and sub-zero temperatures. The electricity went at Low Drumraye and took days to repair. We borrowed gas fires and camping stoves. On our blankets each morning was a layer of frost, and I was afraid that Dale, only fourteen months old, would freeze in her nappies. Nappies hung everywhere inside or froze like boards on the line. The girls brought snow inside to play with it. It sat in piles and hardly thawed at all. Yet, some days, we woke to snow-bright light pouring through the windows, and the country sparkled like an enchanted wonderland under an azure sky.

At the rabbit shed, the water system froze solid and Mike took a blowtorch to the pipes, occasionally penetrating the plastic and spraying the rabbits with an icy shower. "Those ones will die of pneumonia," he accurately predicted.

The days were short and dark, the afternoons spooky and desolate. Late one afternoon, the girls and I headed home under a leaden sky. Snow began to fall heavily, swirling into drifts that brushed the underside of the car. It was at the loneliest part of the journey that the engine stuttered and died when the fuel pump froze. I climbed out and, with Dale under one arm and holding Kim's hand, began to walk back towards a farmhouse a mile or so up the road.

In the near dark, we ploughed through the soft snow with a sharp wind blowing shards of ice off the drifts, pin-pricking our faces. Kim wanted to be picked up, but I could only carry them both for a short distance, so she had to keep walking.

I really thought we might die if we stopped. Kim and I sang silly songs, and, between each one Kim said it was dark and cold and cold and dark, and she wanted her daddy. What a little trooper. Dale huddled inside my jacket, mute, licking snow that fell on her face.

At the farmhouse, I hammered on the door. The farmer's wife opened it and, clearly startled, pulled us into her huge kitchen where a blazing fire burned in a great hearth. She set to stripping the girls and wrapping them in blankets, then dropped the pulley-maid – a hanging drying rack suspended from the ceiling – to drape their clothes on it before whisking it up again. The girls were impressed. I had to thaw my hands under a warm tap before I could massage Kim's icy feet. The farmer's wife draped me with a blanket and made tea but said little.

The telephone lines were down so I had no way of letting Mike know what had happened. Mike was shaken when he came out of the shed and saw the conditions. The ute was higher off the ground with snow chains but, even so, he found driving difficult. He stopped when he saw a car shaped hump of snow at the roadside, and was frantic when he scraped down to the green paint of the Renault. He guessed we would have made for the farmhouse. He had to reverse back along the road as the snow drifts prevented him from turning around. I dashed to the door at his knock, wrenching it open and pushing my face to his

Chapter 23 – Galloway, 1978

wet cheeks.

Back at Low Drumraye, we all got into one bed. At about midnight, we were woken with a farmer hammering at the door. He'd found the Renault and wanted to know that we were all accounted for. "You could die on a night like this!"

At 5 a.m., it was Ross's turn to bang on the door. More power lines were down. The pipes in the dairy had frozen solid, and he had cows to milk. He had a World War II generator that he'd never used. Could Mike help? Mike and Ross broke the ice in more ways than one. Mike would never have to stand on the doorstep of Cairnfield farmhouse again.

It was almost Christmas. A Forestry Commission watchman let Mike have a tree for fifty pence. I decorated it with cotton wool balls and the coloured tinfoil wrappers from a box of Quality Street chocolates. I painted fir-cones and seashells with gold paint and spied the plastic boot from a fishing game someone had given Kim and Dale. It was a perfect Santa boot. (To this day, it comes out to grace our tree.)

It would have been a difficult Christmas had not Carol and Ross invited us to Cairnfield to celebrate, with a roaring fire and traditional fare eaten looking out at a panorama of snow drifts.

"Presents under the tree," boomed Ross as he welcomed us at the door. "Not to be opened without a gin in your hand."

Carol had been one of four sisters who'd entertained troops during World War II. One of them, Margaret, was visiting. When I found out that the sisters regularly performed at Shepheard's Hotel in Cairo, I told them Dad had stayed there in the war. Maybe they had sung for him?

Carol then said, "Margaret and her husband lived in the Sudan before the war."

"Whereabouts? Khartoum?" I asked Margaret.

"Oh, no," she said, "somewhere you wouldn't have heard of:

Medani."

I laughed. "Oh, goodness, we lived there briefly, before we moved to Wad Adam."

"El Adam? The house by the canal? It had citrus trees…"

It was dark when we left Ross and Carol to drive back along the isolated roads to Low Drumraye. The landscape was as glittery as a Christmas card. I said to Mike, "I think wise men and camels might be round the next bend."

Kim stared out, asking, "Where, Mummy? Where?"

Chapter 24 – The Rabbit Run, 1979

Not long after Christmas, we moved into a house we'd bought in the village of Whithorn. I was immediately in my element. An agent for high-end furnishing fabrics operated from her home not too far away, and, when I walked into her showroom, my breath went shallow. Beautiful fabrics have a physical effect on me – I go weak at the knees – but most of all I experience avarice. Fortunately, the windows at Whithorn were very small, because the fabrics were hugely expensive.

The exception was the master bedroom where large windows on two sides filled the room with light. The room had an elegance in proportions far beyond the Scottish practicality of the other rooms. I made duck-egg blue curtains of linen blend to keep the airy feel to the room and complement an unusual pale turquoise and ecru silk rug we had brought from Iran. Until the first night, we had no idea that a flashing sign on the side of the bingo hall next door flared and glared directly into the room.

"We'll get epilepsy," said Mike.

Shades of the Omar Khayyam Hotel, I thought, remembering Cairo.

When I asked the bingo hall manager if he could switch it off overnight, he recommended black-out curtains, "You know, like in the war."

I explained my vision for the room, the moon peeping in as curtains wafted on long summer evenings.

He looked blank. Then muttered about painting the windows or putting in coloured glass. Instead, I made an application to the council, and, to my surprise, the sign came down within days.

I scoured second-hand shops for pine furniture that I stripped with caustic soda. I hated the carpeting, which might have done well in a pub, for it could have handled chips and tomato sauce with impunity. Orange and red swirls chased each other in dizzying contortions around corners and up the stairs. We were too short of money to get rid of the carpet, so I tried to dye it deep red to banish the orange. I started in one corner. It was much harder work than I imagined. I intended to carry on, but I got waylaid by the hideousness of the mint green ceiling tiles in the family room. One evening when Mike was out, I got the ladder and climbed up to see if they came off easily. They did, and I was delighted, believing that the stucco left behind would do wonders with a coat of ceiling paint – a textured look. Kim and Dale woke and came to see what all the noise was about.

"Why is the ceiling on the floor?" Kim said.

"Monty do it, Mummy?" said Dale.

Monty was a half-breed dog that we owned briefly. It was completely crackers, chewed anything he could grab and herded the children whenever they moved. Mike found a farmer to take him, who said an electric dog collar would bring him to heel. He was one pet I did not cry to see go.

The rabbit farm was a family business. The girls were small enough to scamper under the cages to flush out escaped rabbits. Kim came with me to check nests. I'd plunge my hand into a heap of straw and rabbit fur – it was potluck – one dead kitten or sixteen live ones. A rabbit can't raise more than ten, so the extras were passed to does with smaller litters. The rule book says kill the runts, but Mike couldn't and both of us turned a blind eye to the corner of the shed he'd christened 'Rumpdom' where he gave the smallest and weakest rabbits special treatment. Rumpdom grew and grew.

Mating was an unexpected challenge. With 250 maiden does and 25 bucks, some much keener than others, Mike, their

Chapter 24 – The Rabbit Run, 1979

pimp, always came off badly and returned from mating sessions covered with scratches.

Those of the rabbits that chose to live refused to breed or to fatten. The sages said it was the cold, the half-rations, the stress, the new environment. The list of things it might be grew exponentially.

Spring came and the weather improved. We gathered primroses and marsh marigolds. On a walk by Elrig Loch we came across masses of snowdrops. On another walk it was banks of bluebells.

I knew Mike's heart was heavy. He missed Kariba. Not that he ever complained.

In the spring, we got the first rabbits to market; it felt good even though the yield was a fraction of the projected numbers. We reworked our business plan, and Mike negotiated an overdraft with the bank.

The new season brought a wave of mastitis so severe that the vets postulated the young were infected at birth. Or that Mike was a carrier, or maybe the cows. Could we ask Ross if his cows were off-colour? We didn't go there.

Mike contacted other rabbit farmers for advice. John was the most helpful. He'd lived in Africa and invited us to his farm on his parents' property. It was an imposing house in the middle of Forestry Commission land and very remote. The rabbits thrived in a picturesque collection of ramshackle sheds and barns, the yards graced by great tubs of daffodils and bulbs.

Inside, the house was cluttered, haphazard and unbelievably chilly. John's parents were in their late seventies. I had spoken to his mother on the phone and we'd made a congenial connection. She wore three aprons over jodhpurs that might have done service in colonial India. John's father poured us whiskies to go alongside our tea.

John's mother chastised me for arriving in smart city gear when she was in country mode. My jeans were hardly city wear, and I made her laugh when I told her my father so abhorred jeans, I was not allowed to wear them to the dinner table.

Left alone together, she recounted some of her life story.

"Well, you see my dear, my husband and I are either very broke or nearly broke, although there have been periods when we were not-so-broke. We used to own an estate on an island in the Hebrides, and my husband commuted from his legal practice in London. He was always getting marooned on the mainland with me on the island. Anyway, we were in a broke phase and had to sell. We were very sad and, a few years later, in a not-so-broke stage, we decided to buy another house in Scotland. We found this house, and my husband said he was never going to live anywhere else, so we bought it. Then we had a very broke period and had to sell half the house, but the buyers were dreadful people. The wife died and, by good fortune, we were not so broke and bought it back!"

I told her she made me feel much better because we were in a nearly broke phase.

"Oh," she said, "my dear, such things pass."

I forgot my handbag and had to dart back to grab it. John's mother patted me fondly and said she'd spent her life leaving handbags behind:

"My husband thought I should wear mine around my neck, but I felt I looked quite enough like a horse as it was!"

My period was late. I'd made an excuse and slipped out to the doctor's surgery. He was brusque. Had I planned on three? I wanted to explain how I'd defied predictions and had two 'miracle' babies, so had still imagined it was hard to conceive. Maybe he'd seen too many pregnant women that day to offer me congratulations.

Chapter 24 – The Rabbit Run, 1979

Mike looked up as I came in the door, "I was about to mount a search party for you."

"I'm pregnant," I said and burst into tears.

He leapt up, his face alight with delight and lifted me up with his hug. He had the knack of being able to separate milestones from the road ahead.

I needed clothes for my pregnancy. In Kariba, I'd made graceful cotton caftans. I repeated the pattern with long sleeves in thick grey wool tweed. The result was immensely warm and practical and drew amazed stares wherever I went. Mike called it the tent and thought it was of Bedouin heritage. My father was lost for words. I didn't care. It went over innumerable jumpers and swept down to my feet, keeping my legs warm and my woolly socks hidden.

We might just have been getting on top of the infections that had plagued our rabbits when we had a devastating outbreak of enteritis. It ravaged our entire stock. Mike was suspicious that it had started with a new batch of feed. This time the vets were seriously concerned and talked of quarantine measures.

Animals were sent off for autopsy: they had died of gut haemorrhages. But why? A battery of expensive drugs was trialled. Mike called our rep and ordered a new batch of feed. When it turned up, it was the same batch number. Mike was livid, but until more arrived, he had to feed them something. Rumours came from two farms in the south of England with similar problems. Mike grilled the rep.

The suppliers said the EU was to blame. Their regulations meant a change in the antibiotic, and the rabbits needed to get used to it. The vets rubbished that explanation as implausible. They thought it a new disease, much more exciting.

When a bio-security team in hazmat suits arrived and took samples of the water, the hay and made scrapings around the shed, Ross was beside himself, demarcating the muddy track to the shed with bits of fencing, desperate about his dairy cows.

Our rabbit corpses did the rounds of more and more institutions. Their stomachs were raw and eventually the verdict was unanimous. Nothing other than something ingested could have scoured out the stomachs. It had to be in the feed. The supplier said we could pay to have the feed analysed, adding it would be a pointless and expensive exercise, as nothing had changed. In hindsight, I wonder why the vets could not have done that. I wonder why we didn't mortgage our donkey jackets and wellies to do it.

We had become so poor that we started eating what healthy rabbits we had left. Mike butchered the first one, but said he couldn't do another, so we arranged for the butcher in Whithorn to dress them for us. We gave him two rabbits, and he returned one to us. Rabbit pie, pate, roast and stew. I have never eaten rabbit since.

On an overcast day in September 1979, I was laughing and playing with the girls at home when I felt immense unease, and I knew Mike was in trouble. I dialled the rabbit shed. I rang once, twice and the third time he answered. Poor Mike. He had been adding up the figures. We were broke. "It's over, Steve. We can't recover."

We'd lost everything. He was utterly desolate. At last, he said, "What made you ring?"

"I just knew."

Margaret Thatcher had come to power in May 1979 following the Winter of Discontent and begun tough reforms to curb inflation, including raising interest rates sharply. The bank manager was relieved that we were closing up shop and wanted us to euthanise the surviving livestock. Mike, dogged to the end, refused.

Chapter 24 – The Rabbit Run, 1979

Our next visit was to our accountant, who told us how lucky we were.

"Why?" we gasped.

"Because some people take a lifetime losing all they have; you have done it in a year and you are young enough to recoup."

We went to a lawyer, "We want to sue the company that sold us contaminated feed."

"What evidence do you have?"

"The vets say it is in the feed."

He asked us about our business. We told him all our woes.

"Your business was already in trouble. Vets won't stand up in court, they'll obfuscate."

He came around to perch on his desk on our side. This was not to be legal advice; this was advice from the heart.

"Sue Sxxx! The largest stockfeed company in UK! David and Goliath! Ha, that's pantomime! If you had the money to sue, which you don't, you'd spend the next ten years in court and lose. And if, just by a miracle, you won, they'd prove your business was worth peanuts. Go and do something else. Forget it. Put it down to experience."

Ross was mightily relieved and charged no penalty for ending our lease. We couldn't pay all our bills, but we promised we would, except for the feed. Mike kept us afloat doing casual work helping farmers with harvesting and selling off the remaining stock.

Mike scoured journals in the library at Newton Stewart for jobs. Most nights after dinner, he'd have a letter to finish; it took time to explain his C.V. Last thing, he'd walk up to the post box on the corner of the High Street. Some nights, when he returned, I did not know if his face was wet from rain or sleet or because he wept. Once, when the dark was cold and clear, Mike asked me to walk a little way with him.

He took my hand. "Look at the moon," he said, "it's almost full. Imagine the kapenta swirling all over Lake Kariba."

I turned back to the warm light pouring out from the open front door of our house, and, ten minutes later, Mike came in boldly, slamming the door against the cold, to shout, "I hope we find somewhere warm!"

I jumped up to put my cheek against his freezing one for I loved the magic of that heat exchange. We didn't need words. We were good together in all seasons.

Perhaps it was that night Mike's letter took flight from our most remote peninsula in Scotland to land on the desk of an American executive in Dow Chemicals' office in Switzerland. He was responsible for sales of agricultural chemicals in Africa. Mike's C.V. reminded him of an odd bod he'd recruited once before who'd come good.

When Mike left for his interview in Switzerland, it was my job to keep the last remnants of our business ticking over.

"Try not to give Ross a heart attack when I'm gone," Mike had said as he left.

Each morning, I'd settle the girls in the caravan, pull out games and crayons and find cheerful music on the radio, before I slipped out to the shed to feed the rabbits. Frosty nights finished off the sick ones and I needed to get the bodies into the incinerator before Ross did his morning rounds. We had promised him the 'outbreak' was over.

The old incinerator had been built for chicken carcasses, but its big red-brick belly was roomy enough for rabbits. Perched on a rocky mound near the shed; its tin smokestack gave it a rakish air.

It was a particularly cold morning when, seven months pregnant and thankful for my Bedouin tweed with a purple beanie pulled over my ears, I entered the shed, steeling myself

Chapter 24 – The Rabbit Run, 1979

for whatever the light might make real. I didn't mind dead or alive by then, just hated anything in-between. There was just one corpse. A large buck had died and was stretched out like a plank. I stared – most things shrink in death, but not this buck. We had not many bucks, so they got names. His was Big Ben. I donned my mortician's gloves to pick up the corpse. It was stiff with rigor mortis, or perhaps just frozen solid. Bearing him outside, I stepped gingerly onto the path nervous of slipping on the hoar frost.

I pushed the body through the steel hatch of the incinerator as far as it would go, but Big Ben was too long. I pulled him out and tried to bend him in the middle... no chance. I needed to get rid of the buck before Ross arrived, so I mounted the incinerator to ram the corpse head-first down the chimney. It stuck halfway with its hind legs pointing up into the thin morning air. I tried to hoist the buck back out of the shaft, but my feet slid on the ice, my belly distancing me from the scabrous brickwork that snagged at my scarf. My eyes pricking hot with frustration, I climbed down and stood back, holding my arms with their awful black rubber gloves out from my ample girth. As I sucked at the freezing air, I felt my throat closing and my eyes fill.

I was done with the supporting role I had adopted. It wasn't about Mike and his restless eccentricities. I adored Mike, but we had children now. I could not rely on others, not even Mike, not even Greek gods. I wanted dull. I was going to get myself a qualification to be able to support our little family. I didn't want to keep ending up in deep shit.

I straightened my shoulders, pulling off the gloves to light the flame of the furnace. Kim opened the caravan door, calling my name, and I called back that I was on my way. Hands washed, face composed, I joined the girls to put on the kettle and make us some tea.

The Lion Behind the Anthill

Minutes later, Kim cried, "Look!" pointing at smoke billowing past the window. We opened the caravan door and from every crack in the chimney of the incinerator, around the door of the oven and squeezing past the hind legs of the buck, poured smoke. It made it look as if the whole boiler was preparing for take-off. Ross was going to love this.

"Let's go home and have a proper breakfast," I said, quickly packing up, thinking if he did not see my car, Ross might not venture down to the shed. We drove home and I poured myself a large gin. Good work for 9 a.m., I mused Mike would say.

Mike got the job. It was in Johannesburg. I didn't want to go back to Africa, least of all to the country where the objection was also one of conscience, and the job was totally unsuitable. Sales. Mike in sales? A suit job? Someone had to be kidding.

Mike's take was that it was the only job, and it was somewhere warm.

Mike went for training in the south of England. On the second day, a new colleague heard how he'd been farming rabbits.

"I'll tell you a funny story about rabbits. Hay was short last year after the terrible winter, so Sxxx used straw in their rabbit feed. They softened it first with caustic soda, then washed out the acid with alkaline. It worked well until one batch where they forget to neutralise the acid."

"How do you know?" said Mike astonished.

"Oh, we sell them the chemicals. One of their guys told me. Some poor bastard got well and truly clobbered. We were all sworn to secrecy of course. Just wondered if you'd heard anything about it?"

Chapter 25 – Back to Africa, 1980

The last thing I did in Galloway was to give birth to Emily in early March 1980. Dumfries boasted Britain's most modern maternity hospital, which made my experience all the more outrageous. The birth was traumatic, the midwife was abhorrent and the doctor beyond incompetent. When I was wheeled out of the delivery room, the atmosphere was tense. All of us were exhausted. When our posse reached the lifts, the midwife pressed the button, whisked Emily out of my arms and made off down the corridor. I shouted, Mike pursued her, blocking her path. The distraught doctor explained that Emily was just going to be measured and checked. Mike and I insisted she was not leaving our sight. A noisy squabble started.

The midwife, shepherded by Mike back to the lifts told me I was being ridiculous. She had ginger hair and a mole on her right cheek. When I was in labour, she had hissed into my ear, "Stop making such a fuss; this is your third baby."

I had morphed her into a plebeian Cruella de Vil, and she was not stealing my baby. Suddenly, the lift doors opened and out stepped the ward sister. Tall, formidable, starched. She had come to find the new mother she was expecting in her ward. She glared at Cruella, and we knew that without a doubt, there was history there. The doctor, already wishing he'd never turned up to work that day, shrank behind Mike.

"Please explain," she said, and we all threw in. She said I was quite within my rights, extracted Emily from Cruella's arms, and asked Mike to wheel me into the lift.

We came out into a bright maternity ward. Sister had a bed for me in the ward but thought that the private room might suit us better. She wheeled in a trolley and weighed and measured Emily in front of us. She was a stern gem. She ran the ward like clockwork, yet turned a blind eye to Mike, who disregarded visiting hours, and insisted on wetting Emily's head with champagne on his first visit.

I never saw Cruella again, but Sister ushered in the young doctor the next day. He was clutching strips of graph paper and showed me how my contractions had gone off the edge. He apologised. As Emily was my third, it was presumed everything would be straightforward. Doctors are only human. When they apologise, all is forgiven. Although, at that time, I did not know that his attempt to stitch me back together had been disastrous. Emily was beautiful, bonny and healthy which was just as well as ten days later we left Heathrow for our next adventure.

A tide turned as we left the rabbit farm, for so many quirky things happened to put us back on our feet. I think Mike's courage pulled the moon's heartstrings.

Although we might have hankered for a more exotic or quixotic posting than the contentious, expensive city of Johannesburg, it offered us so much.

The day after we arrived in Jo'burg, Beryl and Arthur, friends I had made in Zambia before I met Mike, offered to lend us the deposit for a house. No strings attached. Arthur had been one of several European officers who stayed on in the Zambian army after independence. Returning home with his family after a picnic, he found the army had been Zambianised and all European officers returning to barracks were barred entry. They stood in flip flops, clutching a picnic basket with two grubby, tired children. Refused permission even to get clothes, they'd turned up on my doorstep, and I had put them up at my house in Chilanga until they sorted themselves out.

That's what friends do; help each other, they said. Mike's

Chapter 25 – Back to Africa, 1980

company guaranteed a mortgage for the rest.

That is not to say that the early days in South Africa were an easy ride. We touched down in Johannesburg 'very broke'. Interest rates of over twenty per cent had hiked up our Scottish bank overdraft until it overtook the slumping value of our empty house in Whithorn.

Two dour Afrikaners in dark suits and sunglasses met us at the airport and drove us to the Balalaika Hotel in upmarket Santon. They gave Mike time for a shower before taking him off to a meeting.

We'd had time for a quick hug as Mike left.

"All a bit mafiosi?" I whispered.

"Bloody Dutchmen!" said Mike, and then he was gone; thin, pale and determined.

I closed my eyes and pictured Mike two weeks before – in a stained anorak, loading the last few rabbits into a cage. He'd never been a corporate man. He'd never had a suit job.

Mike was not welcomed, for his colleagues objected to an expat Englishman parachuted into their patch. Except Mike was no expat, he was on local terms like them.

Johannesburg was a bigger, more brash and confident city than I had expected. Motorways and overpasses straddled a panorama of mining dumps, sprawling suburbs, skyscrapers, gardens, trees and greenery. African townships were off limits. I did go once, innocently looking for petrol. The attendant was terribly agitated. "Madam, what are you doing here? Lock your doors and go back."

We bought where we could afford, in Johannesburg's south. The house sat on a kopje. Its high, sloping ceilings dwarfed our shabby, half-stripped pine furniture from Galloway. I likened it to an eagle's nest overlooking the whole suburb, which stretched out in a pleasing patchwork of green. Trees grew dusty as the dry started, scrub shone bronze in the sun. Red tiled roofs, emerald irrigated lawns and aqua-blue glints from backyard pools added random highlights. On winter nights, little grass fires speckled the distance, making the vista mysterious and dramatic.

During the day, sorting out kids and cooking, I'd glimpse the view and sing. Sing opera, sing thanks – sing hallelujah! I'd never felt so dammed fortunate in my life. I was half-way to heaven on that kopje.

It soon transpired I needed a spot of world-class medical care following Emily's bungled delivery in Scotland. One of South Africa's top gynaecologists muttered a butcher would have had more grasp of anatomy than whoever delivered Emily. Without an operation, I would have problems for the rest of my life. Muscle was stitched to skin, layers mismatched. It was, he said, a "Horlicks". He did a repair that left me so tightly stitched up I could not move without pain. The surgeon was unsympathetic, said it would ease with time. I once again called on Sir John. One of his students, by then a top consultant, came to the rescue. He declared the repair technically perfect but practically… The build-up of scar tissue had to be considered before any further surgery could be contemplated. If we intended to have any more children, that would be the very best time to sort the problem as it would heal quickly. Mike had always wanted round numbers. He was thrilled. We felt secure. I was soon pregnant again.

In Johannesburg, I could go to college, so had no excuse not to study for a 'decent bit of paper' and fulfil the promise I'd made as I stood by that blasted incinerator with poor Big Ben's hindlegs so rudely stilled pointing skyward.

In 1980, I enrolled to study for the exams of the Institute of Chartered Secretaries and Administrators. Mike never ever missed a beat and was always home so I could leave on time for my evening classes. He held me as I sobbed after every exam,

Chapter 25 – Back to Africa, 1980

convinced I'd failed, and had the champagne ready for every result. To my enormous surprise, I always passed, winning prizes and distinctions. Mike laughed so generously when I thought there must be a mistake. He always made me feel clever, feel good about myself. He loved me.

We lived frugally, paying a mortgage, repaying Arthur, and paying off the overdraft and bills in Scotland.

I made little mice dolls. At first for the girls, then as presents given out at birthday parties. Mike quietly pocketed one and came back with PVC cylinders for packaging and orders from a gift shop. After the children were in bed, he joined me sewing up the little grey felt bodies until past midnight.

The mice-money paid for a second-hand tent and camping in the Transkei.

Mike took to sales and corporate life as if born to it. He had a pay-rise after six months and then another. He began to relax and delighted in calling me up to meet him for impromptu meals or with tickets for the cinema or theatre. We pinched ourselves to believe our luck.

My letters to Mum and Dad changed. I was bound up in my domestic world and wrote endlessly of my little girls, their ailments, funny conversations and characters. My descriptions bubble off the page, inconsequential, sublime and insubstantial. I am immersed in family… and study.

At the end of 1980, I wrote, "I can hardly bear to let the year go; it has been such a happy one."

Mike's extraordinary versatility had come to the fore again. He never bothered what people thought about him, so he didn't curry favour or partake in office politics. He appeared unassuming yet was immovable – rock solid. He worked hard and was bloody clever without a conventional thought in his head. Mike had never been a corporate man so had no idea how to be one. His approach was his own. The Afrikaners decided Mike wasn't really an Englishman but some hybrid son of Africa, and accepted him.

So it was that Mike stepped into a high-powered, results-driven and cut-throat Afrikaner sales team managed by an eccentric Frenchman. He had morning meetings, fat lunches, after-work confabs. He flew all over Africa, and to Europe. Congo wasn't covered by anyone, so Mike went there to look for business. He retreated, saying it reminded him of his promise to Larry to avoid hellholes.

Alice was born in tranquillity in September 1981, eighteen months after Emily. I felt no pain at all as I had an epidural so that a final repair could be done immediately. I had to stay extra time in hospital, which was just as well as I had study to do. There was a wonderful black night nurse. Her Zulu name meant 'enough'. She was the last of eight children. I told her that we had had enough, too.

The flowers in my hospital room after Alice's birth overwhelmed me. I had become a corporate wife.

We were also on the move again; no sooner had I arrived home from hospital than there were packing cases to fill. Mike was to set up a new office in Zimbabwe, the Rhodesia we had left three years before, and the move was scheduled just after my next set of exams.

When we told our maid that we were moving to Zimbabwe, she screamed, sank to the floor and wept into the apron she pulled from her lap. How could we take her beautiful girls up to a land of savages? We would all get murdered. I said I hoped not.

The company gave us a double moving allowance because we had moved twice in eighteen months. That, combined with a modest profit on the Johannesburg house, cleared our debts.

Chapter 25 – Back to Africa, 1980

And on our return to Zimbabwe, we would be able to access our frozen bank account and the proceeds of the sale of our fishing business in Kariba.

I thought of my jodhpur-legged friend in Scotland. She was right: things pass. We were less broke.

Next, Mike came home bursting with laughter. The company insisted that they furnish our Zimbabwe house because of the instability of the political situation. Our own furniture would be stored in Johannesburg. I had a blank cheque and three days to spend it.

I do love making interiors, so embarked on an unexpected, crazy shopping trip, buying furniture and fabrics, while Mike chose sound systems and a TV, the first we would ever own.

I felt like an old soul in South Africa. Many of both white tribes, Englishmen and Afrikaners, believed their government could hold the chalk line. I knew it was only a matter of time. Apartheid could not last. The end was in sight.

The campaign to free Nelson Mandela was beginning, although it would be another nine years before he finally walked out of prison after twenty-seven years of incarceration.

Much later, I would wonder how different Zimbabwe could have been with such a man.

The white minority government of Rhodesia had finally given way to majority rule in April 1980, eighteen months after we left. The damage to white morale following the downing of the flights over Kariba had been crucial. Moreover, insurgents eventually outnumbered the Rhodesian security forces. Mugabe would have preferred a military victory, to clear the deck of both white and black rivals, but international pressure persuaded him an election was the way to go. As leader of the Shona, the major tribe, he could not lose.

Mugabe had been in power for only twenty months when we returned to the country, yet the early promises of peace, unity and progress had already given way to gloom, fuelled by unemployment, shortages and factional rage.

Serendipity saw the old Zambia clan gathered again. Our friends Dick and Marilyn were still there, and Nick and his wife Helen, had just arrived, also as expats.

We visited Kariba where the harbour was unrecognisable, a concrete jungle. Abisha was there and whooped for joy when he saw Mike and the two men embraced. *Hu Hu* was still on the water, Melo had died, and no one knew where Sorotiah had gone.

The kapenta licensees were all millionaires, with waterside mansions. I felt stupidly envious, until one of the wives sensed it. "You did right to go, Gill. We can't keep this – there is no place for us here."

No one spoke much of the war. That is not to say it was forgotten. Leftover weapons were used to solve leftover grievances, and I couldn't kick a sense of apprehension in the bush. At the top, Mugabe and Nkomo continued their war. It is estimated that Mugabe's North Korean-trained Fifth Brigade, a squad answering directly to him, murdered at the very least 20,000 Matabele civilians during the three years we were back in Zimbabwe, using methods as brutal as the earlier conflict. Except, this time, no international journalists gave a damn. Africans murdering Africans was not newsworthy.

We had two maids. Christansia was tiny, literate and clever. She held her head high, educated her two children and kept men at arm's length.

Not so Enid, a tall, beautiful woman who moved slowly and comely, like a ship under sail on a calm sea. Of her seven children, only three survived. Soft, illiterate and a magnet for

Chapter 25 – Back to Africa, 1980

men, time and time again, she asked Mike to evict boyfriends from the kia, the servant's quarters. Mike paid some to go, others he threatened with the police.

I don't know what had happened to Enid's husband, but I learnt what happened to her mother-in-law. Her husband's family had only delivered half the agreed lobola, or bride-price, when her father died suddenly. Taking advantage of Enid's situation, they refused to part with any more cattle, knowing she had no male relative to demand the lobola be completed.

During the war, when the CTs came to her village to ask, "Who is a sell-out?" No one answered. When they asked, "Who is the worst person in the village?" Enid named her mother-in-law. The terrorists laughed. Was she very bad?

Oh yes, Enid assured them. Then she should pay for her crimes, said the CT leader and, with the butt of an AK47, caved in the door of her mother-in-law's flimsy hut and called on her to come out and face her accusers. The old woman refused. Tinder-dry kindling was set against the hut and splashed with kerosene. The leader lit the match.

Enid could hear her mother-in-law coughing as smoke from the smouldering thatch filled her lungs. At last, the flames took hold, and the old woman burst out of her hut.

"And then, Madam, they shot her."

"Dead?"

"Oh, Madam. Dead. She was all in bits."

I looked in horror at Enid, who was laughing, back in the thick of it, vengeful and vindicated.

"But, Enid, just because you didn't like her… She was the grandmother of your children."

"Eh, Madam, she was a bad, bad woman."

For a few days, I was unsettled. I watched Enid, so gentle with my girls, and then I drew a veil. It could as easily have been her mother-in-law complaining about Enid. I knew the scenario had been played out time after time in the Tribal Trust Lands of the old Rhodesia. In ridding the village of a nuisance, the CTs left the villagers in no doubt about their strength, firepower and brutality. On their heels, the Rhodesian Security Forces were waiting to accuse the villagers of siding with the enemy.

Sometimes, in the morning ahead of the day's chatter, I'd walk through the silent house, smiling to see damp footprints on the tiled floors, big broad ones for Enid and small with arches for Christansia. Flowers hustled the doorways. We had chickens and lychee trees in the garden and our girls ran back and forward between the house and the kia, smelt of woodfire smoke, sudza and a fishy trace of sun-dried kapenta.

Kapenta felt close, but rabbits were a distant memory. When we got word that our house in Whithorn was being vandalised, we were briefly nonplussed. But perhaps because Mike had developed a reputation for barter deals, exchanging tobacco for agricultural chemicals, he came up with the brilliant idea of advertising the house for sale in Zimbabwe currency.

He did that, legally and very profitably, selling the house to a Rhodesian farmer with a son at Edinburgh University. We completely recouped our losses in Scotland. No longer broke at all.

We had our tenth wedding anniversary in Harare. I am not big on jewellery. But the shop where we had bought my engagement ring was still there. I asked them to make me an eternity ring to my design. I enjoy those serendipity moments and life is full of them.

I had continued studying by correspondence. Job offers came in for me as I waited for the results of my final exams. I wanted another year in Zimbabwe for work experience. It was not to be. Sub-Saharan Africa experiences frequent droughts. One

Chapter 25 – Back to Africa, 1980

started in 1982, and, a year later, water rationing was severe. Shower-water was used to wash clothes and afterwards to wash floors. Kitchen water went to keeping some garden vegetables alive. A sour odour permeated the whole house. A basin of water placed outside the toilets at the school for washing hands was so dirty that the kids either didn't wash their hands or did… Kim contracted Type A hepatitis.

As drought depressed the agriculture sector in Zimbabwe, a decision was made to close the office. When Mike's boss asked him where he wanted to go next, Mike answered, "Anywhere, except Geneva."

Of course, he was posted to Geneva – he needed experience in Head Office, it was said. In Geneva, once again, Mike's employment permit did not include 'the wife'.

As we started to pack, a message came. As there was to be no replacement, the furniture we had purchased with the company cheque book was ours to keep.

Chapter 26 – Geneva, 1984

By the time we landed in Geneva, I was not averse to the idea of a tame spell; motherhood had changed me. I unashamedly enjoyed our Swiss francs, for Geneva was the first time in a long time that we had been ahead of the game with monthly financial consistency. I'd grown used to security, for Mike had just received his five-year company pin, a longevity so surprising I had to pinch myself. And the ease, beauty and ambiance of a comfortable life in a truly gorgeous old city was spellbinding.

Life in Geneva really did echo the lid of a box of Swiss chocolates. The plume of the Jet de'Eau rose from Lake Geneva against a background of snow-capped mountains. (The century-old iconic water jet had started life prosaically as an industrial safety valve for the town's hydraulic power plant.) On hikes, the girls and I sang from the *Sound of Music* songbook, collecting alpine flowers in spring. In the late summer, we nodded to men shouldering scythes on their way to cut hay. We went skiing in the winter, had holidays in France, took a road-trip to Italy, camped in Spain.

I joined the American Women's Club, a hive of extraordinarily energetic women who knew that God was on their side. Their confidence, independence and sisterhood blew me away. I bought clothes instead of making them, made friends who lunched, and visited art galleries. In short, I had a lot of fun.

As winter gathered its chill European gloom, Geneva hosted the Fête de l'Escalade, an annual celebration of the failure of the Catholic Duke of Savoy to take the Protestant city of Geneva

Chapter 26 – Geneva, 1984

in 1602. The surprise attack commenced when a few soldiers, furtive and whispering in the dark, started to scale wooden ladders lent against the city walls. Once over the ramparts, they were to open the gates to the Duke's army. But the story goes, the good Geneva matron, Madame Royaume, came upon the ladders and tipped her great cauldron of hot vegetable soup over the Savoyards, foiling the plot and raising the alarm.

Today, children go door-to-door singing l'Escalade songs in exchange for sweets, and, at nighttime, a parade rolls through the town with participants dressed in historical costume. It's wonderfully colourful and merry. Adults pass round warm jugs of spiced wine, chestnuts roast on braziers and children in fancy dress clutch miniature chocolate *marmites* (soup cauldrons) in their sticky fingers.

For me l'Escalade evoked teenage memories of Guy Fawkes Night in England. The two festivals are only a month apart and commemorate the same era, the same protagonists and the same outcome. November the fifth: gunpowder, treason and plot. A day to remember the failure of a Catholic conspiracy in 1605 to blow up London's Houses of Parliament and assassinate the Protestant King James I.

In England, celebratory preparations began with a pile of firewood on waste ground outside our village, weeks ahead of the big night. Often an excuse to dump old furniture and other rubbish, the bonfire pile grew ugly by day, ominous by moonlight and sodden by rain. Ladders were needed to build the pile to a great height and to finally place the scarecrow effigy of Guy Fawkes, the plotters' explosives expert, on top, where the poor chap slouched for a day or two before he was set alight in a blaze of paraffin-fuelled flame and fireworks.

My mother censured kids asking for a "Penny for the Guy"; she drew the line at burning effigies.

Mum was on the right side of history, and Guy Fawkes Night has fallen out of favour in Britain shifting to be simply 'fireworks night'. But the l'Escalade goes from strength to strength in Geneva. Good to think that a pot of vegetable soup makes a more enduring icon than a human pyre.

Next came Christmas. Mystical and enchanting in a cold climate, it's a celebration that doesn't translate well to Africa or Australia. Wax candles flickered in the branches of a real fir tree in our living room, although Mike did insist on a fire extinguisher discreetly behind the sofa. Stores in the city served shoppers with mulled wine, and we strolled Christmas markets admiring rustic wooden gnomes flirting with glittering elfenfolk, past rows of pinecones posing as chubby reindeer and nodding to a red-robed St Nicholas, who carried branches of fir and spruce. All of it made the festival feel earthy, ancient and authentic. Children with red noses, their misty breath floating from open mouths, bounced along with their dismembered mittens dangling and bobbing on strings threaded through their anoraks. I knew it was a far cry from Galilee; much closer to a pagan festival, but that was OK by me.

Geneva gave us an extraordinary three years. Yet, with four small children and numerous guests, delighted to have us within visiting distance, it was frenetic. When Sue, a dear friend from Zimbabwe, arrived, I had someone to confide in. Too busy to pick up a book, I was scared that I could no longer read anything past street signs and the destination on a Geneva Tram. She was wonderful. Her children were slightly older. She'd been there – it would pass.

Mike had a gruelling travel schedule. Once Kim asked me if Daddy was at home or away. Before I could answer, I had to stop and think if I'd seen him in bed the night before.

His regular beat was Egypt, Ethiopia and London, with

Chapter 26 – Geneva, 1984

added circuits round Europe, then on to the United States and back through South Africa. During our first year in Geneva, I was envious when Mike slotted in a trip down the Nile from Aswan to Luxor and waxed lyrical about the Smithsonian in Washington D.C. Gradually, though, the hotel rooms morphed into one, and he sometimes needed the themed opulence of the hotel lobby to remind him where he was. The Egyptian Eye meant Cairo, orthodox icons and textiles had to be Addis. At Brown's Hotel in London, the staff greeted him like family. But I sensed that Mike's pleasure in travelling was waning. He was often too jetlagged to leave the hotel and his travel stories faded into irritations of lost luggage and flight delays.

In all the hurly-burly, I misread small signs that all was not right. When I said the weather was glorious, Mike forecasted rain; when I thought a meal delicious, he said he'd had better. I put Mike's uncharacteristic pessimism and contrariness down to him being pissed off at being in Geneva. Maybe some of the fault was mine. Perhaps I had too much enthusiasm for Switzerland. He'd get over it. Mike was not someone who held onto pique. And, anyway, he'd often apologise, saying he was just tired, that was all.

Next came problems at work. Mike had never been one for paperwork. His stellar performance normally gave him leeway. But when a new manager championed the bean counters and box tickers, Mike snubbed them, flicking them scraps, feigning ignorance.

It finally fell apart on a Tuesday. Dale had just come in from Girl Scouts, and Mike had come home and, instead of coming into the kitchen for our usual hug, he went upstairs, had his shower and sat down in the sitting room with a newspaper. The children were oblivious and noisy. I was confused, distracted, as I served up dinner. His face was strangely expressionless as he insisted nothing was wrong. The next day and the next, he was the same.

Mike had been a zombie for a week when I found myself crying uncontrollably with a girlfriend after I had dropped the girls off at school. She knew exactly what was wrong. Her husband had done the same thing when he started sleeping with his secretary. Didn't I know it was the first sign of infidelity? That left me nowhere to go because I knew that was not what was happening. When she suggested Bible classes, I knew that I was on my own.

Cornered, Mike said he'd had enough of negotiating the tortuous barter deals that made his high-flying reputation. He wanted a change. He was going to resign. What next? The answer was an ambiguous shake of his head. I'm always ready to fill a vacuum, not to be confused with having good ideas. I suggested Australia. Not initially enthusiastic, Mike then thought, maybe – just for a couple of years. After he'd given notice, he slowly came back into himself again. Almost. He was quieter, self-absorbed and a little indifferent. Nevertheless, the excitement of the move gave us all a lot to do, and I thought he was on the mend.

Farewell Geneva. I hated 'to go and leave this pretty sight'. I knew it wasn't going to last forever, but it had been a lot of fun.

Chapter 27 – Sydney and Swank, 1987

We moved to Sydney in time for a second summer in the Southern Hemisphere, bought a house, Mike got a job he didn't like, but it was start.

We were approaching the six-month mark – the time you take stock, take a bow and look forward – when Mike woke up with double vision. It was March 1988; days after his forty-fourth birthday.

The neurologist was a pale but robust chump of a man. He knew what was wrong with Mike: MS, multiple sclerosis. Quite extraordinary, he said, that we'd got away with it for so long. I thought that a strange choice of words – as if we had deliberately concealed Mike's medical history. The neurologist said he could have diagnosed Mike's MS "long ago", had he been consulted.

Déjà vu. I knew Mike had already been diagnosed. I pictured the London hospital and the doctor from Lagos telling Mike he'd get his vision back in a couple of weeks. With a flash of clarity, I knew, the doctor had decided not to point-the-bone.

Almost word for word, came the same reassurance. Mike's eyesight would right itself in a week or so. Multiple Sclerosis was unpredictable, said the neurologist, as he rolled out prescriptions for a cocktail of drugs. The doctor's manner estranged me. The consultation was brief, and he was patronising, his ego bursting out of his buttons. As we left, he called out that he'd awarded Mike the best of the diagnoses he'd got to give, as if he'd kindly dealt it from his gander bag.

We looked at each other, but neither of us skipped out of there delighted that Mike did not have a brain tumour with only weeks to live.

Walking across the carpark, holding hands, we said nothing. From the moment I met Mike, he'd been responsive to my chatter, albeit, once likening it to the burble of a happy mountain stream. I'd jumped on him at that, punching him hard in play, for it suggested he never actually listened and Mike, laughing and lifting me up in the air, had promised that he heard and loved every single word. So, I'd continued to share every niggle, joy and fear. Walking across the carpark, I stuffed back the fraught questions that bubbled up in my throat, and Mike said nothing at all. The silence between us was a chasm. We didn't go for a coffee or go home to cry, we just hugged, then went our separate ways. Each of us so choked; we had to get away to think.

It took me a while to recall a year-old conversation. I'd only met her once. Her name was gone, just wavy brown hair and a wide face. She'd declined the *Kirschtorte* in a café explaining that after being diagnosed with MS, her doctor advocated the protocol of Dr Swank, a highly respected American neurologist, assuring her that if she maintained a very low-fat diet, exercised and took control of her stress, she need never have another symptom. It was not a cure, he said, but if she had the discipline, it was as good as one. She was cheerful and positive; avoiding cakes was, she said, a small price to pay for avoiding a wheelchair.

Excited by the recollection, I rang Mike. He was thrilled to bits. I could hear the relief in his voice, and we prattled to each other as if the horrible morning was behind us. Mike said he'd phone the neurologist.

The invisible cleaver that had fallen between us as we walked across the carpark had risen for a moment before its second chop. Instinctively, I tried to stay its fall.

"Don't ask *him*! Let's find out ourselves."

But Mike made the call.

"Bullshit," said the neurologist; there was nothing Mike could do to change the course of his MS, so no need for pointless restrictions.

Chapter 27 – Sydney and Swank, 1987

Eat, drink and be merry was the message Mike brought home and related with a contradictory gravity that left me bewildered. Being merry was not on the cards. Mike's despair was palpable. All hope had been quashed. Mike decided he did not want anyone ever to know of his diagnosis, not our families, not our girls, not friends. And he'd rather I forgot about it too. (After a couple of years, Mike did tell the girls and friends about his MS, but it would be ten years before his parents were told.)

I was devastated. Yet, some serendipitous magic had my back. I'd called my family before Mike delivered his bombshell embargo, and, though Mike rolled his eyes, it gave me a crucial bubble of love and support.

The very next day, my supermarket trolley faltered in an aisle where I had not a thing to buy. There on the shelf, among the cookbooks, was one copy of *The Multiple Sclerosis Diet Book*, by Roy Laver Swank. The hair on my arms rose. Not a believer, I'll still accept unsolicited divine intervention or a little wizardry.

I saw it as a sign and bought the book, determined that we'd get ourselves together and beat Mike's disease. It was before Google, so I had to put in the hard yards in libraries where I filled ring-binders with journal papers and articles on using diet and supplements to reverse intractable conditions.

Meanwhile Mike, mustering all his reserves, focused on the day-by-day navigation of his new situation, which didn't include talking to me about Dr Swank. He didn't want much conversation at all. That, now, we were not to be a team, was, for me, the biggest shock of all.

It had been Mike's contention that, not only were we a good team, we were champions when the chips were down. We complemented each other in a crisis, he'd said. We'd sometimes laughed and raised our glasses to bring on the next challenge. Be careful what you wish for.

The silence between us stretched to settle like a spreading shroud, depriving us of advocacy, blighting all our rapport at a time when we were catapulted into a new country with none of his old friends to heft the gloom. And no let-up on the mortgage payments. No hush from four girls, whom my mother had once called my "litter" as they tumbled and fought and wept and laughed. Life's messy reality marched on. And, as we know, trouble never travels solo. Bad luck comes in threes, which is why the fourth kicker is so spooky for it heralds the start of another three-timer.

Tragically, Mike's younger brother, Martin, died only months after Mike's diagnosis, hitting his head following an epileptic fit.

Before the year was out, Mike's company closed its doors, his employment too short for any meaningful redundancy.

To cap that off, the easily transferrable disability insurance that came with the job suddenly wasn't, because I, in my naivete, believing we had a duty to be transparent, had told the insurance company about Mike's MS.

When the first follow-up MRI scans came through, the results were far worse than expected. Although the lesions show up as white, Mike obsessed about *black* holes in his brain and their gravity sucked him down, down, down.

And then my brother called from England. Mum had dropped dead. She walked out of her bedroom and didn't make it to the kitchen. She and I had had a pact that we would never leave it more than two years before we were reunited, but, with the sky falling in, I'd not held up my part. She died days after the anniversary of the two years. I miss Mum terribly. She'd kept all my edges together with her belief that Mike and I could rise to any challenge.

Her confidence was unfounded. My inability to accept there was nothing to be done, had tripped us into a bewildering divide.

Chapter 27 – Sydney and Swank, 1987

'To Swank or not to Swank'. I tried compromise, take the pills and 'Swank'. Nothing I said resonated any more with Mike.

I flew solo against a whole team; his neurologist, his GP and a reserve of specialists: haematologists, immunologists, allergists and gastroenterologists, united in their prognosis that Mike could do nothing to alter the course of his disease.

I didn't recognise 'The Black Dog' because such melancholia was beyond my experience. I thought Mike was in shock, that his unyielding pessimism would pass, he'd cheer up and we'd talk the same language once more.

I was thrilled and vindicated when Dr Swank's research appeared in *The Lancet* in 1990, titled 'Effect of low saturated fat diet in early and late cases of multiple sclerosis'.

Dr Swank was not some nut-job who'd written a cookbook but an eminent American neurologist. In 1949, he'd enrolled 150 people with MS on a low-fat diet and followed them for 34 years – yes, years! There was no control group, but Swank monitored the patients who gave up on the diet, and that gave him a comparison.

Of those who stuck to the diet, *not one* ended up in a wheelchair.

Mike consulted Dr No-Bloody-Hope, as I had named his neurologist, regarding my research. He warned Mike that I was being taken in by charlatans. Dr No-Bloody-Hope said it happened all the time because MS came in episodes or exacerbations and, during remission, the poor deluded buggers thought themselves cured! Dr No-Bloody-Hope and Mike were, after all, fellow scientists. They agreed that the worst possible thing that could befall anyone was to be taken in by a snake-oil salesman. Imagine that – feeling better after taking something that wasn't anything. Bloody placebos, you had to steer well clear of anything like that.

And, as for me waving *The Lancet*, he pointed out that the trial was not randomised and double-blinded, so not reliable. And, in any case, such lifestyle interventions were redundant now that pharmaceuticals were available.

I asked Mike if every trial made before those conventions became imperative, was consigned to the dustbin of medical history? Dr No-Bloody-Hope countered with the tantalising carrot that new research suggested a cure was only a decade away; in time to save Mike from a wheelchair. What was the point in Mike punishing himself by restricting his diet and exercising when a pill was going to do it all for him?

Mike opted for every pharmaceutical pill offered, advertised and whispered about. One of the drugs, Beta interferon, made him look like a dead-man-walking with a permanent flu and an even worse mood. After that he tried chemotherapy which certainly didn't improve his pallor. Every new drug featured, oh, so gratuitously, in the MS Society magazine, became a goal for Mike to get his hands on. Conflicts and side-effects were never mentioned until *after* the event. And when I railed against the drugs not doing anything positive, the answer was always the insidious suggestion that he might have been worse off without them.

I researched every drug Mike was prescribed, so I was not surprised when, after one consultation, a specialist held me back for a quiet word, "It's just... just with this new drug, you might have to manage his expectations..."

Really? Wasn't that his job? Were not the side-effects more significant if the perceived benefit was problematic? Why were we and taxpayers paying for such drugs? The irony was that conventional medical consultants were doling drugs out as placebos with little faith in their efficacy.

By the ten-year mark, research had not produced the magic

Chapter 27 – Sydney and Swank, 1987

pills that Mike anticipated would cure him overnight. What did emerge though, in the year 2000, was a book, *Taking Control of Multiple Sclerosis* by Professor George Jelinek. The Australian author was a medical doctor from Perth who had been diagnosed with MS a few years after Mike. Told by his neurologist that there was 'nothing he could do', he'd researched the work of Dr Swank and picked up the phone to speak to the grand old man in the USA. Professor Jelinek's book was his own MS protocol, acknowledging and incorporating Swank's work.

Mike started reading the book. To speed things up, I rang the Professor and asked if he would talk to Mike on the phone. Once Mike had related his medical history, Jelinek told him he was standing on the very edge of a cliff. Mike could choose to slowly walk back from the precipice using diet and lifestyle, but, once he was over, it was going to be almost impossible to climb up again. Following the protocol required perseverance but the results were worth it. No guarantees, but a great deal of hope, backed up by research.

Mike said, "Nice guy."

"That's it?" I said. "Nice guy?"

"Yes, he's a nice guy. Doesn't have MS, though, just thinks he has."

Mike had taken the book to Dr No-Bloody-Hope, who said people like Professor Jelinek never had MS in the first place.

From his prospective, Mike probably felt my peddling a diet belittled the enormity of his challenge. Like packing him off to conquer Everest with nothing but his bathing trunks and a Hawaiian shirt.

What came next were drugs to combat the side-effects of other drugs. Drugs to send Mike to sleep and drugs to wake him up. Diuretics to make him pee and drugs to make him not pee. The list grew and grew yet nothing was ever prescribed to help his depression, because he said he didn't have that.

Neither team won the Swank wars. Mike and I were both losers.

The Swank wars were not the history of everything that happened in our first decade in Australia.

Mike lifted himself up, bought a franchise and ran his own business. His great determination, courage and huge sense of responsibility for his family had not altered. Yet, Mike was not mine anymore, he had changed, and so had I. I'd unearthed the itch, the witch and the bitch in me.

First, the 'itch' – I had to get away. I ran, fast and furious from the misery, taking my ego to seek the sunlight. I ran headlong into a business partnership with an optimistic knave. Nothing licentious. He wasn't a villain, just a crummy entrepreneur on steroids, with an ADHD business manual and a loose conception of integrity. No sooner had he achieved one thing then he was onto the next, no consolidation, no safety net. I fell for it. It was exciting, incredibly challenging, and I was soon a workaholic. It was an environment where I could thrive, talk, be enthusiastic and, above all that, be patted on the head for a job well done. Regrettably, at that juncture, for me a pat on the head was the candy I craved.

Five years later, I was consulting a solicitor to extricate myself from the business partnership I'd rashly put money into.

Second, the Swank debate awakened the 'witch' in me. I started with medical doctors gone just a little bit rogue. Next came Chinese medicine, Ayurvedic medicine, acupuncture, homeopathy, herbalism, meditation and yoga. Soon nothing of mind or body was safe from a shift outside the conventions. With witchery came hope and the remarkable power found in taking responsibility for our ailments.

The 'itch' did not serve our daughters well, and they had to fend for themselves too often, but with the 'witch' came an

Chapter 27 – Sydney and Swank, 1987

energy that we could share. And Mike may have been justified in thinking the coven in his kitchen had gone beyond the pale. Diets came and went. What was in today was out tomorrow. Yet it all added up to a reconnection with earth and nature that pulled us all together when our little family could so easily have been torn apart by the distance Mike and I had put between us. The witchcraft was there to stay.

Alternative medicine has become the way I roll and I still read articles that shed light on MS and Mike's recalibrated brain, although it's now too late to change anything. I've recognised that Mike was unwell when I met him. His genetic predisposition was possibly triggered in Zambia. My bet is the rabies vaccine – since reformulated – for his first neurological episode came not long after when he had brain fog so severe his colleagues were deeply concerned, followed shortly by the start of headaches up the back of his neck. There were many other symptoms over the years, but I was blind to them all. He was so handsome and such a good human; how could he be sick?

It would be a long time before I even connected the strange mute episode in Geneva with his MS. That ten days when Mike could not summon enough brio to even say hello had been a manifestation of the inflammation that had crept about his brain causing havoc with the inexorable destruction of its wiring. *Anhedonia*, a neurological condition that, after a long gestation, can come so fast and furious that it stops the sufferer in his tracks. Physicians had identified anhedonia a century earlier. The word comes from the Greek: an-, 'without' and hēdonē, 'pleasure'. And it's not just the inability to experience pleasure in the present moment; it also wipes out pleasures past and the anticipation of future pleasure. Mike now says that is exactly how he felt.

Mental illness was still under wraps even in the 1980s, and it didn't occur to either of us to seek medical advice in Geneva.

Chronic disease, mental or physical, is a long road. Diagnosis can be scary. Something foreign muscles in and fear ripples out. Like everything else foreign, the more we can understand, the better we can relate. A very welcome addition to the arsenal we need for understanding mental health are writers who can bypass dry terminology and paint a more visceral picture of how it feels.

When I read an article, published in 2020, by columnist Eleanor Gordon-Smith about depression in patients with chronic illness, I had to pause, get up and walk across the room a couple of times before coming back to reread her words. I'd needed a moment for the clarity of her explanation to fully detonate in my mind.

> In that space you get a curdling, spitting resentment of all the things you cannot do. And the only real power left is to say 'no', even 'no' to things that might actually be useful.

That was not all. The article explained that asserting relentless negativity makes everyone feel as wretched and stuck as the patient. And that's what the patient wants. He or she needs people to understand such terrible pain by making them feel the misery.

Mike had put it more succinctly: "You should see it from my side."

It was a phrase that pushed all my buttons at the time, none of them compassionate. That was the 'bitch' in me.

Chapter 28 – The Black Dog

By the time all the girls had left home, I was working for a small charity that helped orphans in Afghanistan. I was perpetually weary, so I threw myself into my work, where pace, challenge and caffeine energised and depleted in equal measure. I loved my job, and it gave me complete flexibility. I called Mike regularly during the day to check on him. If he didn't answer, I could drop everything and dash home. Mostly he hadn't answered because he had his phone turned off, or he was at the local café on his mobility scooter and hadn't heard it ring. Other times, I would find him crumpled and frustrated, unable to get up. Often, I had to call an ambulance just to get him upright, or to take him to Emergency. Fortunately, Emily was with him the day he fell and broke his hip. After an operation and a spell in hospital, Mike was transferred to a rehabilitation unit.

The third day he was in rehab I got a phone call. The doctor had no bedside manner. She was very, very annoyed. Mike told her I was into alternative medicine. Was that so?

"Alternative medicine?" I said, not sure where this was going. "Yes, I am a fan."

"And, because of you, Mike is not receiving any treatment for his condition?"

Ah! Enough! I found my mettle.

"Hold on. Mike has never once listened to me about MS – more's the pity. He's taken every single pill any pharmaceutical company ever suggested..."

"I'm not talking about his MS," she roared, "I'm talking about his depression, which is so profound, it is upsetting everyone here. I will not have my staff and other patients subjected to it because *you* refuse him treatment for his DEPRESSION!"

I could have burst into a maniacal laugh at that point. She wasn't going to get off lightly. I am often tongue-tied and mousified in confrontation but just occasionally my inner warrior takes over while I look on in admiration.

Not one of the myriad doctors Mike had seen in the last fifteen years was remotely interested in his mental state. And when I'd tried to intervene, either it wasn't my business or I was misinterpreting the fatiguing effects of multiple sclerosis.

I think the string of words that I used included: lobotomy, trephination and purging. I said she could try any or all. I would raise no objection. Maybe exorcism would be the go.

Her voice changed. She spoke softly and said it sounded as if the system had let me down. It was, she said, an intolerable situation. Mike had two choices. Treatment – or he'd be sectioned. It was unconscionable that his family or anyone else had to live with him in this state.

The doctor rang the next day to say that, with two of her colleagues, she'd 'persuaded' Mike to accept medication, and she'd researched a drug combination that would give him the optimum result.

Three weeks later, Mike came home on Christmas Eve. He was his old self. It was like a gift from the past. My gorgeous man. Physical disability was unimportant when I had my man. I suppose it was a mix of his genuine relief to be home, the joy of the gathered family, and the pills. The change was remarkable.

It was a brief interlude, though, for Mike had thrown his medication into a bin in the hospital carpark while I was bringing the car to the door to take him home.

A mix of nagging and begging propelled Mike to get more anti-depressants from his GP. They were never as effective as

Chapter 28 – The Black Dog

the first prescription. He'd take the medication for a few weeks then ditch it, and I'd hound him to start again. Mike expressed amazement that I knew every time he stopped. He didn't feel any different so to him the pills were a waste of time.

Mike was much less agile after he broke his hip. The house was a lonely castle full of physical obstacles: stairs and more stairs and a steep driveway. There were horrified physios who said it was a death trap, and older ones who said, frankly, as Mike refused to do any exercise, at least it was a sort of gym.

I knew I was already on borrowed time. I could not leave Mike home alone much longer. He needed a full-time carer. Me. There was no alternative, yet every fibre in me rebelled. I did not want to be home alone with Mike and his misery as he hunted the internet for a miracle effortless cure. I loved my work and resented giving up my small income. Love on a budget might have appealed to Mike and me at one time – a romantic tryst, eking out a snuggly, witty whimsy together. 'Will you still need me, will you still feed me, when I'm 64?' But not now.

Yet it had to be done.

And then I had an idea.

And I fell for my idea.

At first, it waited in the wings, where I could work on it, and I liked it more and more.

My spirits rose. I felt more buoyant than I had for years. I could do this carer gig differently. I had a plan. And I even thought that Mike would like it.

I waited for the right moment to tell Mike about how the time had come for me to give up work and spend more time with him. I chose a day when Emily and Dale were home for the weekend. I didn't want to be all on my own, though I did not open the subject until Mike and I were by ourselves. All was quiet mid-morning when I handed Mike his coffee. My hand shook slightly as I sat down on the sofa beside him.

As I spoke, I wanted his grin to spread slowly across his face, like it used to. I had to be kidding myself… but at least he was listening.

I would become his full-time carer, with a twist. Evoke the A team again.

This would be a year-long adventure, just Mike and me. I didn't think it sounded shocking or blue-sky. Given our history together, it had the ring of familiarity and comfort.

If I gave up my job, we could rent out the house and go walk-about. But not aimlessly. We'd set ourselves a challenge with a goal. We'd write a book together. I'd got the title, *The World in Four Quarters*. We could each choose two islands to visit… for three months at a time.

There was no reaction from Mike to slow me down, so rendition speeded up. I ran away down a smooth, blank slope.

"Has to be places we've never been to. Has to be off-season to keep costs down. My choices would be an island in the Outer Hebrides and St Helena – you know, Napoleon's exile…"

I paused here. Mike's expression was unfathomable. So, I moved to the exciting bit. "There's no airport on St Helena, so we'd need to get a boat from Cape Town. We could spend a few days there…"

I'd saved that teaser till last. He'd get to set foot back in Africa.

But there was not a glint in his blue-grey peepers. Perhaps my words had spooled out too fast. So, I stopped for a moment, and, when I saw his flawless brow pucker, I thought it a positive sign and persevered…

"At St Helena they'd put you and your wheelchair in a sling on a zip line to get to shore." Still meeting a dry-stone brow, I quipped, "Bit like they hoisted our Citroen when we went to the Orkneys!"

Chapter 28 – The Black Dog

Then I shut up. I knew he would take a few moments to respond. I wished I hadn't mentioned the car swinging off the ferry on a derrick like a sack of potatoes. Yet despite that gaffe, my heart was beginning to thrum happily – my own spiel, spoken out loud at last, excited me. Maybe he'd choose Reunion or Madagascar. I'd purposefully chosen islands so he could not choose countries in Sub-Saharan Africa. He'd been to university in Trinidad, so perhaps he'd opt for the West Indies. Can people stay on Lundy Island, I wondered? That was near his hometown of Barnstable in Devon. So many possibilities… After I had spoken, I waited, on edge, my breath hostage.

Mike's eyes, incisive and grave, bore through my shifty look and he said, with deliberation and emphasis, "A – I don't want to go to either of those places and B – we have NO MONEY so WE can't GO anywhere or DO anything."

His answer should not have surprised me. I could have anticipated it word for word. Yet the shock of my precious dream, vanishing as he spoke, as fast as mercury escaping a broken thermometer, blew me away.

It took a moment to understand that the strangled hollering was mine. That my fists were flailing at the knots of the wooden floorboards, and that I was on my knees, no longer on the sofa. Histrionics is not my style. My protests are usually silent, sullen affairs.

I felt Mike levering himself out of soft cushions to reach me. MS gets in the way of even the simplest acts. The warmth and tenor of his touch had outlived Mike's loss for words. But he could not stretch his long arms quite far enough.

"Please," I heard him say, quite softly, yet slicing through the din. "Please, get off the floor."

Feet came thudding down the stairs.

"Dad, what did you do?"

"Nothing," he replied to Dale. "Absolutely nothing." Truthful to a fault.

Emily arrived and gasped "shit" as she caught her breath and, to no one in particular, said, "I thought Dad had fallen over." And then, "What is it, Mum? What's happened?"

There was undoubted relief in their voices. Relief that it was me on the floor and not him.

As a child, I'd grown up in Northern Ireland, where every loud bang I heard was the IRA. For my girls, since early adolescence, every thud has been Mike falling – falling downstairs, upstairs and in my lady's chamber. He could fall from standing still like a dead man. Out of chairs and especially out of baths. From showers and off toilets, crashing to break bones and bleed red on insensible whiteness. It was all so familiar yet never failed to shock.

Even today as I write, heavy matter tumbling sets me shuddering in the house where he does not live, and, in my daughters' houses, where he has never lived, they too panic. Our reactions too quick for logic to intervene just as Mike's were too slow for him to save himself.

Dale stroked my arm. "Just stay here, Mum, for a minute, don't get up."

Emily bent to hug us all in turn and put on the kettle to calm her own beating heart.

Later, on the sofa, sipping tea, my breath was still uncertain where to go – like a newborn, rewiring for life in the open.

It was time for me to repeat to the girls what I had said to Mike.

Mike reached out and took my hand. That sweet gesture, genuine and warm, felt awkward and my hand sat crooked. I could have moved closer and fixed it but, well, frustration isn't always flexible.

Vaguely bewildered, Mike repeated he had no idea why I was so upset for he could not envisage anyone choosing to visit

Chapter 29 – Variations on an Idea

St Helena, a God-forsaken blip of an island in the mid-Atlantic, in winter.

"While to Mum, an Atlantic gale on a far-flung isle sounds like fun!" said Emily, bursting a fissure of tension. "How did you two ever get together?"

Mike and I exchanged a rueful glance, the glimmer of a smile surfaced, and I relaxed a smidgeon. Not much, though, as I was contemplating my strategic mistakes. Had I chosen Jamaica and Zanzibar, I'd have better captured his imagination.

Amid the lighter chatter that ensued, I stared down at those knots on the floor – the grain swung smoothly round the complex, dark snags. I resolved that I wouldn't ask the bugger again. *The World in Four Quarters* was but a detail in the real plan. Renting out the house and living simply off the income was possible – I just had to tailor it differently. I also had to start talking it out loud. In keeping the whole thing secret and launching it like a rocket, I had invested too much in the colour of the nose cone, the naming of the voyage.

I'd use Africa as bait. And I exchanged the impossibility of writing a book, which I'd never done, for volunteering to mitigate the paperwork burden that bedevils grass-roots charities. There I had some experience.

We owned our house in Sydney. We were not 'broke', although we had little in the way of a cash buffer; Mike's long illness and my incompetent business forays had seen to that. Mike's flat admonition did frighten me, though, for my resolve was fragile, and I was scared of money. I knew cornering myself to be the only answer. I lacked natural courage.

I gave six months' notice at work and put up the house for lease. I told Mike we were going overseas. The bait was Botswana: we both wanted to see the Okavango Delta, a vast wetland sanctuary for game, and then I'd try volunteering, perhaps in Zimbabwe or Zambia.

Chapter 29 – Variations on an Idea

Three months later, at the end of 2008, when the family arrived home to celebrate Christmas, my successor had been appointed at work, and the house lease was signed. No one in the family questioned me much about taking Mike to Africa, and I had another three months to think about visas and find some volunteer work.

Whatever tensions beset Mike and me, we are still a good family together. The girls talk over each other, switch conversations, yell and howl with laughter; are given to tears of joy or the occasional clash, which passes like a summer storm.

Once the wine was opened, we relaxed into family brouhaha and acknowledged how much was needed to get the house ready for tenants without actually doing much at all. Dale suggested, "Let's start with the books."

We directed our gazes to the bank of IKEA bookcases. All were crammed with colour – paperbacks stacked on top of hardbacks, order and disarray, fat spines and the lean, the sloping, listing tall boys jostling with upright thicker grandees. Before Google became omniscient, books held connections as well as knowledge. Inherited, bought, gifted, nicked, each one had a story. And the odd book never returned to its rightful owner held you ever accountable because that was undisputedly a sin.

The girls sorted the books, piling, swapping, putting some aside for Alice who was in London.

A tremor spooked me. Why was I rattling the bars of the cage? Why could I not be the good carer, a job guaranteed accolades all round, fake contentment until it became a habit

Chapter 29 – Variations on an Idea

and create a small niche for myself within that framework?

I left the hubbub to sit on the deck. With the hot sun on my bare arms, my mind drifted back to Gwena and my first Christmas with Mike. My first African Christmas.

Mike came out to join me, and I said, "Remember our first Christmas?"

Most times, if I brought up our intrepid past, he'd hold up his hand and ask me not to talk of it. So, it felt good to watch a smile play on his lips and hear him say,

"Ahh, Gwena. How could I forget Gwena?"

Gwena held a special place for us.

My mobile rang. It was one of my best friends, Karen. We'd met a month after I arrived in Sydney.

"I'm at the airport," she said, "I've left Geoff."

"Karen, you can't leave on Christmas Eve!"

She'd been married to Geoff for over forty years. He'd been having an affair for at least the last two.

"Why not? Christmas wasn't going to be a barrel of fun."

She'd booked a flight to New Zealand where her son Pete and his family lived on Waiheke Island, off Auckland.

Karen continued, "Will you come over for a couple of days... after New Year?"

I booked my ticket for New Year's Day. The family was home to look after Mike.

On New Year's Eve, Mike did two things. He polished off a bottle of wine before sundown. Kal, Kim's partner, held up the empty bottle in disbelief, it had been a particularly nice Pinot he'd bought to share. Secondly, Mike consumed a great many anti-cholinergic pills; a drug to stop you peeing every ten minutes.

I woke in the night to Mike's groans.

"I can't pee," he said.

I had no idea he'd taken pills so I got a jug of water and ran the bathroom taps. "Drink," I said, "You must be dehydrated... all that wine." Later I phoned an emergency doctor who promised to call in at 10 a.m., the time I was to be at the airport.

Kal said, "Just go, Gill, we'll look after Mike."

So, I did. When I called from Auckland, Mike was in hospital, his bladder in spasm from the pills. The hospital said he was comfortable, and they'd keep him until I got back.

On the ferry to Waiheke, I yawned and wished I, too, had not embraced the New Year with such vigour. Never mind, I thought, I'll have a couple of lazy days listening to Karen's murmured regrets, vale for a marriage. I'll pour libations of wine and gin and proffer tissues.

How wrong I was. Karen was a woman spurned. She was a white-hot mix of rage and lust. Leaving Geoff was not going to define her life; she would not play the wounded wife. This was one hell of an opportunity, not to be wasted. Karen had walked out of her house, her job, and her marriage. The only way forward was up. She had, she said, been transported on the wings of angels out of a lifeless relationship into the arms of a loving son ensconced on the world's most beautiful island. Supported, wanted, loved. Now 'a woman of independent means', she looked younger and more radiant than I had seen her in years.

I sat cross-legged on the end of Karen's bed, and we talked into the night.

"Let's have a midnight feast," she said, sustaining our chatter with wine and nibbles.

By day, we wandered headlands and sandy beaches. Once we rolled down a slope of long grass, screaming like toddlers for there were no spiders or snakes to worry about in New Zealand, the sun was shining, and this was time to blow off the cobwebs, put on the glad rags and live. Since only twelve months before,

Chapter 29 – Variations on an Idea

Karen had been a yoga guru advising me that it was time for us to go into the forest and contemplate, I was thrown slightly off-balance. No more navel-gazing, it seemed.

"Join us on Waiheke," said Karen, "we can start a new colony."

I could have thought here is your island. But I wasn't ready for paradise. Waiheke was olive groves and vineyards; long empty beaches and sunsets. It was heavenly; cold in winter, though?

Karen smiled, "Fresh, like champagne. Log fires, music and laughter."

I loved travel, yet Waiheke just did not appeal. I quietly labelled it 'an old people's home anchored in the Huaraki Gulf'. Yet I did question myself. Why did I need travel to be a bagatelle of dirty buses, sweaty armpits, sign language and manageable disasters?

Back in Sydney, I collected Mike from hospital.

Two weeks later, he was back in again. Out. In. Out. In. Urinary tract infections grew more and more intractable.

When he got sick, Mike simply closed down and went to sleep.

I sat by his hospital bedside in Emergency and read my book. Sometimes, it was just for a few hours, other times, he'd be admitted.

Once a doctor said, "I see Mike's neurologist is in Emergency right now with another patient, so I'll get him to come over."

I opened my mouth to say don't, but it sounded churlish, so I composed myself and breathed deeply. I looked to comatose Mike and knew this was going to be my conversation with Dr No-Bloody-Hope. That sucked.

"Hello, hello! And how's Mike today?"

"He's not happy…" I said.

"Happy," he snatched my word. "Happy? Ha! I've been treating Mike for twenty years, and I've never seen him happy! Not once!" And off he went, chortling, to himself.

God, how I disliked that man. Mike had told him so, and he'd replied I had 'shoot-the-messenger-syndrome'. He said I had bundled up my anger at Mike's predicament and directed it at him. He confided that it happened to him all the time, and said he had broad shoulders.

On another Emergency admission, a young doctor, twirling his stethoscope, said, "Mike will be on dialysis within six months. Just preparing you."

Trips to weekly dialysis were an addition to things I didn't want to do. So, I frog-marched Mike, with his Zimmer-frame, to see Catherine Chan. That Mike agreed to see her is a measure of how scared he was.

Catherine had been bedridden with MS as a young woman. She had fought her way back to living symptom-free without any knowledge of Swank, but on a similar trajectory. She was a naturopath and I'd taken Mike to her years before and although he'd rejected all she had to say, the girls and I had become her patients and thought she was an extraordinary healer.

Catherine used iridology for diagnosis. We told her nothing before she studied Mike's eyes. When she put down her torch, Catherine said, "This is truly serious. You are peeing blood."

Mike was so astonished that he followed her protocol, threw away his antibiotics and took her herbs. He didn't have a UTI for another five years and has never been to the dialysis unit.

The next time we were in Emergency, Mike had fallen head-first down a flight of stairs, hurting his neck. The doctor looked up from his notes to ask me about future plans. I told him the exciting news that we were off to Africa.

I could see flickers of consternation. A consultant was summoned and, after a whispered conversation on the other side of the curtain, I was asked to step out of the cubicle.

"Are you trying to kill your husband?" the consultant said.

Chapter 29 – Variations on an Idea

Just like that. His eyes centred in his wire-rimmed spectacles like an irritated cartoon pontiff. He did not pause before his sermon. Mike was not a well man. Not well at all; heading for dialysis, with advanced MS and various comorbidities. He turned to his assistant who reminded me of a vintage noddy-dog on the back shelf of an old banger – the ones with fuzzy spray-on coats. Quite so, said Fido, nodding.

The consultant turned back to me. "I would be very concerned for your husband's welfare… well, not would be, I *am* concerned. Your plan sounds… rather *is*, very unwise. He would not survive it."

I blurted out, "Oh God, no, I don't want to kill HIM, I want US to LIVE."

At that, they stopped focusing on me and turned to each other, both nodding, speaking for my benefit. There were places where Mr and Mrs Shaddick could live together in a safe environment. Yes, yes, what a good idea. There were even some disability units going up nearby. Units attached to nursing homes were ideal in their situation as it would make the inevitable transition easier. Yes, indeed.

Better still, why not beside the crematorium, I thought.

This was not the first time I'd been steered towards a disability unit. The question made me sweat. At an interview with a social worker at one hospital, I had tried to deflect the inevitable recommendation by quipping, "I know that we will have to downsize and move to a disability unit…" when she interrupted me.

"Oh, I'm so sorry, Mrs Shaddick, how remiss of me, I was not aware you had a disability."

"No, not me, Mike."

She pounced. "So dear, why do YOU want to live in a unit for the disabled?"

I loved that woman.

With the two consultants gravely weighing up their duty-of-care, I stood tight-lipped, white flags fluttering in my stomach. What if Mike did slip into the Okavango Swamp or was trampled by an elephant in rut on the road to Kariba? Both scenarios Mike had joked were the way he'd like to go, adding, "And just leave my ashes in Africa."

I pictured myself being picked up by Interpol, who would note that, as well as the absence of widow's weeds, the wife was not even clutching a made-in-China urn. My mind turned distractively to wonder if Chinese urns were big enough because their clothes sizes were always on the small side.

Would a legal beagle in a coroner's court, after noting there were no witnesses to the death, reveal the serious concerns of the consultant for Mike's welfare? Would Dr No-Bloody-Hope reference my pent-up anger? And the deceased's GP, Dr In-God-We-Trust, would he remember 'the wife' was difficult, persistently asking for drugs for her husband's non-existent depression?

What if Mike took *himself* out in Africa? In my defence, I could prove he was suicidal. He had a manual from EXIT, a DIY organisation championing euthanasia in his desk drawer and about twice a year, he told me with all the benightedness of a flat joke, that he wished to die. I had the mental-health team on my speed dial, and they'd been several times to our house. Professional don't-do-it-ers. They'd spend ages interacting intently with Mike; I'd make tea and, when everyone had cheered up, they'd leave.

After we came home from the hospital, jolted by the consultant's admonition, I settled Mike, then dialled New Zealand.

"Karen, is the offer to join you guys in Waiheke still valid?

Chapter 29 – Variations on an Idea

We have to be out of the house in six weeks…"

"Of course, and you can meet Ken. I'm about to move into his place…"

It had been a whirlwind romance. Ken was kind, compassionate, and the rest would come later.

Chapter 30 – Waiheke and Other Interludes, 2009

As I booked our tickets for Waiheke, I mused that it was once more the need for first-world safety that directed us to New Zealand, initially to have a baby and now to live a sheltered dotage.

Mike was understandably confused when he found he wasn't heading for his beloved Africa but rather over the ditch to New Zealand. He'd asked why we didn't just stay in Sydney. But I had already pulled that carpet out from under our feet.

Dale said she would come to Waiheke, too. She was studying, could do her master's course online, and said, "Mum, you can't do this on your own."

The tiny run-down bach we rented on Waiheke Island had a stunning view. Waiheke itself was quirky: the local cinema had a drop-down fabric screen in a hall full of old sofas. There were organic shops and mudbrick houses as well as the grapevines and olive groves.

Dale explored the island in the manner of a perpetual forward scout, finding uncommon spots to share. Once it was a wild beach near Clear Point, steep and stony, our only company the dissolving detritus of a dead dolphin waiting to be taken home by the next big tide. As we approached, the noise of pebbles rolling reluctantly up the beach and down was so visceral and thrilling it gave a new voice to the shore. Not a playful sound, more a tempestuous rondo orchestrated by a cantankerous conductor. Sometimes a wave did not just rattle the stones, it galvanised the whole beach to buck and gyre, setting pebbles demonically dancing all along the shore.

I was mesmerised by those tossing jackstones being picked

Chapter 30 – Waiheke and Other Interludes, 2009

up and settled down in a new spot. I laughed with joy, for Dale was holding my hand, grinning, and the wind was in our hair. I knew Waiheke would only last until the next wave dislodged, unsettled, turned me over and took me away, reminding me to live in the moment.

I itched to redecorate the bach and make it mine. Wherever you put me down, I need to recreate the space before I can settle. In the grimmest of rooms, like tacky motels, I can't help but wonder, "If I were stuck here, how would I make it look?"

After a week or so, I relaxed and played the more dutiful wife, which was perhaps why I noticed that it was snowing in Waiheke. Whenever Mike sneezed or nodded his head, white flakes swirled around the bach. I shaved his head and shuddered. An internet search suggested it was a yeast or fungus growing on dandruff. So, armed only with the ingredients of the kitchen cupboard, I started a new regime for Mike's pate. Lemon juice, tea tree oil, apple cider vinegar, olive oil and lavender – and lots of massage.

After only a couple of days, his head emerged, beautiful, clean, shiny. He loved the daily treatments with fragrant oils; this was one alternative therapy Mike did not deride. Next, I scored a free sample of Aloe Vera exfoliant and massaged his face, taking off decades of old cells, the man was just getting younger by the day.

I got more ambitious. For years, Mike's chest had been a bit spotty. I made an exfoliant mix from the kitchen cupboard. Brown sugar and olive oil looked to do the trick. I sat him on the sunny veranda and began to rub his chest. After a few minutes, he said he was not enjoying the experience as much as the other treatments. He said it felt rough on his skin. It began to dawn on me that perhaps I should be using soft brown sugar and not demerara sugar crystals, I rubbed a tad more gently. By the time

251

Mike called a halt, we were both covered in a sticky film of sugary olive oil.

"Get it off!" he roared.

I said I would get some warm water, but, with shaking intensity, he said, "Quickly, quick, get this stuff off me."

So, I grabbed the hose, all the charisma from Gill's Skin Care Clinic violently swept away. Mike stood up dripping and shuffled off for a shower while I sluiced the veranda, floating off armies of foraging ants. Word had got out about that manna from heaven: first dandruff flakes and dry skin and now, a few days later, sugar water.

I boiled up green tea bags and fresh thyme to make a gentle calming solution for his skin, and boy did he need it because when he emerged from the shower, his chest was covered in tiny, livid-red diamante cuts as if he'd been targeted by a miniature pellet gun at close range. I told him he was fine. There were pains to beauty, and all that.

The next day, I had to concede his chest did look very uncomfortable. I nipped down to the pharmacy for a fistful of soothing remedies to apply.

By lunchtime, Mike was raging red all over and there was a rash creeping up the sides of his face. I began to wonder if I had inadvertently given his yeast or fungal infection its best day ever.

Mike said he needed a doctor. I said I should not have put sugar on his skin.

"If sugar did this, I will swear off it for life," he said.

I suggested an aspirin. Applied more cream. "I think it might be a 'healing crisis'," I said sagely.

Poor Mike looked at me. But wait, his scepticism was laced with something of that old camaraderie we'd shared in so many places.

"Indeed, it is a crisis, fire ants have nothing on this. I want cortisone, antihistamine, steroids and sleeping pills. I want to go to the vet. Now!"

The doctor gave him all of those and antibiotics. She professed she had never seen anything like it. So perplexed, she went and got her husband, also a doctor, and he didn't have a clue either.

Mike did not tell her what I had done. He told me in the car on the way home that he didn't want me arrested.

Karen and I escaped our minimal domestic duties for long lunches in the vineyards that strained our modest incomes and make me smile to think of them, while Mike took his buggy down the street to a small café in the village and read the paper. We showed up weekly for Thirsty Thursday at Carlie Farley's and trivia at the pub.

Life was disconcertingly pleasant – and more and more expensive.

Mike had been down to the beach on his Zimmer and seemed more engaged with life. He certainly looked a lot healthier. I began to think maybe we could still do something together more exciting than Waiheke. I googled how long it took to walk around the world. The answer was about three years. We could do it in stages, I mused. Cheat a little. No, cheat a lot. Trains are nice. At that pace, we'd meet the locals. It did not matter how many years it took. We could even go back to Sydney for visits. I could write articles. A book?

I mooted the idea, dinner-time conversation, sowing seeds. Keeping it light. Then I took it a step further. "What about seeing how far you can walk in a day?" I said, and followed up by suggesting that we could modify his Zimmer with bigger wheels for rough ground. Anything mechanical appeals to Mike – I could see his mind turning. A day or so later, I lured him with wine and chocolate onto the short coastal path that led over to the village. It wound along some cliffs in front of a row of baches.

It was a gorgeous day. A light breeze and the occasional white cap out to sea. After a patch of short grass, we got onto the path. At first, all went OK. Mike, invested in the idea of fitting bigger wheels to his Zimmer, was chatty and my spirits soared. Only, I had forgotten how much the path narrowed. Soon it was hard to keep both of the frame wheels level and Mike kept listing. He persevered. He was very slow, but it was early days. This is just an experiment, I told myself.

When he started cursing the stony ground and muttering about the ruts, I realised his spirits were flagging, so I sprang ahead to a picnic table to whip out the wine.

Mike sat down heavily. He said the sun was too hot, and he was tired. I thought about the opening of Martha Gelhorn's book, *Travels with Myself and Another*, where she says traveller's tales are not made out of the stuff that goes right. I reminded Mike that these challenges were what made it exciting. He looked at me dolefully, and we sat in silence until he remarked that the outing would not have been any less exciting with cold wine and solid chocolate.

I said we were at the point-of-no-return – I knew he'd appreciate the old airman's phrase – we could push on to the road where Dale would come and pick us up or turn back. Mike actually grinned a little and said, "Press on, McDuff," got to his feet, grabbed his Zimmer and fell over.

Was it the heat? The wine? Or because he was very tired? Whatever it was, he chose to tumble not onto a soft sandy spot or into the tufty grass, but right where the picket fencepost of a bach was set into a square of concrete. His skull hit with a horrible crack, and he let out a bellow of pain.

Out of the bach rushed a lady who took one look and said,

Chapter 30 – Waiheke and Other Interludes, 2009

"My husband's a doctor. I'll get him."

I thrust the bottle of wine into my backpack.

We helped Mike, moaning softly, to sit up and lean against the fence. I hovered while the doctor held gauze to his head, lifted the wad, tut-tutted and pressed it back.

"He'll need stitches."

He started to ask Mike questions. What day was it? That sort of thing.

"Seems a bit out-of-it," said the good doctor. "Concussion?"

"Oh, it's 'cos he has MS," I said. "Sometimes takes him time to answer."

The doctor looked up at me, and then his eyes flicked wide open.

"What's that?" he said, pointing at Mike's Zimmer-frame lying in the grass. "Was he here on that?"

I didn't elaborate on the training program.

"Oh, it was such a lovely day, he just thought he'd like a walk," I lied.

I could feel Mike's eyes on me. He did not have concussion; they were quite steely.

"But… why here? Why not on a pavement!" said the doctor, quite forcefully. The three of us manhandled Mike through their house and into a car for the short drive to the clinic. There was no doctor on duty, so our man said to the nurse, "Oh, don't bother calling anyone, I'll stitch him up," and while she went off to get the sutures, he grilled me again on what on earth had possessed me to let my husband use his Zimmer off-piste.

At this point, the clinic doctor appeared. She asked Mike whether he'd had any recurrence of the strange rash. Mike looked at me, and she followed his gaze. I had a feeling that these hospital notes were going to make interesting reading if I was ever to end up in that coroner's court. Especially as the path had bordered a cliff.

Six months into our year in Waiheke, Karen called for rescue from Ken, and I loaded her luggage into our pick-up and dropped her at the airport. Dale had finished her degree and would leave in the new year.

Mike announced we should move permanently to Waiheke. I was aghast. I wanted adventures, not a new base camp. I blurted out that, when it came to living in New Zealand, we'd been there, done that once before. I reminded Mike that he'd refused to live in a pleasant safe country full of lawnmowers, adding, "Nothing much has changed."

Mike agreed but said we had changed. We were now old farts, so it would be easy to settle in New Zealand the second time around.

The idea that it was a country for old farts *and* full of lawnmowers made it even less appealing, I said.

The debate did not get off the ground for, in mid-December, history repeated itself and Mike had an unexpected summons that would whisk us out of New Zealand. He was to start a plasmapheresis trial in Sydney, a process of syphoning out his blood plasma, removing antibodies and returning it. He had to be back in Australia the following week for pre-trial tests. He was on top of the world.

"Tell those people to pack up; we need our house back," Mike said.

There had been talk of plasmapheresis, but I thought it had been discounted, as there was virtually no literature to support it.

I knew it was Mike's journey to endlessly research possibilities, but was there no filter? I swear, he would have accepted a brain transplant without question.

I pounded Waiheke's wildest beaches. I likened my situation to some bizarre game of *Snakes & Ladders*. Falteringly, I'd climbed as far as Waiheke and just gone whoosh down a big long snake back to the beginning. Worse than the beginning;

Chapter 30 – Waiheke and Other Interludes, 2009

right off the board. Where were we going to live?

Christmas was ten days away. I found a room advertised in a share house in Sydney for a month. There were two girls and two boys in the house. We hardly saw them except to exchange pleasantries, but, at the end of the first week, one of the girls, let's call her Maggie, asked to have a word. Normally, she explained, there was a selection procedure, but we had not gone through the process because the booking was just for a few weeks. She felt, had we been more transparent, they would not have accepted us. I looked at her in amazement. I'd said we were a retired couple, what else was required? She remained silent. And then it dawned, a Zimmer-frame parked in the porch, a walking stick hooked onto banisters, pee bottles forgotten in the bathroom.

There was no walking her back.

"It's a dynamics thing," she said. "You and your husband do not match our criteria."

Her smile, acquired for a job in HR, never slipped.

"The house is unanimous; you are not welcome."

Given the circumstances, Maggie said, she had no choice but to ask us to leave and wanted to know how soon we might do that. For reasons that totally elude me now, I didn't tell her to get lost. My fragile ego didn't want to stay where we were not wanted.

I rang Karen. She was up the Eiffel Tower in Paris with her granddaughter. I asked if I could call her ex? Geoff ran a holiday resort on the Central Coast where we'd stayed many times.

"Go ahead. Doesn't bother me!"

Geoff was an hour away. He greeted me warmly on the phone, we joked about Karen at the Moulin Rouge, and he said it was quite extraordinary, he'd just had a cancellation. "Come on up," were his words.

It was strange to turn into the driveway and not have Karen dash out, bursting with laughter, to thrust a glass of wine through the car window. The next day, I watched Geoff mowing the lawns and cleaning the pool. Each time I stepped out of the unit, he bolted. I said to Mike that I felt a summer frost. He replied, "You're being over-sensitive. It's lovely to be back and Dale will be here tomorrow."

I am an early riser, even on Christmas Eve. There was a was soft tapping at the door. The conversation was whispered, not because Mike was still asleep, rather because it was tricky, and dawn lends exchanges a hush. Geoff opened with our long friendship and led into his new lady friend being highly-strung. I was one of Karen's very best friends. I stared at Geoff and saw a slightly furtive stranger trying desperately to stick his verbal sandwich together. I left space. Geoff fell in, his voice rising. It had frankly been hell for him since we arrived. It was their first Christmas together – this very day a year since the split with Karen. Would we mind terribly… leaving… as soon as possible?

This second fiasco was a joint venture. Geoff and I had slipped unthinking into our old friendship.

I packed up, texted Dale not to come and booked a cheap motel room in Sydney – the place was opposite the share house we'd left so unceremoniously, for my brain was so frazzled it was the only name that came to mind. I swore a lot on the trip back to Sydney. Mike found the whole thing incomprehensible.

Dale arrived at the hotel and said, "Mum, let's go for a walk and find a branch to make a Christmas Tree. All we need is something green, and I've got some cottonwool balls."

Emily had left to spend Christmas with Alice in London, and Kim was in Vancouver where Kal was on sabbatical. My mobile rang: my cousin John, an uncomplicated, warm and familiar voice. He'd heard on the grapevine that we were back in

Chapter 30 – Waiheke and Other Interludes, 2009

Sydney. "What are you fellas up to for Christmas lunch?"

I said brightly we'd organised a picnic. Well, said John; why not bring our picnic to them for they too were on their own. That Christmas with John and Sa was as cheerful, memorable and magic as any pre-planned Christmas day could have been.

A few days later, Mike and I left Sydney to drive to Camelot, Karen's house near Dubbo. While packing up the car, the other girl from the share house ran over to ask why we'd left so suddenly. When I explained, she apologised and gave me a hug, none of them had a clue about Maggie's ultimatum. Maybe Maggie had some trauma from a disabled relative. We will never know. I started to cry as we set off for Wellington, five hours west of Sydney, and Mike said I must have picked up a cold.

I felt more grounded once I was in Karen's house. Before we left Sydney, I'd collected my sewing machine from storage. When Finn, Kim's first son, was born, she'd insisted I make a quilt. Hesitant at first, I'd enjoyed it so much, I made another with gypsy caravans for Karen because her grandmother told her she had the coal-black eyes of a gypsy child. Kobi would have a Waiheke quilt because Kim and her boys had visited us while we were on the island. As I set up my sewing machine on the veranda and started placing scallop shells and seagulls, I felt the prickling tears of the past weeks, begin their retreat to a deeper haunt.

Karen returned from Paris. She said what fun she'd had trying to remember what she'd put on the immigration forms. I looked at her. The trouble with getting past old is we are on the hunt for signs of dementia in our friends, a bit like looking for the moats after the Sermon on the Mount.

"Yes," she elaborated not at all, "we can put down anything we like."

Like what, I asked, my brain always duller than Karen's.

"Like philosopher, artist, writer, thinker. Tinker, tailor. Whatever we like."

God, how I loved that woman. A woman to lift you like an elevator out of whatever chain of down-thought you'd got stuck into. Unpredictable and joyous. A gadfly sent to prick and puncture and postulate and pleasure us all. You could never rest on your laurels with Karen around.

Each week I drove Mike to Sydney for his plasmapheresis treatment. We'd have one night in a hotel and drive back in the afternoon. It's good to be off country roads before dusk to avoid kangaroos and wombats yet because the five-hour journey took seven with Mike who needed frequent stops, I'd inevitably find myself tensed-up and peering into the dark, while Mike slept soundly beside me. I was soon utterly exhausted.

I rang the hospital to ask if they had any arrangements with nearby hotels for discounts so we could stay two nights on each trip.

"Your Medicare card says you are living in Wellington, NSW, is that correct?"

I hesitated. I had no recollection of changing my Medicare address to Wellington.

The voice took my pause as confirmation. "Try Blue Gum Lodge. It's subsidised accommodation for country patients and carers."

Mike's doctor said he'd be relieved to have Mike staying closer and recommended Blue Gum for the duration of Mike's treatment, which stretched to five months.

Chapter 31 – Blue Gum Lodge, 2010

The day I drove us to Blue Gum Lodge, I was very, very tired and sore too. My physio had warned that Mike must stop using me as a prop. Leaning on me had become his habit.

"But I'm only balancing," said Mike. He 'balanced' so hard, sometimes we both went down.

When I found the Lodge was beside the rehabilitation hospital where Mike had met his match with the doctor who'd outed his depression, my mood plummeted.

Perhaps that was why, when I looked at Blue Gum, I saw an ugly building, the colour of wet puke mortared with blanched flesh. The large lattice carport, painted regulation sour cream, had a notice: 'Drop-off only – no parking.'

As I unloaded Mike's Zimmer-frame and our bags, my stomach was churning snakes, and the words 'Drop-off, drop-off' were grubbing around in my head. Why wasn't it drop-off and pick-up. Drop-off, drop-off… down the snake, over a cliff… I was suddenly mad-as-hell.

I marched in past an ever-unattended Formica reception desk, strewn with old mail, topped with a tiered wire holder of drooping leaflets. The energy-saving dim was perfumed with synthetic pine; the corridor walls were limpet green. I clutched a key with a numbered tag, counting off the doors until I had a match. The room was functional, clean and dreary with grey blinds at half-mast. I looked around for any redeeming feature, even something truly offensive would have done. Something to relieve the desperateness of innocuous decor. And then there was a crash behind me in the corridor and I turned to see Mike on the floor fighting off his Zimmer. Before I had time to react, there was the pounding of flappy feet and a flurry of laughing people reached out to pull him up, right the aluminium frame and dust him off.

"Up you come, laddie."

"There you are mate, no damage done."

I stepped back, folding into the shadows. Out of sight, I could still hear them.

"Walker's fine!"

"Just walk beside him, Frank."

"I think tea's in order."

"Oh, here's Misha, she's got a walker too, you two can have races."

Will they ever stop, those merry blasted gnomes that have come out of nowhere – their asinine comments spiralling into my brain, clogging my throat with their compassion. And all as creaky as he is, with their saggy tee-shirts and trackie pants, bared cracks and bald pates.

There was no pick-up from here. It was the end of the bloody line. As I hadn't appeared, and Mike, delighted with the attention, made no enquiry as to where I was, the pilgrims shuffled off down the corridor, leaving me alone in the gloomy room. I was unable to decide who best to murder, myself or Mike.

When it was quiet, I stepped out. Across the corridor lay the ablutions. Toilets and showers. I stared at wet footprints and a rumpled towel topped with toiletries.

It crossed my mind, I could just walk out and drive away. Mike wouldn't miss me, for I, his warm, chatterbox lover, had become a crotchety, mortician's clone. He would undoubtedly be better off, even better cared for. The only thing stopping me was that it seemed a lot to lay on the girls. So, instead of turning left, I turned right, rearranged my frowns and pursed lips into some more lively semblance of me and slid quietly to the sunlit lounge.

People were still fussing over Mike. One was explaining what happened. He was just coming out of the shower and had heard an almighty crash, and there was this poor man all tangled up in his walking frame. To place myself in this scenario without a whole heap of explanation, I quickened my pace to Mike's side and said, "Oh, I heard you fell, you poor old thing." I hoped they might think that he had gone ahead, and I had only just caught up with the situation. But none of them were fooled.

There were no fools in Blue Gum Lodge. It was layered through with inconsolable sorrow, horror and resignation yet there was more grace, empathy and solace in one small square of real estate than I could have imagined. My eyes could not see any of those things at first, just fussy people who made me feel bad when I didn't think I could feel any worse.

Mike adjusted more quickly to Blue Gum than I did. I was forever trying to get the hell out of there. The ever-changing mêlée of other inmates meant there was always someone to chat to Mike, make him tea, share a biscuit and an anecdote. Each one told their story, why they were there. I didn't have a story. I thought Mike's upcoming treatment spurious, and we didn't really live in a country town. So, at first, I could not connect even to share the biographical rite of passage, the key to the community. Mike, on the other hand, felt entitled to belong, for he had a very sad story.

Some saw my impatience as Mike took ages to eat his lunch. Kind souls would say, "Off you go Gill, we'll make him a coffee." And I would fly out… Just to breathe. Just to not have to communicate and chat with all those nice people. Not to live in institutional servitude.

Entering Blue Gum Lodge fired a crucible of anger igniting my resentment of Mike's refusal to talk or to countenance any input from me about diet or protocols; his pursuit of pills and his insufferable penetrating gloom. My deep sense of loss and pain were not charitable; they stoked my fury at the medical profession and at Mike for his acquiescence. My Greek god had sold his soul for a mess of pharmaceutical pottage. He'd believed industrial pharmacy would deliver one pill to cure him instead of a shareholders' bonanza of prescriptions to alleviate symptoms. My beautiful, darling man – how could *you* be so naïve?

Prowling the perimeters of Blue Gum, I found a separate building attached to the Lodge by a covered walkway. The sign said, 'Recreation Room'. I tried the locked door. I peered through the windows, cupping my hands into a tunnel. A big room with a small kitchenette, some tables and tilting towers of stackable dog-brown chairs. The manager said she'd be pleased to see the room used and gave me the key. I lugged my sewing machine out of the car and settled in.

Every spare moment I escaped to sew, leaving Mike in the company of others. I kept the room locked. Occasionally people's faces pressed to the glass, their hands up like blinkers, looking like donkeys. I ignored them, until one afternoon, a tall skinny girl in bright clothes knocked insistently, and when I opened the door, she was in like Flynn.

"So glad to find you. I've been peering through the glass at the wonderful work you are doing."

She had an American accent. She fingered a quilt I was designing that traced the history of Vicars Woollen Mill for my cousin John. "How long have you been an artist?" she asked.

I blustered that I wasn't, and her brow furrowed.

"Well, of course you are."

And off she went.

Had she sung the 'Ugly Duckling'? I couldn't recall Danny Kaye's exact lyrics, so I improvised:

Chapter 31 – Blue Gum Lodge, 2010

You're a very fine artist indeed!
An artist? Me, an artist? Ah, go on!
And she said yes, you're an artist.
Take a look at your quilts and you'll see.
And I looked, and I saw, and I said
I am an artist! Wheeeeeee!

At least next time I travelled, I'd have something to put on my immigration forms. I must remember to tell Karen, I thought.

The girl came back. "We all need distraction in this place. I've arranged for you to do a talk in the lounge. I'll get wine and nibbles."

I gave in, being a rude bitch was tiring, so I showed off my quilts and explained my creative streak was therapeutic. Both men and women gathered around. Some told me they'd been peering through the glass and seen me completely absorbed. A flash of guilt.

After that, I stopped locking the door of the recreation room and established a small retinue of regulars. I was at last a resident, and it was my time to hear the stories first-hand. It was mostly women who stopped by. Some brought knitting. We'd talk of handicraft, and we weaved our tales in and out of whatever tragedy had brought them to Blue Gum Lodge. That was the common thread; there was always a tragedy.

Some came just to sit in the quiet, too conflicted for the sunshine of the lounge. Before, I'd have been irritated for I preferred to be on my own. But there had been a shift, I needed company too. When they did speak, mostly I had no idea what to say. Sometimes, I just put out my hand. Sometimes, I knew they were in a private hell, not ready for the touch of a stranger. Sometimes, it was quite the other way. They'd cry and I'd cry, too, and we would hug as if way back we shared DNA, which, of course, is true. Often, a cup of tea took its ineffable place in the hierarchy of mankind's good deeds.

I, who had grown a heart of stone, felt palpable relief when I recognised compassion still stirring, for it signalled that I was still capable of commiseration. Yet, it was unsettling, I was nervous, I could feel the dam inside me, and I knew I must not weaken; my reserves were there for my beautiful girls for they had stayed constant. Mike was beyond my reach and yet I could never let him go.

People from country areas stayed at Blue Gum to receive outpatient treatment at Sydney hospitals. Those were mainly cancer patients. Others were relatives summoned, often hastily, to be at the bedside of their sons and daughters, fathers and mothers, admitted for accidents, heart attacks and horrific trauma. Boys spinning motor bikes or tumbling from drainpipes on their way to knock on a girlfriend's window; a girl who'd crashed out of a tree trying to rescue a cat. That was the last tree she'd ever get to climb. Horrific road accidents. Last rites and farewells, machines to turn off and reflections on the future of the living dead. I did not know that so few could carry so much sorrow or that strangers could comfort strangers with such intimacy.

There was so little to say. Lies and bullshit didn't have much traction, for no, it wouldn't be all right. It wouldn't get better. No, I could not imagine anything more awful. One woman had had months to come to terms with her son's accident. She spoke of her husband, of her other children. Of herself, how she had got the call and followed the helicopter down to Sydney. "Haven't been home since! Makes you wonder, doesn't it? They all cope. I keep telling my husband which clothes to bring me now it's getting colder and it's as if he never saw me dressed," she said, smiling. "Life will never be the same, but I have to pull it all together differently. Nothing else to be done, is there?" She was funny, practical and a good companion – her eyes dark one day

Chapter 31 – Blue Gum Lodge, 2010

and light the next.

Another couple faced the loss of all their children, one by one, through some wretched genetic misprint. Unspeakable shit happening and lives changing. Fate's intervention and a lesson in humanity.

The shared litany of woe, of courage and acceptance should have been deeply depressing, but, in some strange way, it was too immediate, this level of suffering, too raw for that. They were at the coal face, blasting and hacking, and all the truckloads of suffering, of depression and of regret, were too far ahead to comprehend.

Helicopters ferrying critical patients to the Royal North Shore Hospital passed low over Blue Gum Lodge. At night, I'd wake long before the airborne flutter was clearly a definable thrum and tense up as the big birds closed in, my breathing shallow before leeching out when the vibration of the rotors had passed overhead. I'd wait until the sound quietened altogether and imagine the bright lights of the hospital helipad. A stretcher, IV bags held aloft. It was hard then to sleep for, as like as not, before dawn, there would be a light brightening under our bedroom door and hushed, confused conversations in the corridor. A posse of summoned relatives lurching in, who had dressed hurriedly, jeans pulled over pyjama trousers; the slender sinews of their hope gnawed by fear.

And in the morning, another room occupied, a box in the fridge marked with a new name and often no one there. They'd have turned around and gone to wait at the Intensive Care Unit. We would all be asking each other who knew what the story was. Scrapped filings of sorrow drawn to the magnet of calamity. Realigning ourselves in the hierarchy of trauma.

One morning, after a night when not one but two helicopters had drummed past, Mike said, "It's because of Rhodesia."

"What is?"

"The helicopters," he said. "That's why they upset you so much."

He'd hit the mark. My mind was with the critically ill arriving at the nearby helipad, yet deep down it dug up Casevac helicopters flying overhead in Rhodesia with badly injured soldiers from nearby combat.

I turned and looked into those Atlantic grey eyes. Those penetrating, gorgeous eyes. When we were in love, I used to wonder, which most beautiful, his eyes or his mouth?

I shivered.

"Maybe," I conceded. Rhodesia was a place Mike never spoke about. He'd closed that door because for him, the past was too painful ever to visit. How strange he made the connection?

Maybe Mike thought a lot more about Rhodesia than I knew. After all, Rhodesia, undoubtedly our most reckless endeavour, was Mike's high noon.

That night, my fractured sleep opened a sluice gate to the past. Rhodesian dreams are full of unpredictable visions, like photos in a crucible, twisting, burning and then capricious, unfolding to reveal the brutal space and gentle place where we had had so much life.

Chapter 32 – Respites and Rescues

Dale arrived at Blue Gum Lodge with a leaflet picked up from the wire rack at the front door.

"Mum, do you know about these people?"

I looked at the glossy pamphlet. Nice, neat, pleasant women with even teeth smiled at me.

"Carers NSW," she said, "They give advice and counselling for carers. Do you want me to make you an appointment?"

I raised an eyebrow and shook my head, "Oh… Thanks, I'll have a read later." I could not imagine how they'd help.

Dale persisted, "Mum, it's at Pallister House. Over there…" She pointed out the window, "Of all the places it could have been in Sydney, it's in plain sight. You have to take that as a sign." Dale is keen on signs.

Pallister House, built in 1892, had been there, done that. A circular carriageway outside the front door was all the dignity left to the old lady. Its gardens were now under hospital foundations. After mansions fell out of fashion, Pallister did its turn as a girls' school, and then an orphanage. Next it was leased to a clique of healthcare groups.

If there had been stones along the path, I'd have kicked a good few, and that trivial action would have taken me out of myself, but the featureless grey strip cutting across the last decent piece of grassy lawn was my path to self-absorption.

Inside, the building had been refashioned. Remnants of the old house tolerated only as tokens to the past, not integrated into any new elegance. The receptionist took me upstairs to a high-ceilinged sliver of a room once perhaps part of a boudoir, I mused as I waited, a place for women to withdraw to or in which to sulk. It was bare like the rooms of Blue Gum, devoid of flair, furnished with bland Formica. On the table was a box of tissues. Strangely, those tissues held my gaze, a crumpled Matterhorn rose, peaked and snowy, from home-brand box mediocrity. I thought of Switzerland, before…

In came the counsellor and introduced herself. Dale had made the appointment and given her some background. The counsellor called Mike by his full moniker, Michael. "No, no…" I said, "it's Mike. He hates being called Michael." And those few words made him briefly mine again.

"And how long has Mike had multiple sclerosis?"

I could feel a knocking in my skull. I didn't want to say what he would have said, what he said every time he'd been asked for the last twenty years: "Forever, I've had it forever." It took an effort to say. "He was diagnosed in early 1988, five months after we arrived in Australia. We'd been living in Switzerland before that."

Stop there, Gill. That's all you have to answer. But her big pale eyes were on me, and she bloody well paused, left a space.

"… but he says he's had it forever," I added.

And with that I was undone. The pain of two decades. The loss of my Greek god. I could feel my face crumpling even as I straightened my shoulders.

All it had taken was the mountain of tissues and a void.

"Go on," she said.

Why go on? I had answered her question. Go on?

I didn't know where to start, except I knew it had to be at the very beginning. Yet how? Words were impossible for I was melting, turning to water. In front of strangers in this cheerless room, tears flooded from me, my jaw ached and I bawled. Embarrassed, spooked, I grabbed the Matterhorn, then snatched again and again, the alps of tissues rising at my fingertips.

I don't know what they made of it. They, because the lady

Chapter 32 – Respites and Rescues

with the pale eyes called in reinforcements, two more of her own, more tissues, water. A cup of tea that sat undrunk. This was not the time for tea; once I found my voice, I had to finish. Misery is awfully boring, lacking the adrenalin of trauma. No one wants to hear it all, so given this opportunity, I didn't want any interruption, I wanted the whole thing out.

I don't think those ladies could understand, or were that interested in, the minutiae of my saga. They acted on what they saw.

They talked in acronyms, over my head. Paperwork to short circuit. Telephone calls to make.

I was not expecting any solution. Yet I knew it had been cathartic, and I stared down at the bin by my feet, where all my frustrations had ended up in an insubstantial swamp of paper ranges and canyons.

Pale eyes asked when I had last had respite.

I didn't know what that was.

It took a few minutes before they believed me that no one had ever told me about the respite scheme that gave support to carers – not Dr No-Bloody-Hope or Dr-In-God-We-Trust, or anyone at the MS Society.

Well, I said slowly, they were there for Mike, not me. I doubt if Mike… even if they mentioned… And my daughters have always stepped in…

They asked me why I had not spoken to my own GP, and, when I said I didn't have one, Pale Eyes looked taken aback.

Then she said, "You don't get any uninterrupted sleep, do you?"

"Hardly," I replied, "not in years."

That I must take respite, time out, was the unanimous evaluation. Keep in touch, but physically detach for at least three months, more if I needed.

The paperwork usually took months, but deeming this a crisis situation, they would endeavour to get Mike into a nursing home for respite when he finished his treatment.

"You won't need to find accommodation before your tenants move out, so I think that would help, too?" said one of them. Of course, that helped, though it also reminded me that in the end, willy-nilly, I was destined to be back home as a full-time carer, alone with Mike.

"At this point, you must help yourself before you can help anyone else," said another.

"And when you do move home, you are eligible for help. Carers will come in to shower Mike and assist you," said the first. "You should have had that help already."

And then came the dispensation. "Could you go overseas?" asked Pale Eyes.

I stared at her. She grew wings, lifted off the ground and smiled at me from the high plaster ceiling.

"Maybe," I said.

I glanced at my watch. I had been there all afternoon.

I walked back to Blue Gum Lodge in the dusk. The first bats flew over and a few spots of rain made dark circles on the macadam in front of me. The calm after the storm. I felt lighter. And I was. For I had left my sad tale on the Formica table at Pallister House to join an invisible library of sad tales shed there.

The next morning, when I came out to the carport in front of the Lodge, I looked over to where a soft breeze shifted the trees dappling the wet-sand-between-the-toes patina of the old brick walls of Pallister House. What a difference twenty-four hours could make.

"Drop-off only – no parking."

Drop-off was exactly what I was going to do. I did not say much to Mike. He did not say much to me.

Chapter 33 – The Long Drop Off

I booked a flight to London with a stopover in Vancouver to see Kim and Kal. Kim was finishing her Ph.D. to a deadline, so I could only stay a few days. I was welcomed with open arms, and a riot of Canadian spring sunshine.

My onward flight was cancelled when volcanic ash from eruptions of Iceland's Eyjafjallajökull volcano shut down European airspace. Kim put down her pen, we hired a car and set off for a glorious week on Vancouver Island.

When we got back to Vancouver, Emily phoned from Sydney to say Mike had booked himself on a flight to Dar es Salaam in Tanzania. The respite home was, Mike said, all very nice but actually a police state. He was going to see Nick, his old friend, now divorced, who lived in Dar.

All of us applauded Mike's newfound spirit. Dale and Emily drove Mike to Sydney airport with 60 kg of luggage, his monster electric buggy and his Zimmer-frame. Way over his baggage allowance, he needed help repacking.

Emily found he had six one-litre bottles of moisturiser. "I'll let you keep one," she said.

Dale, too, had advice. "Not your hair clippers; finding a Tanzanian barber is a cultural experience you must not miss. Or your speakers. Tanzanian marketplaces have cheap speakers – special price for white man but still a bargain."

Going for a farewell coffee, Mike lost control of his buggy, tipped over a table, showering cappuccinos and pinned a terrified young dark-suited businessman to the wall.

That sorted, Emily said the last sighting was of Mike driving his monster buggy determinedly through the departure gate; he never looked back.

Alice met me at Heathrow. At the tiny flat she shared with her boyfriend in North London, I slept on a fold-down sofa in their loungeroom. I could only get to the bathroom and kitchen through the bedroom she shared with Chris.

"You can stay for as long as you like, Mum," said my gorgeous girl.

It wasn't too long before I said, "I think, Alice, it would be a good idea for me to take you on a holiday. Where do you want to go…?"

"Turkey!" she said. I flipped back to the south coast of Turkey with Mike on our way back from Iran. Where was it – Antalya, Alanya, Adana? I remembered only bliss.

"I'll ask Chris if you can use his computer to make the bookings," Alice said.

He was reluctant. I understood. He was home from work and using it. He muttered to Alice. She whispered that I had to be really quick and not use too much data.

He moved to an armchair, flicking through a magazine. I scanned Ryanair for flights, then dashed through the bedroom to the kitchen to confer with Alice. Towns beginning with 'A' began to spin. Not all had airports. Chris was shifting in the corner, wincing each time I sat down to struggle with the unfamiliar computer. I tried to listen to Alice calling out dates – while wafts of Thai curry curled through to join that fuggy, particularly London smell of Roman legions, Thames water and railway soot. I pressed the final key, and… Oh hell, I had booked us to Alicante in Spain. I went through to the kitchen, "How about Spain instead?"

"What? No, I've been to Spain. I said Turkey."

I went back to the living room. Chris was re-hunched over his computer. I explained that I needed to get back on. I could only change the booking for a flight on the same day. That narrowed the field. I booked Morocco.

Chapter 33 – The Long Drop Off

Dinner was sombre. Alice didn't want to go to Morocco. Morocco wasn't far enough for Chris.

We stayed in a lovely though modest guesthouse in Fez. We did have fun... made memories. After Alice flew home, I stayed on and backpacked, fortunately oblivious to the modern lore that solo European woman of my age only went to Morocco for toyboys. Ahh... I had been irritated when the mountain guide I'd hired, pulled off a remote dirt road and wanted 'kissy, kissy'. I was wearing a headscarf, raised my ring, pulled out photos of Mike and the girls and looked severe. He could not possibly be serious.

I travelled Morocco by bus and train and squashed into innumerable 'Grand Taxis'. I saw nomads in black felt tents high in the Atlas Mountains and slept on the floor of one dilapidated mud-brick farmhouse alongside mites that burrowed into my skin causing a rash that would revisit for years to come to remind me of that uncomfortable night. I hitched a lift at one stage because I could find no other option and turned up to a remote police station when my phone ran out of battery, causing a surprising amount of commotion followed by great curiosity and kindnesses beyond the call-of-duty. Eventually, I arrived weary in Tangier to fall in love with the city. Each morning, I walked out of my cheap, spotless lodgings in the old town and crossed the square to a coffee shop with an unchanging coterie of old men. By the third morning, my coffee waited on my table, the men nodded in greeting, and I sat in the sun and felt blessed.

I was sitting at that coffee shop when I suddenly desperately missed Mike. It took me by surprise, hot tears filling my eyes. Mike would have loved Tangier. The Rolling Stones had visited in 1967 and a local bar was rumoured to be the inspiration for Rick's Bar in *Casablanca*. I wanted the Mike who took my hand when I least expected. The Mike who was so wise when I got my knickers in a knot. The Mike that I knew loved me. The Mike that listened to my every silly story and wild idea. The Mike who encouraged me, made me feel smart and beautiful. The Mike who said we make our own luck. The one who thought we were a good team. The irreverent, funny anarchist who hated authority. I missed his intellect; the shared books, music and ideas. Now we had nothing to share. I ached for what had once been mine and felt so overcome that I went back to my room to email him, pointing out that at least we now shared the same continent.

He replied that he intended to remain in Africa if I would promise to visit him once a year? I said yes. Of course, I would say that. It was not the moment to punt realism. Mike's Africa was not there anymore. Small enclaves of aged and beleaguered friends had their own problems; pockets of expats were transient. And sick men have to pay a lot of money to get visas.

Yet, I wonder if, with more energy and imagination, I could have taken him back to Kanja or Gwena, where the villagers would have been happy to look after an old white man who wanted to drop his fishing line in the Zambezi, drink a little beer and stare rheumy eyed at the sunset. But that is more the premise of technicolour film directors to achieve.

On a clear day you could see Spain, my next stop, where I was to meet my friend Trish and her daughter, Elizabeth, in Granada. Travel can make or break a friendship, but there was not that risk with Trish. She had been the first friend to know about Mike's MS. She'd found out when she'd invited us to lunch. Mike was late, and when he did arrive, Trish commented, "About time! Gill couldn't settle. Wouldn't even have a bloody drink till you got here."

Mike, to my absolute amazement said, "That's because I have MS, Trish, so she worries about me."

Chapter 33 – The Long Drop Off

Without a moment's hesitation, Trish said, "Oh, we've got a friend in England with that. Red or white?"

I wanted to hug her, but that would have spoilt perfection.

Now in Europe together, Trish, Elizabeth, and I circled round the Iberian Peninsula, finishing in Lisbon, another city I fell in love with. My friend Karen, I mused, fell in love with men, I fell for whole cities.

There were one-liner emails from Mike in Africa and a longer one asking me to lodge a travel insurance claim after he'd made his way to Kariba, shared several beers with Mervyn, fallen down his steps and ended up in the hospital where Dale had been born so many years before. Longer messages came from the girls trying to keep track of their wayward parents.

Back in London, where Alice worked for an upmarket property company, she'd made her boss laugh with 'when mother-came-to-stay' stories. He mentioned a Belgravia property waiting for renovation, "Your Mum can move in there. It's far better occupied than sitting empty!"

Trish and I flew from Lisbon and arrived in Heathrow on a beautiful sunny day, caught the underground to Hyde Park and walked with our backpacks, arriving at the pretty mews house just as Alice rocked up with the makings of dinner and a bottle of wine. The dining room table rose up from the floor at the press of a button. Another button slid back half-a-wall to reveal a fridge and shelves of expensive glassware and china. The curving staircase was killer marble, and the spa bath was wasted on one.

I was there for six weeks and did wonder if I could have just hunkered down for a year or so. Friends came to stay. I pounded the streets of London, visiting old haunts, drifting through galleries, hunting Australian baristas – the world's best coffee makers – and propping up the bars of historic London pubs with Alice and Chris.

To my delight, London's iconic Victoria and Albert Museum were presenting their first ever exhibition of British quilts. Walking into the exhibition felt like a surprise party put on by a huge extended family I'd never met.

Quilting wasn't solely a woman's craft; quilts from men in Wandsworth Prison spoke volumes. One used a tiled floor to inspire a hexagonal pattern, the sunlight through the bars, another. Soldiers were taught quilting to keep them off the bottle, using old scraps of military uniform and insignia to quilt in convalescence. In a home for unmarried mothers, the girls cut out hearts and then quilted one half to the blankets of their babies. The babies were taken off for adoption, and the mothers lived on in the forlorn hope that one day they'd unite the two pieces and find their lost children. That made me cry. Those hearts split in two.

I left London and did one last loop around UK visiting family and friends before turning for home. Our tenants had moved out, and I had to get back to Australia. I'd blocked out worry for five long months, and now it came back to nibble at my conscience. I had 'dropped out' without solving anything. Yet a smile bubbled up, I'd had a ball, spent time with Kim and Alice, and even returned Mike to his beloved Africa.

After a tearful parting from Alice, I was at the gate waiting to board my flight home when I read an email from Kim. Her Sydney university had put out a call for accommodation for two young Dutch students. She had registered my interest. I was irritated that Kim saw being a housekeeper was my future, as if juggling Mike's regime was not sufficient. I emailed back and said thanks, but no. I am not a people person. I like my space. It was out of the question. Yet, even as I protested, I thought of Blue Gum Lodge, and a wedge of possibilities snuck in.

Kim responded, "Mum, your options are limited. You need

Chapter 33 – The Long Drop Off

money. It's confirmed, they arrive in two weeks. I've put your name up on the Sabbatical Homes website. So, there will be more."

Our house had been empty for weeks. The plants on the deck had dried, died and desiccated. Indoor furniture was outdoors, upstairs furniture downstairs, every picture in a different spot, even curtains had been switched. And there was junk – an old microwave, broken chairs – and when evening fell, I discovered scarcely a lightbulb that worked, with not a single battery in any remote.

I was jet-lagged and a little deflated. I poured myself a glass of duty-free wine and thought how Karen had instilled in me the need for a mantra. I could not summon up much initiative, so I just said, "I can do this." And those words would prove invaluable at jump-starting my gumption and gusto. I can do this!

I can't travel without acquiring books, and I shook off my despondency there and then by putting them on the empty bookshelf. The heart was back. I could do this.

The next day, I reordered the house with the radio for company. A discussion came up about depression within families… I stopped to listen. The gist was that one hundred per cent of people who lived with depressed people became depressed.

Fuck, I said to myself. Was that me?

I went to the garage to get my boxes of books. I had to re-read Eckhart Tolle and be reminded how to deal with the sad story we repeat over and over, embedding it in our brain, feeling sorry for ourselves. After five months away, I had to be very careful to leave my sad story where it belonged, on the Formica table at Pallister House.

Chapter 34 – Rooms to Let

I bought a beat-up Toyota Townace van thinking it would work better for Mike's buggy than a car. It had stickers galore – 'No Fracking', 'You can't eat coal' – and several rainbows. I rocked up to collect my Dutch students from the train station late at night and ushered them to the windowless back of the van. Oliver and Jort, both polite and softly spoken, looked askance. There was no light in the back of the van and communication with the driver was through an opening just big enough for me to see out of my rear-view mirror. I hadn't bought the van with guests in mind.

I think the boys were relieved to reach the house. After I'd shown them their rooms, they pleaded starvation. Venom was the topic as they tucked into the midnight feast that I rustled up. I laughed lightly, saying spiders did their best to avoid us; the ones in the house were not the deadly kind. They asked if I sprayed the house for spiders. I explained, I didn't use insecticides.

I did add, just because no one wants to hear their deepest fears are completely groundless. "It's not a good idea to go barefoot at night, especially after heavy rain."

Oliver quipped, "But you have a policy of no shoes in the house?"

I shrugged with a goofy smile.

Relieved, tired, fed and with a beer in their bellies, the two lads trooped upstairs. They were nice, and I felt triumph in a minor key; maybe this idea would work after all. Then they reappeared, one clutching a clear specimen jar with a yellow lid.

Jort had found a large black spider under his bed.

My first thought was what the hell possessed him to go scouting under his bed. He'd chased it with a bit of cardboard.

Chapter 34 – Rooms to Let

He apologised – the spider did look worse for wear – sinister, though, even in repose.

"Oh, it'll just be a house spider," I said, swiping the jar. "They are nocturnal, hardly ever see them – s'pose cos we're asleep." My flaky laugh echoing as they furrowed their brows.

With daylight, the boys were madly enthusiastic about the house's proximity to the rest of the wildlife – we live opposite a national park – and in no time they were pursuing lizards and birds with rangy telephoto lenses.

Ten days later, I had additional guests – Ingrid, an academic from Scandinavia with her husband, Erik, and a small baby, Lars. They had not expected a chilly autumn in Sydney. It's champagne weather, I said. Taken aback by the temperature of the house, which never reached the constant of 25°C they were accustomed to, I suggested wearing something over their T-shirts. They looked at me in amazement and said, "But *inside*?"

Every radiator was dialled to the max. When they went out, I'd fly round the house turning everything off. Australia has some of the most expensive energy in the developed world. They'd come back, strip off their jumpers and shiver.

They marvelled at the clothesline in much the same way that I might look at Leonardo de Vinci's flying machine. They would, they declared, just use the dryer. It was a spider haven, crisscrossed with webs. They were horrified. I explained it was hardly ever used. Was it safe? Were there spiders inside it? Erik went back to survey the clothesline; contemplating how to set the lines to 'wrinkle free' or 'iron ready'.

Erik confessed that paternity leave was challenging. Ingrid went daily to the university and left him with the baby.

"I think I will go crazy! I have nothing to do when Lars is asleep."

He prowled the house, finding things to fix. The washing machine waltzed, a tap dripped... make that two taps. He observed that the TV speakers were not the right match, the CD player had a background hum, and the light in the larder flickered before it came on.

"It is very annoying; do you have a new starter for that fluorescent light?"

He rearranged my furniture. He liked things in straight lines. Ornaments, too. Squint pictures drove him crazy.

Outdoors, Erik really came into his own. He found moss on the driveway and happily power-hosed for hours. The paint flew off nearby fences in strips.

"Just a little repainting, I think," he called out. He hosed underneath the deck. "I think it has not been hosed for a very long time."

Never, mate. It's been up 25 years and never been hosed.

A rhythm developed and I had time on my hands. I decided to make a quilt for Mike. Mike hated anything fake: epaulets, false pockets, were an anathema to him, so it had to be a proper quilt – bed-sized.

No table was big enough, so I started on the floor. Erik came to chat, and the baby cooed. I began with fish eagles, Mike's favourite birds, Lake Kariba and Gwena. Then Kanja, the little house where Mike fished the Zambezi from the veranda.

Making Mike's quilt became a race against time as the baby at first sat and stared, then flopped forward to wriggle and eventually could crawl, putting me into hasty retreat.

All my guests were intrigued by the quilt. It introduced them to Mike, whom I knew would one day reappear. I knew he would be back for his girls.

Mike and I had been apart for nearly eight months, and I had been with my guests for three when, as I predicted, Mike

Chapter 34 – Rooms to Let

messaged, asking to be picked up from the airport a few days hence. He arrived missing a tooth from the fall down Mervyn's stone steps in Kariba.

Driving home, I asked Mike about his flight, his trip, our mutual friends in Africa. He responded in monosyllables, re-tuned the radio to classics, put back his chair and closed his eyes.

The guests were happily chatting on the veranda, juggling boiled eggs and telephotos, bouncing the baby and crunching cereal. I introduced Mike. He was tired. A hush fell over the house.

I was busy over the next few days re-establishing Mike's routine and was taken aback when Erik asked for a word. Mike, he said, had told him I'd turned his house into a hostel, and he'd been turfed out of his bedroom, the one they were in. They had contacted the university to find other accommodation. They had loved staying but now could not impose.

"No, no," I said. "Mike's in the little room so that he has less room to fall. He was joking."

Erik looked abashed, "Gill, the real problem is he is the saddest man we have ever met. Too sad to live with."

Erik added that Ingrid felt depressed after only forty-eight hours. The other guests too agreed that the house was suddenly somber. It was better for them all to find another place to live and leave me in peace with Mike. Erik was sure it would be better if it was just the two of us...

The two of us!

I had the number for emergency respite. I told the truth: Mike was unsafe at home. I lied about needing new grab rails fitted. I got a place for him that day. I also got a consultation with the home's doctor. With Mike beside me, I told the very young medic that without anti-depressants, Mike was borderline catatonic. Mike refused to take his anti-depressants, and I was no longer prepared to live with him in that state. It was a choice Mike had to make.

I drove home alone, stopping to buy wine to share with my guests and, after some awkward questions, the house settled.

Mike accepted my ultimatum and, two weeks later, made another homecoming. He stared at the quilt I had made him and tears sprung to his eyes as he traced the outlines with his fingers. He swore it had not been in his room the first time, but it had. He wanted it hung up so he could look at it every day.

And that was it. Mike took his pills and talked to our house guests. To Lars's baby bouncer and push chair, we added a Zimmer on each floor and walking sticks.

There were still hurdles. Mike played solemn music at breakfast. I'd ask him if the guests on the deck appreciated his dirges, and he'd say, "It's my house."

I'd start to apologise and find them more focused on the birdsong and their own conversations than Mozart's *Requiem* wafting out the kitchen window.

I was more insistent about Mike tottering with his pee bottle from his room to the bathroom. He said, what was the difference between that and the baby's brightly coloured potty which Erik wielded. A world of difference, I muttered. Mike said, didn't I mean an age of difference?

Mike's own mantra, 'It's my house', meant he helped himself to whatever food took his fancy, to the mild consternation of my guests.

He also had an inability to distinguish his clothes from any others.

"Excuse me, Gill, but I rather think Mike has one of my socks."

I recognised one sock on Mike's skinny ankle but not the other. Presumably he had another pair like that in his room.

Chapter 34 – Rooms to Let

Once, he appeared at breakfast muttering that his jeans had shrunk. I sat, prickling with sweat on a cool morning, wondering how long I had before the guest realised she was short of Levis.

Self-absorbed with the reignition of my habitual irritations, it took me a little while to realise that the guests saw Mike as a different person. Not the stubborn, lugubrious shadow of a lover who drove me to distraction; rather a creaky old cowboy dealing with a horrible disease. They saw a family man who loved and was loved. A sagacious man. Although Mike needed time to arrange his brain to speak, the guests hung on every word. Although he relied on repeated witticisms that made me flinch to hear them, to a new audience they were wicked repartee. And as we had a new audience every few weeks or months, he was on a roll.

Moreover, in the company of others, we behave ourselves better and that went for both of us.

Nearly all our guests were travellers with their own tales to share. When I summoned the shadows of our past, Mike no longer turned away. In company, he was happy to own our adventures again. To laugh at the tales of fake gold bars, a hotel in Cairo that once was a palace or our disastrous rabbit-farming days.

The house developed a continuum, so Mike and I never had to explain ourselves. There was always a crossover of guests, and old guests loved to put new guests in the picture about the landlady and her challenged and idiosyncratic husband and the four daughters. The four daughters were pure gold. Pretty, funny and usually a lot closer in age to the guests than Mike and I. Guests who stayed longer than a few days would count off on their fingers how many of the four they had met.

Friendships were made between us all, friendships that have lasted across years and continents.

More grandchildren arrived. Both Kim and Emily had baby girls in 2012 – quilts for Aila and Rocket. (In 2017, Rocket's brother Fox joined us and another quilt.)

Grandchildren meant we could rustle up a crowd of kids on demand. When Emily organised a surprise birthday party for one little boy, his parents were as thrilled as their son.

Mike became the still centre of the house; always on the deck to enjoy a conversation or read a book while others sat convivial around him. Guests offered him tea or coffee, and he never refused. He never turned down food, for he was never on some crazy diet adopted by his dotty wife and daughters. All food was good food to Mike.

Even on his off days, when Mike repaired to his guise of gloomy and morose old codger, the guests saw him rather as taciturn and eccentric, something like a living legend.

The tears of a Shakespearean actress were not fake as she bade him goodbye. She said she would miss him terribly.

When we threw a leaving party with vodka and kasha for a Russian professor, I wanted us to sing 'The Song of the Volga Boatman', but Fedor told us that was very old-fashioned and instead we sang a more modern Russian love song, which still sounded pretty doleful. I printed out the words and Mike joined in the singing. When I looked over and our smiles connected, it flipped my heart.

We had a neuroscientist whose specialty was people who, after a knock on the head, could pick out family members but identified them as aliens. That gave me food for thought one night, looking at Mike who'd just made guests laugh out loud at something he'd said. Had my alien come back to me or me to him?

A doctor came to inspect the accommodation. He had a wife and two small children.

Chapter 34 – Rooms to Let

"Yes, we will move in. I need a three-year lease."

"Oh, no," I said, taken aback. "I can't commit to that; we might not get on."

"Oh, we will get on," he said. And after a couple of weeks of inaugural chaos, we did get on.

The first hurdle was how to handle the TV that went on at 6 a.m. until bedtime while wherever I looked, a small child held a noisy computer game. The floor of the larder disappeared under sacks of rice, boxes of sauces and packet-noodles. Neon-tinted transparent suction caps grew like fungi on the tiled kitchen walls. The benchtops vanished under a battery of appliances, including an enormous rice cooker and an egg boiler modelling as a fat clucky hen in yellow and pink plastic.

Australian wildlife still held sway over technology and a cricket on the wall brought the circus to a stop. The children, lifting their heads briefly to find a real-life monster, screamed, bringing panicked parents rushing to their side.

While insects of any description caused mind-boggling uproar, birds were OK. I'd return from my morning walk to find the outdoor table covered in breadcrumbs, lorikeets happily hopping on their short legs and my guests in heaven. The sky would darken as flocks of white cockatoos, magpies, currawongs, and lorikeets, descended on the house to squirt white shit everywhere in an invasion that would have thrilled Hitchcock.

There was no escape, even the top veranda became an obstacle course of drying racks sporting smalls and fluorescent cleaning cloths. In the laundry, a complicated mop contraption sat ready for Ying to start cleaning the floor, and once she'd done that, an enormous iron with a steam tank was waiting in the wings.

Petite, slender, bright Ying soaked clothes endlessly, cooked hugely, played games with her children and was one of the loveliest people who ever stayed with us. It was only after a week or so that it transpired she was a medical doctor herself.

With Mike, Ying was endlessly patient. When he fell, I, with gritted teeth, would haul him upright and dust him off. But, if Ying got there first, she would achieve the same outcome gently, allowing him time to right himself, calling for one of the other guests to help her lift him. If he was bruised or cut, she had creams, plasters and compresses. Mike was in heaven.

Out of the blue came a phone call asking me to go back to work for twelve months. I stalled, then rang back and accepted. I had given up work because I could not leave Mike at home alone. Now that we lived with a resident doctor and other guests, he was not alone. I confess, I never asked the surrogate carers, I just waved to them as I went to work, and no one blinked an eye. And, when my year was up, I had made myself 'space' within the day, so I could do what I had always wanted to do and start writing a book.

The house proved endlessly flexible. Daughters arrived on the doorstep and found a nook until a room became available. Old guests came unexpectedly, sure I had a bed somewhere. I'd protest that I didn't have room, but I always found them one.

There were parties for people leaving and parties when they came back; meals where everyone cooked a dish, and, of course, there were festivals – Easter and Christmas and several shots at New Year. The house had cycles of calm guests and noisy ones. What everyone had in common was a story.

No one had a story where life was perfect. Often great sorrow had come unbidden from the wings. Heartache and hardship didn't play fair.

My admiration and great affection for many of my guests who shared their stories, far outlasted their brief stays. I could not have imagined how good it was for my soul to live in a transient colony, the big house adapting endlessly to its occupants. I

Chapter 34 – Rooms to Let

thanked my lucky stars I was not in a one-bedroomed unit for the disabled.

At first, I had been quick to confess that spiriting Mike off to New Zealand had been a fiasco, a run from reality, which had taken me to the brink and dented our wobbly finances. In time, I saw a different synergy. I owned the fiasco as the revolution we needed. Blue Gum Lodge was my nadir and our salvation, a place where Mike found people even worse off than he, and I learned how living with strangers was better than living alone.

Opening up our house and welcoming guests from all over the world was the next best thing to the travel. It brought the world to our doorstep, generated an income and gave us a daily destination.

Mike kept taking his anti-depressants. And if my guests could see him as lovable, well, perhaps he was…

Life is not a movie, and it will never be the same kind of loving. No more travels together, no more sharing every silly thought. I cannot stop missing him. I cannot stop imagining how it might have been. But I cannot imagine loving anyone else.

And so, even though life may not be perfect, let us not stop it being an adventure and let us find *a path out of every ditch.*

Epilogue

Memories from our early years recharged me when the lights went out after Mike got sick. One, in particular, breathed life back into my soul.

I could choose to feel warm air on my skin and smell the polish that Mary rubbed into the concrete floor of our house in Kariba.

It had been a sultry noon. I'd sat reading, sometimes glancing beyond our two scrubby acacia trees, to where the view leapt over the Kariba Gorge to the more-blue-than-green hills of Zambia beyond.

I'd looked up and caught sight of his profile. The sun behind silhouetting him as he stood, leaning over, absorbed by papers on the table. A sudden lump in my throat choked me. I loved him so much.

"Mike," I said, distracting him, "I know it's so silly, but sometimes I feel scared that I might never have met you. It was so random. What if I hadn't gone to that party? What if..."

He'd turned, smiling, shifting his focus to find me in the shadow.

"It's not silly," he said so softly, gathering his words. "I've had that thought, too." And he came to sit beside me, taking my hand in his. "You know you'd planned moving on from Zambia to the new job in Libya... well, I've wondered what if my Land-Rover had died or the pontoon was out. What if *I* hadn't made the party?" He chuckled gently. "So, if I'd missed you in Zambia, what on earth was going to take me to Libya? Not a place for an entomologist, it's all bloody desert. I decided that perhaps I'd have taken a holiday – toured North Africa on a whim. Then I'd have met you there. If I'd missed you in Lusaka, I'd have found you in Tripoli."

Leaning back, he stretched out his long legs, our hands clasped between us.

"And, if it hadn't been Tripoli, then think some gin joint in Casablanca, some airport tarmac… It's OK, Stevie, we would always have met." He squeezed my hand. "It was kismet. It was written in the stars."

Then Kim had woken from her afternoon sleep and stumbled out to join us. She was a year old.

And, with that, the world straightened up, restarted, and moved on.

Such a whimsical conversation; all about love, luck and illusion. Such exchanges sew lovers together… and long after the thread has perished, pinholes of light remain, holding a place in the memory.

Acknowledgements

Mike is now in a nursing home. He is a favourite of the staff. A huge achievement for a man who can hardly talk or move. So handsome still, with barely a wrinkle, but with lots of whiskers. No longer piebald, they are all white. The African quilt is on his wall, and he still watches *Casablanca*.

I am ever indebted to Mike for his love and loyalty. There was never a dull moment when we were a team chasing adventures. Mike considers his daughters to be his crowning achievement. Kim, Dale, Emily and Alice have stayed the distance and shared the costs of the journey. They are just the best!

I owe a special thanks to many guests, for their conversations about wayfaring life's tricky pathways and for the liberties I have taken including them in my memoir.

Dr Charles Okumu, a guest from Kenya, recommended Kwame Nkrumah's classic book, *Neo-Colonialism: the Last Stage of Imperialism*, which is as relevant today as when it was written. And my lovely Iranian guests, Abbas Azarmehr and Sara Mohmmadzadeh, were ever willing to talk about Iran.

I've mentioned David Howarth's book *The Shadow of the Dam* and was thrilled to discover Julia Tischler's more recent work on the dam, *Light and Power for a Multiracial Nation*, which she kindly shared with me. Hans Hansen's account of surviving the shooting down of *Hunyani*, Flight 825, *The Deafening Silence*, is challenging to read as are Ian Pringle's books, *Murder in the Zambezi*, and *Green Leader*, which give much detail on the disaster and it's aftermath. I am grateful to my brother, Robert Stevenson, who published my parents' correspondence, *Love Letters from World War II*. Andrew Humphreys' great book,

Acknowledgements

Grand Hotels of Egypt in the Golden Age of Travel, was another source of detail.

I am indebted to Professor George Jelinek for his kindness and for all the encouragement he has given to people with multiple sclerosis. I gratefully acknowledge Elanor Gordon-Smith's Lifestyle article which appeared in *The Guardian* on 5 November 2020, on depression in chronic illness.

Thank you to all our old friends. Mervyn lived on in Kariba while Lesley and their daughter Kim moved to the West Indies. Their son, Paul, tragically died in a road accident. Dick and Marilyn continued to live in Harare and Nick is now back in England.

Trish lives in Queensland. With a heart of gold and a very pragmatic view of life, she recognised that Mike usually did the opposite of whatever I asked of him, advice I should have listened to earlier in the piece. Karen, whose infectious optimism should be bottled, now lives in South Australia. Karen married Geoff for the second time in 2023, an event which surprised everyone except Karen, who just knew it would all work out.

I was lucky to have friends who kept nudging me on. Anita Sekely, Alison Dodd and Kate Norbury. Ros Burton, herself a writer, was generous with her time and advice. Thanks also to Linda Subert and Teresa White who gave me early feedback.

My warm thanks to author Ashley Hay for her encouragement and to my agent, Irina Dunn, who pushed me to the finish line. Thanks to my daughters for their adept input from gruelling edits to cover concepts. And, finally, thanks to all at Interactive Publications, and in particular to Dr David Reiter, who generously put so much time into the manuscript.

www.ingramcontent.com/pod-product-compliance
Lightning Source LLC
Chambersburg PA
CBHW060832190426
43197CB00039B/2564